I0797082

Carlo Gambino

Books by
FRANK DIMATTEO and MICHAEL BENSON

Carmine the Snake:
Carmine Persico and His Murderous Mafia Family

Lord High Executioner:
The Legendary Mafia Boss Albert Anastasia

Mafia Hit Man:
Carmine DiBiase, the Wiseguy Who Really Killed Joey Gallo

The Cigar:
Carmine Galante, Mafia Terror

Red Hook:
Brooklyn Mafia, Ground Zero

Carlo Gambino:
Boss of Bosses

Books by FRANK DIMATTEO

The President Street Boys:
Growing Up Mafia

Books by MICHAEL BENSON

Betrayal in Blood

Lethal Embrace (with Robert Mladinich)

Mommy Deadliest

A Killer's Touch

A Knife in the Heart

Gangsters vs. Nazis:
How Jewish Mobsters Battled Nazis in Wartime America

Moguls:
The Lives and Times of Hollywood Film Pioneers Nicholas and Joseph Schenck (with Craig Singer)

Mafia Secrets:
Untold Tales from the Hollywood Godfather (with Gianni Russo)

Hollywood vs. Nazis:
How the Movie Studios Took On Nazis Infiltrating Los Angeles

Carlo Gambino BOSS OF BOSSES

FRANK DiMATTEO and MICHAEL BENSON

CITADEL PRESS
Kensington Publishing Corp.
kensingtonbooks.com

CITADEL PRESS BOOKS are published by

Kensington Publishing Corp.
900 Third Avenue
New York, NY 10022

All Kensington titles, imprints, and distributed lines are available at special quantity discounts for bulk purchases for sales promotions, premiums, fund-raising, educational, or institutional use. Special book excerpts or customized printings can also be created to fit specific needs. For details, write or phone the office of the Kensington sales manager: Kensington Publishing Corp., 900 Third Avenue, New York, NY 10022, Attn. Sales Department; phone 1-800-221-2647.

ISBN: 978-0-8065-4423-6

ISBN: 978-0-8065-4425-0 (ebook)

First Citadel hardcover printing: March 2026

Printed in the United States of America

10 9 8 7 6 5 4 3 2 1

The authorized representative in the EU for product safety and compliance
is eucomply OU, Parnu mnt 139b-14, Apt 123,
Tallinn, Berlin 11317; hello@eucompliancepartner.com.

Carlo Gambino was a hard man to write about because he lived the life of an old-time gangster—quiet and under the radar. But he ruled like a king. People think they know about him, but if you weren't in his family or circle, you don't know shit.

The feds did a good job following him, but a lousy job of finding evidence that could hurt him. Even with their surveillance and their shadows and their informants they couldn't figure him out. They couldn't put him in jail.

But I can tell you from my personal experience, from going along with my father and meeting him and having dinner every Thursday night during the summer of 1974. We met at the Dixie Tavern, Todo Marino's restaurant in Brooklyn.

He was polite and passionate about this life. When we met he would school me like a teacher. He was powerful but not a tyrant, small in frame but a huge presence. It was a summer I will never forget—my summer with Don Carlo.

Thank you, Dad, Ricky DiMatteo!

CONTENTS

"Judges, lawyers, and politicians have a license to steal. We don't need one."

—Carlo Gambino

Carlo Gambino

INTRODUCTION
The Ultimate King of the Hill

HEY, IT'S ME, UNCLE FRANKIE. Here to tell you about Carlo Gambino, Boss of Bosses, *Capo dei Capi.* I knew him a little, when I was young and he was old. He was a small man who radiated no danger.

He reminded me of a kindly grandfather, with smiling eyes and a soft voice, almost always speaking Sicilian. Us guys, born in America who knew some Italian, didn't understand all of it. These old-time gangsters—and Don Carlo had been straightened out in Palermo—had their own language, a quiet language, the language of the secret brotherhood, the language of unthinkable profit.

The Big M word has been thrown around a lot, too much—but this was it, the real thing, *la Mafia*!

So, he might have been small, and maybe he looked kind in a sort of vacant way, but everyone knew that underestimating Gambino could be a fatal mistake. He understood the Big Picture, largely because the Big Picture was of his own design.

Next to maybe Meyer Lansky, who was less ambitious, Gambino was the smartest gangster of all time. Not just smart. He was wise. He knew when to hang back, when to be patient. He spoke like a prophet.

Although he believed in the sanctity of Sicily—where the dusty soil grew poor crops but bestowed on its native sons near-magical criminal abilities—he was smart enough to know that the power of organized crime in the U.S. was not limited to the Sicilian Mafia, or Italian mobsters for that matter.

The American Gangland was a melting pot, different ethnicities and religions. Or the lack thereof. WASPs were mega-powerful and hadn't a dimple of ethnicity in them, all white bread and American cheese. Yet they could get together and rip people off on a mass scale.

Gambino sought allies and placed spies within organizations well outside the Five Family system. At the peak of his power, he had a deal with the outlaw motorcycle clubs. They could do what they do, move tons of crank, terrorize the countryside on their Harleys, just as long as they kicked up.

Newfangled inner-city gangs, Spanish kids as sharp as blades, Irish gangs all strutting like Cagney, rock-hard organized criminals of all ethnicities, they all got a regular visit from the big boys, to explain what's up, and pick up the envelope.

Don Carlo's rise to the top of the Mob heap, becoming the ultimate king of the hill in a deadly game of attrition, is itself a tremendous achievement. And his ability to remain at the top, boss of bosses, right up until he breathed his last, is a story of multitiered financial investment and amoral ambition.

Gambino's climb to the top of the ladder came on the backs of dead men. And just about every man who chose to be an obstacle between Gambino and his ultimate goal ended up prematurely on ice with a tag on his toe.

In this book, you'll be reading about many murders. All but two of them benefited Gambino. That little man with the long, hooked nose played a deep game.

Like Marlon Brando as Vito Corleone in *The Godfather*, Gambino held court as people came to him to pay respects and ask favors. He would grant some wishes, refuse others. His ring was all slobbery from being kissed so often.

To get to the front of the line, one had to tell a Gambino soldier what the problem was that he wished to have fixed, and if it seemed in the father's wheelhouse, they let him through. A guy who wanted Don Carlo to cure their wife's cancer was told to get out of line and go see a priest. A guy who needed help paying the medical bills was sent through. Holding court was very important to Gambino. It was his, and his secret society's, *moral justification.*

That was one side of Gambino. Another side (and there were many) was the guy who worked organized crime like a puppet master pulling strings, sometimes one at a time, other times pulling many strings at once.

He had factions holding hands to do his bidding, and factions quarreling to distract them from what was really going on. He had a percentage of every fucking thing in New York City and beyond, in control of the docks, in control of the airport, in control of garments. His game was so deep that even his closest associates didn't always know where they stood.

And he did it all very, very quietly.

It has been said that Don Carlo spoke softly because of a speech impediment, a slight lisp. I didn't notice it. I just got the impression that being the quietest of all-powerful men somehow made Gambino feel good.

He knew that he struck terror in the hearts of his enemies, and the fact that he did it with a whispery voice and a small smile just made the terror that much richer. Anyone could be a villain. Carlo Gambino was a super-villain, and in many communities, a superhero, too—a granter of wishes, a solver of problems.

And he did it without flash. In fact, the opposite. There was no outward indication that he considered himself as anything but regular. Even later in life, when he could clearly afford anything, he wore no jewelry, never dressed with any style, never drove a luxury automobile, and continued to live in a middle-class home on a busy, noisy Brooklyn thoroughfare. His only concession to his wealth was his Oyster Bay summer home, and even that wasn't showy. He had a boat, but it wasn't the Coast Guard cutter it was rumored to be.

Gambino once employed a secretary named Joseph Cantalupo, a made man who was around Gambino a lot and got to see Don Carlo in all kinds of situations.

Later, Cantalupo turned rat, which is how we know his feelings about Gambino. What we learned was that Gambino's behavior wasn't an act. The Boss was always low-key, always private. There was nothing in his manner to indicate that this man was a wielder of tremendous power.

Joe Bonanno—another Sicilian, but a prince born to power—completely underestimated Gambino. During the time when Albert Anastasia was the head of the family, and Gambino his underboss, Anastasia regularly disrespected Gambino, raised his hand to him, scolded him, and sent him on errands. Bonanno saw this as weakness, when in retrospect we see it as patience.

Gambino made Anastasia pay for his insults with his life, and he himself took over Anastasia's world, which he brilliantly expanded into a global force. Mob life was like a three-dimensional chess game, and Gambino its master. His enemies often thought they were winning, right up until the moment the lights went out.

Because I come up now and again in our story, let me quickly tell you about Uncle Frankie, your friendly narrator. I was born in 1956 in Red Hook, Brooklyn. My mother got married in 1954 to a pro boxer named Alfonzo "Funzi" Milone, from Coney Island, Brooklyn. She grew up in Red Hook, Brooklyn, on Baltic Street, between Henry and Hicks, but moved to First Place (that's a street) when she was thirteen. She had a girlfriend who dated Joey Gallo and lived in the same building as Frank "Punchy" Illiano.

When she was a young woman, my mom took the train to Coney Island all the time. In the summer, it was not only fun to be there with the beach and the amusement parks, but those were the days before air-conditioning, and it was ten degrees cooler at Coney Island than in Red Hook.

There used to be a place for dancing underneath the boardwalk, with a jukebox. My mom loves to dance. One time she was dancing with a guy and Funzi cut in. He asked her a few times for a date. She finally went out with him, and he told her he was a boxer.

He told her he was a semi-pro because he had to work a real job in addition to fighting, but his record shows he was a full-fledged pro (although not necessarily well paid) who fought on the undercards of major shows.

Funzi fought as Al Milone and had a 16–15 record, taking on all comers. He started out fighting at the Fort Hamilton Arena, at Ninety-Ninth Street and Fort Hamilton Parkway, in a spot that is now underneath an entrance ramp to the Verrazzano-Narrows Bridge. He fought in Philadelphia, at the Fifth Regiment Armory in Paterson, New Jersey. He fought at the St. Nicholas Arena in the city, and at the Sunnyside Garden Arena in Queens. At the peak of his career, he fought twice at Madison Square Garden.

Things might have proceeded more quickly between my mom and Funzi, if it hadn't been for the policies of my grandfather, which were strict. She was just seventeen (if you know what I mean) so she had to be sneaky. She was expected to be home by eight thirty, nine o'clock. If she was too late, my grandfather would lock the door, so she'd have to pound and my grandmother would come down and let her in.

"It was rough," she says.

On the other hand, if she wanted to go shopping she much preferred going with my grandfather, who couldn't say no and bought her whatever she wanted.

When she was nineteen, Funzi asked my mom to marry him. My uncle and his wife took Mom and Funzi to get married, and they moved to Bay Fiftieth Street in Bath Beach to live with Funzi's parents and his sister Lucy.

Mom soon learned that Funzi didn't like to work. He liked doing his roadwork and training for fights, but bringing home a paycheck wasn't his thing. They divorced when I was a baby.

When I was five and Mom was working as a bartender, she met Ricky DiMatteo, another boxer. I came along on their first date and loved him right away. With my small but wholehearted blessing, they married and he became my dad.

Like many boxers who were real-life tough guys, Ricky took work with "the boys" as a bouncer in Mob-run bars. That was how he met Larry Gallo, leader of the Gallo gang on President Street in Red Hook.

Ricky started out as Larry's bodyguard and went on to become a trusted member of the President Street Boys, surviving two Mob wars, first when the Gallos took on the Profacis and again when, after a change in administration, they took on the Colombos—same family with a different boss.

I began hanging out with the President Street Boys when I was a little boy, and by the time I was fourteen (and already at my current height) I was driving for the guys and being initiated into the Life.

I did a lot of things and I saw a lot of stuff during my time as a gangster, but I got out with my head still attached to my neck, and today I'm a loving father and grandfather.

I channeled all my experiences—play with the cards you're dealt, pallie—into a publishing venture, a magazine of gangster stories and pretty girls called *Mob Candy*.

From there I wrote my biography, the great *Growing Up Mafia: The President Street Boys*.

After that was a hit, me and my writing partner Mike Benson have been telling Mob history my way, based on firsthand street knowledge, in books like *Carmine the Snake* about Carmine Persico; *Lord High Executioner* about Albert Anastasia; *The Cigar* about Carmine "Lilo" Galante; and *Mafia Hit Man* about Carmine DiBiase, aka Sonny Pinto, the man who really shot Joey Gallo (that Scorsese picture, *The Irishman*, was a great movie but it was full of shit).

My most recent book was called *Red Hook*, the history of my neighborhood, ground zero for Mob activity for just about the entire twentieth century.

Now I'm writing about Carlo Gambino, a man who accrued power like a black hole sucks in planets.

And, as you'll learn, Carlo Gambino once saved my life. Not an exaggeration.

CHAPTER 1
Born into the Life

CARLO GAMBINO WAS BORN on August 24, 1902 (some sources say 1900), in the Sicilian capital of Palermo, a metropolitan area with close to a million people set in a basin formed by the Paprieto, Oreto, and Kemonia rivers, on the island's north shore. It was a place where carts were tugged by donkeys, and the streets were hard-packed dirt. Population at the time of Gambino's birth, about 300,000. It was also the time of a big crackdown on Mafia activity in the city. The event was more entertainment than crime-fighting. So many mafiosi were rounded up and tried simultaneously that they had to build a jail cell right in the courtroom, and during the trial the forty or so suspects were stacked up in there asshole to bellybutton. It was all a big show and nothing much happened.

Palermo is surrounded by mountains. Mount Pellegrino can be seen from just about anywhere in the city or its outskirts. From its summit, there is a spectacular view of the city, the Gulf of Palermo, and beyond that the Tyrrhenian Sea.

Gambino was born *Palermitano* and remained that way his entire life, an expatriate insisting on the old traditions even as he planted roots in the New World. The people of Palermo spoke in an Italian dialect, a language all their own, so different from standard Italian that many Italian-speakers couldn't understand it. Maybe they could pick up a word or two here and there but they needed a translator to get the full meaning. This Palermitani dialect was the only language that Carlo Gambino would ever speak well. He would always need to surround himself with homeboys. No one else understood him.

Throughout his life, particularly as an old man, Gambino spoke of Palermo, of the summer street celebrations like the Feast of Santa Rosalia, Palermo's patron saint, which always seemed to be held on the hottest days of the year. Summers in Palermo were long and hot anyway. Palermo was not just one of the hottest cities in Italy, it was one of the hottest cities in all of Europe. The temperature could approach one hundred degrees Fahrenheit any day from May till September.

Gambino's family was mafioso, in a crew operating in Passo di Rigano, one of eight *mandamenti* (administrative districts) of Palermo. Gambino's home city was home to one of the busiest ports in Sicily, where there was much cargo coming in and out, all to be skimmed.

He was the son of Tommaso Gambino and the former Felice Castellano. He had two brothers, Gaspare Gambino, who remained legit, and Paolo, who went into the Life with Carlo.

From a very early age, there were people who couldn't reconcile Gambino's personality—reserved, shy, soft-spoken—with his ambitious career in the Mafia, an organization so powerful that it was thought of as a second government in Sicily, a rival to the Italian government, which seemed parasitic and remote.

After writing Mob history for years, I'm amazed at how many childhood friends end up becoming powerful gangsters. Friends of each other, I mean. Meyer Lansky met Bugsy Siegel when he was a kid, and he met Lucky Luciano when they were teenagers. Carmine Persico was already tight with Gerry Lang and Andrew "Mush" Russo when my mom knew them as teenagers.

But no childhood friends ever rose higher than these: As a small boy, Carlo's best friend was Gaetano Lucchese, who was a year older. They had to cross an ocean to do it, but both rose to the very top.

As kids running the streets, Gambino and Lucchese idolized that era's Sicilian Boss of Bosses, Don Vito Cascio Ferro, who had gone to America as a boy (actually fled as he was wanted for murder), became an original Black Hand terrorist in America, made a mint, and returned to Sicily dripping power.

Don Vito demonstrated—as Bugsy Siegel, Mickey Cohen, and Joey Gallo would in later years—that the danger he represented, twenty hits, all of that power, allowed him to mix easily with the power elite. In this case, not just celebrities and intellectuals but Sicily's judges, bankers, and moguls.

Anybody who was somebody wanted Don Vito at their party. Deals were cut, corrupt to the bone. He was flamboyantly charitable and discreetly greedy, other characteristics that little Carlo would one day emulate.

Don Vito's legend crossed paths with another fellow who'll be long remembered, Detective Lieutenant Joseph Petrosino, a New York City policeman who relentlessly battled the Black Hand, which is what they called the Mob in America in those days.

For a brief but impressive stretch, Petrosino was the number one enemy of Little Italy mobsters. He was the force's first Italian-American lieutenant and detective, as pure as the driven snow, unbribable. He formed the "Italian Squad" of the New York police, an elite corps of Italian Americans who went undercover to combat the Black Hand hoodlums.

During Petrosino's New York City offensive, Black Handers were scooped up left and right. While he was on a roll, Petrosino also founded the bomb squad and the canine squad, the first such squads anywhere in the United States.

Stupidly overconfident with success, he took his battle overseas. He tried to yank up the Black Hand organization at the roots. In 1909, when Carlo was seven-to-nine years old and Gaetano nine, Petrosino sailed to Sicily to lay waste to the underworld.

Well, it didn't work out that way.

Petrosino arrived in Palermo on March 12 but his visit lasted only hours. Petrosino went from the pier to a hotel, and from the hotel to a restaurant. He'd just finished dinner and was on his way back to his hotel—strolling near the Piazza Marine, only a few yards from the statue of Garibaldi—when two men, hands in pockets, approached him from behind. Each pulled their rod and emptied their guns into Petrosino's back. The policeman was dead before his face hit the pavement, which it did with a sickening thud.

The hit made newspaper headlines globally. Petrosino's body was returned to New York City and his funeral packed the streets. (Today, to honor the brave but none-too-bright cop, there is Lieutenant Joseph Petrosino Square at Lafayette Street and Cleveland Place in Manhattan.)

The whacking of Petrosino is important to our story because it was Don Vito himself who executed the hit. Reportedly, Ferro drove to and from the hit in a horse-drawn carriage with a member of the Sicilian Parliament, a man who may have been the second gunman and later offered Don Vito an airtight alibi.

The news of Petrosino's short-lived visit was greeted by the boys of Palermo, including Carlo Gambino and Gaetano Lucchese, with shouts of joy.

Carlo and Gaetano wanted to be just like Don Vito when they grew up.

Carlo Gambino was sad when, at age nine, Lucchese took a boat to America with his family. (And there would be much joy about ten years later when Gambino arrived in New York City and rejoined his old friend, this time on the streets of Brooklyn.)

Gambino stayed in school until he was a teenager, briefly attending the equivalent of high school (called *liceo classico*) before dropping out and dedicating his life to the magnificent Palermo underworld.

In America, in late 1919, while working as a machinist's apprentice at a munitions manufacturer, Lucchese lost his right index finger and part of his thumb. The accident convinced him that working a legit job was for suckers.

A few months after the accident, Prohibition came, organized crime took over booze production and distribution, and young Gaetano Lucchese joined the bootlegging gang of Salvatore "Little Caesar" Maranzano, out of East Harlem—the neighborhood then known as Little Italy.

Maranzano, at the dawn of the Prohibition era, was a Mafia unicorn. He had a college education. He was multilingual. He'd studied for the priesthood. He wasn't just smart, he did smart things. When Mussolini came to power, and threatened to wipe out the Mafia, Maranzano told hoods in Sicily to flee the purge and come work for him in America. According to one source, eight thousand Sicilian men did just that and were smuggled into America to man Maranzano's operations.

Because of Lucchese's accident, it has long been reported that his nickname was "Three-Finger Brown," after future Hall of Famer Mordecai Brown, the Chicago Cubs pitcher whose mangled right hand allowed him to throw a nasty curveball. Truth is, *no one ever* called Lucchese that.

The story is that a cop filling out a fingerprint card after a Lucchese pinch wrote down "Three-Finger Brown" as an alias, just to be funny, because two of the fingerprint boxes were blank.

But the tag stuck with him, at least in law enforcement paperwork, for the rest of his days.

Gambino became a made man and took the oath while still in Sicily. Because the best Mob jobs in Sicily were already taken, Gambino decided (or was told) to go to America, which for a young and smart criminal was a rich land of opportunity. In America, he was told, he would find a wide-open pathway to power and riches.

It would be wrong to state that Gambino fled Sicily. Mussolini's purge hadn't yet started when Gambino came to America. Like so many others, Gambino came here to pursue happiness. Prohibition was already in its second year and the business opportunities presented by the growing black market of booze must have been irresistible to a smart fellow like Gambino.

* * *

Mafia soldier Carlo Gambino entered the U.S. illegally on December 23, 1921, a stowaway on the Italian ship SS *Vincenzo Florio,* an iron-screw steamer built in 1880 and designed to handle cargo. Maybe "stowaway" is the wrong word. He was an undocumented passenger. His accommodations were luxurious. Gambino was the only passenger on the voyage, and, because of his connections, the crew found it wise to not ask too many questions.

It could not have been an easy trip. The *Florio* was only slightly longer than a football field and less than forty feet wide. The ship was named after an Italian entrepreneur, a member of one of Italy's wealthiest families, and one of the world's first race car drivers. Palermo was the steamer's home port, and it regularly traveled the Atlantic. The *Florio* was near the end of its sailing career. It had served as a block ship for London Admiralty during World War I. Only months after delivering Gambino safely to America, it was retired and broken up for tons of scrap.

Gambino jumped ship at Norfolk, Virginia, wearing a brand-new suit. He had many relatives already in the country, with factions of the clan in New York and Massachusetts. As he set his first step on American soil, though, he had a piece of paper in his pocket upon which was written the address of his cousins, the Castellanos. His mom's maiden name was Castellano. He made it to New York and there took a job working for his uncle's trucking company.

His first home in America was on Brooklyn's Navy Street, only a couple of blocks from the Navy Yard Basin and the docks of Wallabout Bay. His constant companion during those early days in America was another cousin, the son of his mother's sister, Thomas Masotto. Cousin Tommy spoke Carlo's language and for the rest of his life would be one of his most trusted companions.

Gambino rejoiced over his reunion with Gaetano Lucchese.

"What the hell happened to your hand?" was no doubt Gambino's first question.

But the childhood pals got to hang out for only a few weeks before

Lucchese went to jail for three years for stealing cars. The pair might have developed their own thing if Lucchese had remained free. With Lucchese in the cooler, Gambino needed companionship and joined the city's largest crew, that of Alfredo "Al Mineo" Manfredi.

The brainy Gambino almost immediately began hanging out with the upper echelon. For a time, Gambino reported to Mineo, who had his own crew that operated strictly in Brooklyn. Mineo reported to Salvatore "Toto" D'Aquila. Through the 1910s, when Mineo was in his thirties, the Brooklyn operation ran unopposed.

After that, there were moves on Mineo's turf. Organized crime is a survival of the fittest game, and survival depends on being on the side that is winning. Once Giuseppe "Joe the Boss" Masseria acquired power to rival D'Aquila's, Mineo, and Gambino beneath him, both maneuvered themselves in attempts to make a smooth transition to the new administration when Joe the Boss inevitably took over. Gambino, a master at this sort of thing by this time, pulled off the awkward move with quiet grace. As we'll see, Mineo didn't pull it off at all.

Sal D'Aquila, the cheese importer, first boss of the crime family that would become known as the Gambinos, was killed in 1928 at age fifty. D'Aquila had taken his wife to the doctor, and while she was tended to, he stayed outside and worked on his auto's motor at the corner of Avenue A and East Thirteenth Street in the city. He was accosted by three gunmen who fired five times in total and left him dead in the street. The killers fled on foot. With that, Joe the Boss earned his nickname.

Gambino remained on Mineo's crew right up until Mineo was whacked in the middle of the afternoon on November 5, 1930, one of the first casualties of the Castellammarese War. Three killers hired by the Maranzano crew rented a first-floor apartment in the Bronx. The apartment had a view out the window of the courtyard to a fashionable apartment complex on the nearby Pelham Parkway. The location was chosen because Joe the Boss had been seen entering and exiting the complex a few days earlier. (Joe the Boss was not the only bigwig who'd been at that complex. There had been a meeting of Joe and his top boys, attendees including Lucky Luciano and Vito Genovese.)

The gunmen staked out the spot for days. Joe the Boss never reappeared, so they went for the next best thing. Thirty-seven-year-old Mineo came strolling by. Alongside him was thirty-four-year-old Stephen Ferrigno, who lived in the complex with his invalid wife and four kids. Without bothering to open the window, the assassins fired shotguns and killed the two men.

It was one of the first salvos in what came to be known as the Castellammarese War. (Although no one was ever charged in the double hit, years later, in 1963, Joe Valachi, while singing his little brains out, told the world that one of Mineo's killers was Girolamo Santuccio. The assassins' nest was also reportedly manned at one time or another by Valachi himself, Nick Capuzzi, and future boss Joseph Profaci.)

The press called Mineo a big shot in the numbers game. Ferrigno, they wrote, was involved in bootlegging, gambling, prostitution, extortion, and controlling the longshoremen's unions.

One day Gambino is working for Mineo, the next day for Masseria. Silky smooth.

Joe the Boss sent young Carlo Gambino to Boston to oversee bootlegging operations there. The move was disruptive to Gambino's life, but he had relatives in Brockton, which made the transition easier.

While bootlegging in New England, Gambino met many future superstars, members of Masseria's operation that would go on to bigger and better things, including the all-time great, Salvatore Carlo Lucania, who came from Lercara Friddi, Sicily. In America he was known as Charlie Luciano, and then, after surviving a kidnapping during which he was tortured and left for dead, as "Lucky."

Luciano was a childhood friend of the great Meyer Lansky. They were both hustling on the same street corners. At that time, a Jewish boy on the street alone had to be careful not to be mugged by Italian and Irish gangs. When an Italian gang, led by the boy named Salvatore Lucania, surrounded little Meyer and demanded his money, Meyer said, and I quote, "Go fuck yourself." Lucania took one look at this kid and saw a kindred spirit.

Sicilian-born, but knowing little of the language, Luciano found himself adaptable, capable of compartmentalizing, able to live in the purely Sicilian world of omertà and vendetta, and also in the modern American world, with a wide variety of money-making opportunities that in the Old World would have been considered taboo.

He lived enveloped by paradox: Organized crime thrived when networks of criminals worked together, yet those same criminals distrusted one another. Operations were often botched because of infighting. How could you get these meatheads to work as a team when they were playing quickdraw in the street?

Regarding his first meeting with Lansky, Luciano recalled, "We both had a kind of instant understanding." The first thing Lansky and Luciano did was halt the war between the Jewish and Italian boys, and team up those crews to take on the Irish gangs. Later they would put their heads together again and come up with the Five Family system and Murder Inc. Lansky lived a long life and was never convicted of a significant crime. Law enforcement was beyond frustrated.

Lansky and Gambino have often been compared to each other—they both built networks, but there were deep differences as well. Lansky spoke perfect English, mixed well in a variety of social groups, and didn't think of himself as a criminal, just a businessman whose product happened to be illegal. His motto was "It's always better not to shoot." Gambino was criminal to the bone, and in his own indirect way, vicious.

When Prohibition came, Lansky and Gambino each designed systems of creating, moving, and selling booze far beyond the capabilities of other men. It was while selling Boston rotgut that Carlo Gambino showed his genius. He had the ability to keep the details of large operations in his head. Nothing needed to be written down. No need to create unnecessary evidence.

Working in Massachusetts, Gambino not only had to set up a complicated system that worked, he had to do it in a world with its own Mob troubles, with its own history of guys getting whacked and replaced by guys who got whacked.

Generally, the power in New England at that time was Castellammarese, land of the Bonannos. But there were large Irish gangs, too, who could be pains in the ass if they thought they were being disrespected.

There were always rival gangs shooting each other, small-minded hoods who fought over street corners. Gambino, who was large-minded, knew that keeping them in line was key to maximizing Mafia profits.

In a chaotic world, Gambino demonstrated that he had a quiet and orderly way of thinking to go with his quiet manner. By the time Gambino returned to Brooklyn, he had enough money to buy a house, get married, and start a family.

CHAPTER 2
Blood of My Blood

THE UNCOMFORTABLE TRUTH about Carlo Gambino was that his marriage was incestuous. He married his first cousin, a Castellano. Gambino's father had also married a Castellano. These were no wild and weird flings. Far from it. The Gambinos and Castellanos were so determined to keep the money and power in the family that they didn't let outsiders in—not even by marriage. *Sangue di mio sangue.* Blood of my blood, was the motto.

Young members of the family *had* to marry a cousin. The Roman Catholic Church condemned such marriages, but for the Gambinos and Castellanos the practice went on for generations. It kept the power in hand but diminished the bloodline. Luckily, all of Carlo's children would be fine.

(Years later, Robert F. Kennedy had a genealogy made of Carlo's ancestors and was shocked by what he learned. He complained to the Church about it and asked that they stop the practice. A Justice Department memo refers to the "peculiar marriages" among the cousins.)

On December 5, 1926, Gambino was wed to eighteen-year-old Kathryn in Brooklyn. Kathryn's parents were Joseph Castellano and Concetta Cassata Castellano. She grew up in a row house in the old Little Italy, the uptown version, on East 101st Street. Her father was Italian-born and had been in the U.S. for eight years when Kathryn came along in 1908.

Best man at the wedding was Kathyn's brother Paul, who was the groom's first cousin, good friend, and business associate. Carlo and Kathryn would go on to have four children: Phyllis, born 1927, Thomas, born 1929, Joseph, born 1936, and Carl, born 1944.

Although Kathryn was never seen nor heard participating in any gangster activities, she was always a friendly and attentive hostess for her husband's many and varied visitors over the years. Gangsters always spoke of her in reverent terms. She was clearly a saint with room reserved in Heaven. As was typical in many marriages back then, she was in charge of the praying.

When Gambino's visitors were members of the Law, which sometimes happened, Kathryn's demeanor didn't change at all. She was the same lovely hostess, offering espresso and some cookies. One FBI agent recalled Kathryn inquiring about his family. And, of course, no matter who was visiting Carlo, she had the grace to withdraw quietly so the men could discuss business.

For Kathryn to build their nest, Carlo would purchase a home in Midwood, Brooklyn, on Ocean Parkway. That street has the honor of being the widest street in Brooklyn. It is about five miles long and runs from the southwestern edge of Prospect Park to Brighton Beach, which is east of Coney Island along the same sandbar. The street was built in 1866 to provide a beeline from Prospect Park to the ocean—thus the name.

Gambino would never have to worry about neighbors trying to look in his front windows. The other side of the street was about a hundred yards away. The main part of the road is six lanes wide with a grassy mall on either side. There are also two service roads for streetside parking, and on each side, America's first bike paths. Those paths were originally designed as bridle paths for horseback riding but changed around the turn of the twentieth century. When Robert Moses carved expressways into Brooklyn after World War II, the topmost portion of Ocean Parkway turned into the Prospect Expressway.

It was a noisy place to live, but the Gambinos must've loved it. For the rest of their lives, they stayed on Ocean Parkway for most of each year.

CHAPTER 3
Castellammarese War

GAMBINO WAS NEVER A GUN, but during the Castellammarese War he "fought" on the same side as Vito Genovese, Frank Costello, and Luciano. While others were out hunting, Gambino thought things through and whispered instructions.

He was by this time an expert at all levels of the bootlegging business. He could distill, distribute, smuggle, and sell. When competition needed to be discouraged, he knew people who could do that.

He could advise ship captains on how to evade offshore law enforcement. He knew the roads. He knew where police were to be avoided and where highway patrols needed greasing. As a persuader, he was silent and smiling—but he always got his message across. He knew guys, he explained softly, who weren't as nice.

The subtlety of his approach impressed Luciano. Despite his youth, Gambino was fatherly, and he meant that in all of its meanings. He was too valuable to be put in harm's way. Joe the Boss, on the other hand, had lived in harm's way for years.

Masseria, by the time he was boss, was used to having bullets whiz past his ear. The first attempt on his life came on August 9, 1922, when he was ambushed as he came down the front stoop of his home on Second Avenue in the city. Six shots were fired in drive-by fashion by two shooters. All missed, but Masseria's straw hat looked like

Swiss cheese. The getaway car ran smack-dab into Murphy's Law as, in their attempt to get as far from Masseria as they could as fast as possible, they drove directly into a crowd of striking tailors who'd packed the street in front of a large building called Beethoven Hall at the corner of East Fifth and Third Avenue.

The desperadoes fired into the crowd to disperse it, and one tailor died. The shooting sequence lasted long enough for Masseria to recognize one of his assailants, rival bootlegger Umberto Valenti.

Valenti was a snappy dresser who always cut a sharp profile, and Valenti knew it—so perhaps he was relieved a few days later when Masseria invited him to a sit-down in a restaurant at the corner of East Twelfth Street and Second Avenue in the city.

"We shall discuss our differences," Masseria said, and Valenti showed up on time. The men ate, and ate, and ate. And they talked. They had a lot in common.

Masseria was out on bail on a murder charge. Valenti knew all about how that felt. He had been arrested for a 1914 murder (Fortunato LoMonte) but was acquitted at trial. When they were finally full, they exited the restaurant together and two Masseria gunmen fired twelve to fifteen shots at Valenti, who clawed at his chest and stayed on his feet to the curb where he leaned on a cab driven by a hack named Zuckerberg.

Valenti got his hand on his own gun but lacked the strength to grip it. The cabbie threw open the door of his taxi but Valenti collapsed and died on his running board.

Masseria's gunmen weren't troubled by collateral damage. In whacking Valenti, they also shot a street cleaner in the throat and an eleven-year-old girl, Agnes Egglinger, in the chest.

The sloppy gunmen ran through the basement of a tenement on East Twelfth, then over the back fence and through another apartment building, emerging on Thirteenth Street.

The payback nature of the Valenti hit was too obvious for the police to confuse, and Joe the Boss was almost immediately arrested and charged with murder.

Masseria was in a jam. He was already free on $15,000 bail for the murder of a hood named Silva Tagliagamba in Little Italy at what was known as Bootlegger's Curb (curbside service selling rotgut at Grand and Mulberry Streets).

Gambino, when he switched from Mineo to Masseria, had proved he could change allegiance without breaking a sweat. Now he would show he could do it again and again.

While the Castellammarese War was still raging, guys getting squibbed on both sides, Gambino once again hopped the fence. He saw that the side he'd been on, Masseria's side, was going to lose.

All you had to do to predict the winner was count the stiffs. Sixty members of the Masseria crew all died in the same year. If the path to the top required toasting to Castellammare every once in a while, so be it.

Without emotion, Gambino betrayed Masseria, joined Maranzano, and made friends with his new allies, Joseph Bonanno, Joseph Anthony Doto, aka Joe Adonis, and the Olive Oil King, Joseph Profaci.

One version of the story, one with a measure of evidence, was that Gambino switched sides during the Castellammarese War, but only after his brother shed blood on his behalf.

In early 1931, with the war at its bloodiest, Maranzano sent Joseph Valachi (who would later become famous as the Mob's first big-league rat) and Steve Rinelli out hunting, so they cruised the Flatbush section of Brooklyn looking for members of the enemy to pick off.

While cruising around they saw a guy in a luxury car and, thinking him a target, shot the guy, one bullet taking off a chunk of his ear—but leaving him otherwise unharmed.

It turned out the wounded man was Paul Gambino. To make up for the error, Maranzano offered Carlo a good job with his crew. So, sensing that Joe the Boss's days were numbered, Gambino went to work for Maranzano.

That's one version of events.

Another version, according to Joseph Bonanno, who didn't always tell the truth, the subject of that hunt was Carlo Gambino himself, who was still with Joe the Boss. That much seems feasible, but Bonanno then takes it another step: that it was Gambino's childhood friend Gaetano (now known as "Tommy") Lucchese who ordered Gambino taken out.

It seems highly improbable that Lucchese would sponsor the hit on his friend. As history would prove, there was plenty out there to satisfy both of those Palermo street kids. Bonanno seemed to think it was a miracle that the men later became close friends, their children marrying. It was as if Bonanno didn't know Gambino and Lucchese had done crimes together long before they could shave and thought he could get away with the lie.

The Castellammarese War officially came to an end when Lucky Luciano had Masseria whacked. It was April 15, 1931, and the place was Gerardo Scarpato's Nuova Villa Tammaro in Coney Island, on West Fifteenth Street, the current site of Banner Smoked Fish seafood market.

Childhood friends Benjamin "Bugsy" Siegel, Meyer Lansky, and Lucky Luciano still put their heads together as adults. They'd had a clandestine meeting with Sal Maranzano in the Bronx Zoo. There, while feeding peanuts to the elephants, they came up with a plan to take out Masseria.

On the fateful day, Luciano asked Masseria to join him for dinner at Scarpato's in Coney Island. The men ate, and ate, and they drank Italian red wine. The feast lasted for three hours. Luciano patted himself on his belly, belched, and left the table to go to the can and take a piss.

As soon as Masseria was alone at the table, four gunmen—Bugsy Siegel, Vito Genovese, Albert Anastasia, and Joe Adonis, what an all-star cast!—burst into the restaurant and aerated Joe the Boss.

Joe danced and writhed in the ultimate game of dodgeball, but he was struck by six bullets, at least one of which was fatal. Fourteen more slugs broke glass and tore up the restaurant wall behind Masseria.

Luciano came out of the restroom and left the restaurant before the police arrived. For the four gunmen, it wasn't a silky-smooth getaway. When the getaway driver stalled the car, Bugsy slugged him. But everyone escaped anyway. (The driver was lucky Siegel didn't shoot him. Bugsy famously disliked putting his hands, even his fists, on other men. He saved his hands for the broads, he said.)

The Masseria hit, and its violent aftermath, proved to be a pivotal moment in Mob history. It helped to put into place the Mob leadership that would remain for most of the remainder of the century. I know this because my uncle Joe Schipani was a driver for Lucky and told me so.

With Joe the Boss off the board, Lucky Luciano had Sal "Little Caesar" Maranzano's ear, and he started talking.

Looch said, "You be boss, I'll be underboss."

Maranzano said, "Sounds good." He spoke through the side of his mouth.

Maranzano, the college graduate who spoke several languages and thought himself smarter than other hoods, bought Luciano's plan hook, line, and sinker. Of course. Luciano had no intention of being underboss. Undertaker was more like it.

Maranzano, on the other hand, didn't want Luciano to be his underboss any more than Looch wanted the job. It was all for show. Even as he was saying, "Sounds good," he was formulating a plan to bump off Luciano and Vito Genovese. With that powerful pair out of the way, Little Caesar felt he could regroup and maybe take his time executing the rest of his enemies. The plan never got off the ground. It was thoroughly unreasonable to suppose it would.

"I'll just fucking kill everybody," was a common sentiment in power-hungry guys who came unhinged. Maranzano's plan was to have an Irish gunman named Vincent "Mad Dog" Coll hit Luciano and Genovese at Maranzano's office on the ninth floor of the New York Central Building overlooking Grand Central Station.

But things did not go as planned. When Tommy Lucchese caught wind that Luciano and Genovese were being targeted, he informed Luciano. And so, the tables were turned. Luciano called Albert "Mad Hatter" Anastasia, the Lord High Executioner of Murder Inc. fame.

Anastasia was an animal, a physically intimidating man, a sadist, a mass murderer. He couldn't have been more different from Carlo Gambino. And Anastasia was one rung above Gambino in the pecking order. The Hatter was one of the original guys, a kid whose first smuggling job was getting himself ashore in New York in 1917. He was born in 1902 as Umberto Anastasio in the fishing village of Tropea in Calabria, Italy. He and his brother Anthony were working the crew of a ship crossing the Atlantic and jumped ship in New York, then went to work on the Brooklyn piers, where over time the man now known as Albert came to control Brooklyn Local 1814, which repped longshoremen employed by stevedore companies. Ostensibly a dressmaker and milliner, the papers called him "the Mad Hatter," after the *Alice in Wonderland* character. He was convicted of murder in 1921. It looked like his Mafia career would be a short one until he avoided the electric chair when a key witness abruptly returned to Italy. Anastasia was acquitted at the retrial. He went from the Sing Sing death house to the streets.

Lucky Luciano turned to Anastasia when he needed someone dead.

"Albert, I need you to intervene with Maranzano," Luciano said.

"Anything you want, Boss," Albert said.

"Visit Maranzano's office before the Irish gun gets there."

Albert assembled a team.

"Before you fuckers go, I got a present for you," Anastasia said.

The gifts were hats, brand-new broad brim, broad-band, crisply crowned fedoras made in Chicago.

"After we squib the guy, lose the hat on the way out," Anastasia said.

"Huh?"

"Just do it," Anastasia said, so they just did it.

Anastasia's team left Murder Inc. headquarters, aka Midnight Rose's Candy Store in the East New York section of Brooklyn, at 2:45 p.m. on Thursday afternoon, September 10, 1931, and rode in a car to Maranzano's Midtown Manhattan office.

They pounded authoritatively on the door.

"Open up! We are the police!"

Inside, Maranzano was fretting. He knew that knock came from a pro gun, and the targets, Luciano and Genovese, were yet to arrive. In Maranzano's office, eleven men were working. Someone answered the door.

The invading men had handkerchiefs over their faces and the broad brims of their brand-new hats pulled down.

"Line up against the wall!" one of them said. Maranzano went pale and felt cold sweat soak through his shirt. This wasn't an Irish gunman from out of town. They had their faces covered, but you could tell by the way they moved they were Brooklyn through and through. One of them had huge hands, the hands of a strangler.

The office workers did as they were told. Maranzano made a move to join them.

"Not you!" the guy with the hands said.

With their target alone, they riddled Maranzano with hot lead, killing him instantly. No one else was injured. The killers were in no hurry. They lost their hats and walked calmly out the door.

As Albert and the other gunmen left the building and stepped out into the hubbub around Grand Central, on his way in was Mad Dog Coll, the Irish guy from out of town who'd been paid $25,000 to whack Luciano and Genovese.

Coll arrived upon a scene of chaos: targets not there, his client dead, killers already flown, cop cars screaming toward the scene. The pro killer pulled up his collar, did a quick about-face, and disappeared into the stream of pedestrians.

Maranzano's murder was witnessed by a thirty-one-year-old prizefighter from Brooklyn named James Santuccio, who claimed to have been in the building for innocent reasons, and probably should have told cops he kept his eyes shut because they immediately took him into custody and held him as a material witness.

Telephone operator Grace Samuels also witnessed the action. She was smart and said she didn't know nothing about nothing because everyone spoke Italian, and she didn't.

Anastasia's genius became immediately clear. Investigators picked up the discarded fedoras, all bearing a label reading:

MADE IN CHICAGO

Cops told the press that the hit was most probably done by "guys from out of town. Probably long gone by now."

For Prohibition-era detectives, the files in Maranzano's office turned out to be a gold mine, listing the ritzy clients and establishments along Park Avenue that were in Little Caesar's booze network.

They also found Maranzano's diary, which contained the names of politicians, lawyers, and immigration officials with the Federal Nationalization Bureau. The book was found on the sidewalk outside the building, dropped or planted by fleeing gunmen.

When the customers listed in Maranzano's diary were questioned, they answered with eyes wide and innocent. None of these people had *any* idea why that guy they hardly knew would have their number in a book.

With Maranzano gone, Vincenzo Giovanni Mangano, aka Vincent Mangano, aka the Executioner, became the head of the family. Mangano (pronounced MAHN-gano) was now Carlo Gambino's boss. Anastasia became the Mangano family's underboss.

Mangano was hand-chosen by Luciano. He was born in Palermo in 1888. At first, his brother Philip was his underboss, but Philip wasn't up to the task—too busy with gambling and broads—and was eventually replaced by Anastasia.

Mangano lived in Red Hook, Brooklyn, and owned the City Democratic Club in Brooklyn. (It had a political-sounding name, but in reality the place was your usual storefront hangout for hoods.)

Like the other original fathers, Mangano still maintained ties with the actual Sicilian Mafia. He came with the Sicilian stamp of approval.

His rackets included booze, dope, and the smuggling of illegal aliens from Italy. He'd been in the U.S. for less than four years, yet here he was, a Boss.

Mangano was aloof, a rich man with clean fingernails, having little or no contact with the sweat and grime of the piers that buttered his considerable bread. He'd made his bones in Sicily and hadn't broken a sweat since. He left the labor and grime to Anastasia.

As for Gambino, he would have to work under Anastasia for twenty-six years before Gambino turned on him. We'll get to that. Hint: It involves a barber chair.

Carlo and Kathryn attended all of the correct events. On September 18, 1932, Gambino attended the wedding of Joe Valachi and Carmela "Mildred" Reina, the daughter of Gaetano Reina. The father of the bride was sadly unable to make it because he'd been whacked on February 26, 1930. Reina was leaving his *goomada*'s (his mistress's) apartment when Vito Genovese himself opened up on his head with a double-barreled shotgun, another casualty of the Castellammarese War.

The Valachi/Reina marriage was a real Mob wedding, with the young couple collecting thick envelopes from the many hoods who attended. The reception was at the Palm Gardens at Fifty-Second Street and Broadway.

While running booze in New England, Gambino had cop trouble. On November 13, 1930, he was pinched in Lawrence, Massachusetts, and charged with forgery. Also arrested at the same time were Joseph Brandino of Brooklyn, Salvatore Cusamano of Revere, Massachusetts, and thirty-six-year-old Frank Tiro of Boston.

A week later, Gambino, Brandino, and Cusamano had their charges dismissed and were released. Tiro was held on two charges of being a fugitive from justice from Bridgeport, Connecticut, and Portland, Maine. Gambino did not stay out of trouble for long.

On Tuesday, December 8, 1930, he traveled to Brockton, Massachusetts. Two of his friends, Peter Vitelo and Salvatore Ross, were in trouble and he was heading north to see what he could do to help.

Vitelo and Ross were part of a coast-to-coast "flim-flam" crew. They were con men, and scheduled to appear in Brockton District Court. Gambino's presence was supposed to be quiet, but it got louder when a Brockton man named Luigi Perichello told police that he recognized Gambino.

"He tricked me out of a thousand dollars two years ago," Perichello told police.

Gambino was subsequently arrested and charged with larceny. He was held on $3,000 bond and scheduled for a court hearing on December 13. Soon thereafter, a fifty-four-year-old Michael Maffeo of Roxbury put up bond for the release of Gambino and Frank Tiro, who was still being held after his arrest in November.

The move came back to haunt Maffeo when he was arrested and charged with a "straw bail" violation (a takeoff on "straw bale," a phrase more common when horses were still used for transportation). The straw-bail law was a city statute that many lawyers were not aware of. It was very old and had not come up in decades. The statute was ignored as it was considered obsolete. Maffeo did not offer cash to pay the bail but rather signed a statement that he owned property valued at $46,000 in Roxbury. It was later ascertained that Maffeo owned no such property. He was charged with perjury. In short, this team of (alleged) con men conned Brockton authorities into releasing two of its members. Maffeo pleaded not guilty and was held on $15,000 bail.

When Gambino got in trouble, legal help swooped in, and he returned with a snap of his fingers to the grueling work of supplying the masses with a gloriously potent product, access to which they were otherwise denied.

On December 8, 1932, Gambino was again arrested, this time in

Brockton, Massachusetts. He was charged (again) with swindling a local man—not Luigi Perichello, but another—out of a thousand dollars in a "handkerchief and pill scheme." He made bail and skipped town. In 1934, he made this charge go away by returning to Brockton and paying back the money.

CHAPTER 4

The Depression Years

WHEN PROHIBITION CAME TO AN END around Christmastime 1933, and Happy Days were there again, most bootlegging operations folded up, their operators moving on to other rackets.

But Gambino saw the repeal of Prohibition as an opportunity. Just because the government was back in the business of taxing alcohol sales, that didn't mean that people wanted to pay that tax.

Gambino figured he could continue selling illegal booze, tax-free, and take advantage of governmental greed. Gambino already had an elaborate bootlegging system in place and instead of dismantling it, he expanded.

Distillery equipment was for sale cheap, and Gambino bought it up. As a front, he purchased companies that used grain alcohol commercially (a varnish manufacturer, for example), and repurposed them.

He also set up a hijacking network and routinely stole whole trucks full of alcohol. Gambino was always careful to make sure the booze he sold contained no wood alcohol—that stuff could kill or blind you—and he saw no future in poisoning his customers. His booze might've left consumers headachy in the morning, but it never killed anyone.

By 1935, Gambino owned all of the illegal booze within a one-hundred-mile radius of New York City. He became a very rich man.

* * *

Mangano began to lean on Gambino, his youthful caporegime. Not that the boss understood it completely, but he knew that everything Gambino touched turned to gold. And when things went wrong and there were unexpected fuckups along the system somewhere, when things shook out, Gambino was always on top. He was a brainy little bastard, Mangano thought.

Gambino was an ambitious guy, but he was always sensible. He must go up the ladder to the top of the Mob world one rung at a time, and he must do it by removing obstacles without making enemies, a task that took finesse, and more than a little patience.

Gambino was confident that Anastasia himself would eventually take out Mangano. Anastasia was rapacious for power, and he had no intention of peaking as underboss. The two men, Mangano and Anastasia, didn't get along and grew to loathe each other. They got into physical fights.

Mangano would get jealous when Anastasia took orders from a boss of another family, which happened anytime the Commission handed down a murder contract to the Murder Inc. boys in Brownsville. Mangano on several occasions attacked Anastasia with his fists before being overpowered and thrashed by his vicious subordinate.

Mangano slunk away from these encounters, outdone by his more vital subservient again. Gambino knew enough to stay as far from these confrontations as possible, and that the situation would work itself out. Eventually, there would be only one man between Gambino and the top spot in the family, and he was fairly certain that person was going to be Anastasia.

In gangland, the 1930s were marked by violence, the Castellammarese War being just one example, which led to Luciano and his brainy pal Meyer Lansky devising the Five Family system. Vincent Mangano, who took over Maranzano's crew, was one of the original Five Fathers.

Power in the city of New York was divided five ways, representing sections of the city and representation from the mafioso cities of

Sicily. Each family had a father and the fathers served on a commission.

In order to whack a made man, you had to get approval from the Commission, and if that permission was granted, an outside organization affiliated with none of the families (Murder Inc.) carried out the kill.

The fact that Gambino remained a bootlegger after Prohibition was repealed wasn't lost on the government. In 1934, a U.S. Treasury Department, Alcohol Tax Unit, report read, "Since the coming of Prohibition, there has been in the City of New York and vicinity and extending into the State of New Jersey a notorious, daring group of bootleggers known as the Gambino outfit. The principal members of this outfit are: Carlo Gambino; his brother Paul Gambino, and their cousin Anthony Gambino."

Gambino's next arrest came on October 8, 1934, when he was charged with evading paying tax on alcohol sales, and for selling booze, wholesale and retail, without a license. While he was in custody, it was realized that he was a fugitive from justice in Massachusetts, having skipped on his bail. He waived extradition and was returned to Brockton. It was at this time that he paid back the money he'd swindled. The Massachusetts charges against him were officially dropped on February 28, 1935.

Gambino's bootlegging ring thrived until the summer of 1936, when 650 gallons of the "cleaned" bootleg alcohol were discovered and seized in a garage at Fourth Avenue and Fifth Street, in the Gowanus section of Brooklyn. The indictments alleged the ring operated a chain of stills and "cleaning stations" to convert denatured alcohol into potable alcohol.

According to Assistant Federal Attorney James D. Saver, the ring was the largest in the country, distributing the bootleg booze to Maryland, New Jersey, Philadelphia, upstate New York, Manhattan, the Bronx, Staten Island, and of course Brooklyn.

The defendants maintained a series of "drops, stills, and cleaning plants" on Long Island, in New Jersey, in Pennsylvania, and in New York from Houston Street northward to Monticello.

The corporation running the bootlegging operation was listed as Lauro Brothers, Inc., 107 Navy. Of those under indictment, the one most associated with Carlo was Joseph Gambino, who listed his address as 2244 Bay Parkway. Others were Paul Masotto, Salvatore Guglielmini, Leo Handler, Sol Mandalari, Julius Caetta, Lea Lovallo, Zealy Gerber, and Frank Lauro.

On the legit side, in December 1936, Gambino and cousin Paul Castellano opened a new family-business venture, the Independent Meat Market on Quentin Road in Brooklyn, north of Marine Park. For decades, Castellano would identify himself to authorities as a "butcher."

In June 1937, Gambino and Morris Jenkins of Chicago were arrested in that city and charged with the attempted hijacking of a tank truck on a Port Richmond railroad siding that was carrying eight thousand gallons of pure grain alcohol. The bust, made by the feds, involved shortwave radio interceptions, Dictaphones, and wiretapping. Though the feds had hoped to round up all the bootlegging big shots, the initial arrests involved only ten rumrunners, and Gambino was among them. The tanker was outright stolen—it was substituted with a near-identical tanker, this one holding legitimately acquired denatured alcohol.

On July 15, 1937, Gambino was indicted by a federal grand jury on bootlegging charges. The feds bragged to the press that they had busted up "the largest bootleg liquor ring operating in the country." Gambino was one of thirty-five men (plus one woman) named in the indictments.

Bench warrants were sworn out immediately by Judge Robert A. Inch for those under indictment. U.S. marshals accompanied by fed agents and armed with the warrants spread out over the tristate area in search of the wanted men and woman, about a quarter of whom were said to live in Brooklyn.

The defendants were charged with a conspiracy to redistill

114,000 gallons of denatured alcohol as whiskey. The estimated tax on such a haul was $300,000, which of course no one had any intention of paying. The indictments also charged the defendants with possession and transportation of tax-unpaid alcohol.

In a ballsy move, Gambino and Morris Jenkins, the man he was arrested with in June, sued the U.S. government. They claimed that when they were busted by fed agents on June 15, the agents confiscated $2,500. Gambino and Jenkins now wanted the money back, and the matter went to U.S. District Court. Judge Oliver B. Dickinson presided at the hearing. He ordered Edward C. Dougherty, supervisor of the Alcohol Tax Unit, to retain possession of the cash until the prosecution of the case was complete.

Also in 1937, twenty-two-year-old Big Paulie Castellano married Carlo's teenage sister-in-law Nina, who was barely pubescent when the two became sweethearts. The marriage was a lasting one, bearing healthy sons who helped with the family businesses.

Big Paulie was born Constantino Paul Castellano. As a boy he built a red "wheel of fortune"—not as fancy but the same idea as the one on the game show—which he called "La Rosa Wheel."

He used it for gambling purposes and reeled in degenerates. Maybe the thing was rigged. Maybe the odds Castellano paid were on the short side. Maybe both. One way or another, cash went from the gamblers' pockets into his.

Like most hoods, he dropped out of school as soon as he could. His dad taught him two skills: one, how to be a butcher; and two, how to run numbers.

In later years, when he oversaw a lot of shit, Big Paulie would be known as a "white-collar" boss, running operations that could be accomplished without soiling one's shirt. This was a guy who would one day place a top heroin dealer on the board of directors of a major grocery store chain. But when he was a kid, Castellano was just another street thug.

He first got in trouble when he was still a teenager. On the Fourth of July 1934, he and two friends charged into a hat store in Hartford, Connecticut, with guns out.

"This is a stickup," Big Paulie said.

They scored fifty-one bucks out of the cashbox. The mini-heist seemed to have gone well, until they learned that someone at the crime scene had jotted down the license plate number on the getaway car, which happened to be Castellano's vehicle.

Cops told Castellano that he could get a light sentence if he named his accomplices. He told the cops to go fuck themselves and ended up spending three months of a one-year bid behind bars.

CHAPTER 5
The Big One, World War II

DURING APRIL 1939, the "Big Alcohol Plot" trial began, with the seating of the ten-person jury, eight women and two men. Federal Judge George A. Welsh presided in a Philadelphia courtroom. There were initially twenty defendants. Three pleaded guilty. Seventeen stood trial.

On May 4, the jury convicted Gambino, along with Philetus Smith, Salvatore Guglielmini, Peter Pillon, Harry Brown, and Aaron Purdue. Two and a half weeks later, Gambino was sentenced to twenty-two months in jail and fined $2,500. His was the harshest of the sentences. Guglielmini, for example, got only eight months and a $250 fine.

Lawyers swooped in and the legal machine was slow. It wasn't until February 1940 that the federal charges against Carlo Gambino were dropped, dismissed by Judge Grover M. Moscowitz. Gambino was represented by Louis J. Castellano—all in the family.

The dismissal, which included all forty-two defendants, came because the evidence that led to the charges was obtained by an illegal wiretap. This was based on a brand-new law. On December 11, 1939, the U.S. Supreme Court ruled that evidence gathered by wiretapping was not admissible in a court of law. (This law has since been amended to allow wiretapping if installed with a warrant from a judge.)

Before the charges against Gambino were dropped, Louis Castellano applied for a review, either by the court or by himself, of the minutes of the grand jury hearings that led to the indictments. To prevent that from happening, fed prosecutor James D. Saver admitted that the evidence against Gambino was obtained exclusively from wiretaps. Hearing that, Castellano moved for dismissal, and got his wish.

Gambino and his lawyer cousin may have thought they were off the hook on the bootlegging front, but the government decided not to give up. In March 1940, Gambino was again indicted, on basically the same charges, but this time reliant on evidence that could be used in court. Of the forty-two people indicted the first time, only ten were indicted this time, but Gambino was one of them.

"These indictments," Saver said, "are based exclusively on sworn testimony of witnesses. The new indictments estimated that approximately one million gallons of denatured alcohol was cleaned of its poisonous ingredients and sold by the bootlegging ring, defrauding the U.S. government of about three million dollars in taxes."

In later years, Gambino got a reputation, at least partially deserved, as a malingerer, a guy who faked illness to avoid legal prosecution. Later, it would be heart trouble that kept him out of court—and jail. This time it was a different body part.

On March 10, 1941, Gambino was scheduled to appear in the federal courtroom of Judge Marcus B. Campbell, a distinguished-looking man with clear, kind eyes and a well-trimmed gray mustache. Gambino and nine others, all underlings, were charged with federal tax evasion.

Assistant U.S. Attorney James D. Saver was a distinguished prosecutor of mobsters, commies, spies, and terrorists. He'd been prosecuting cases out of the Southern District of New York since 1926.

When court was called to order everyone was there—except Gambino. Saver explained to Judge Campbell that Gambino had entered New York Hospital in Manhattan to correct a "kidney condition."

"Your Honor, my information is that he might be hospitalized for upwards of a month," Saver said.

"I believe the defendant has willfully acted to bring about the postponement of this trial," the judge replied. He then forfeited Gambino's $1,000 in bail and rescheduled the start of the trial for May 7.

Gambino was out of the hospital and in court for the May start date. The prosecution demonstrated how Gambino—who was referred to in the newspapers as "Carl"—had used tank trucks to divert untaxed alcohol from a Brooklyn varnish company. He was convicted on all charges. Judge Campbell sentenced him to the identical sentence he'd received the previous year: twenty-two months in the federal penitentiary and a $2,500 fine.

By July 1941, the U.S. government did some recalculation and decided that Gambino owed more in taxes than originally estimated. U.S. Attorney Harold M. Kennedy filed a joint government suit in Brooklyn federal court, claiming that Gambino and six others had failed to pay $1,365,000 in taxes since 1935. The suit added to that figure a 5 percent penalty, and 6 percent annual interest. The six others named in this lawsuit were Carlo's brother Paul Gambino of Bogart Avenue, Bronx; John Petrone of Arthur Avenue, Bronx; Jesse L. Weinberg of Broadway, Manhattan; Leo Lavello of Twenty-Eighth Avenue, Brooklyn, and Sol Clemenko of Linden Boulevard, Brooklyn. The lawsuit was scheduled for a September 3 court date. The case was settled out of court. Gambino coughed up something to the government, details unknown, and then went right back to doing business.

It was during the 1940 Christmas season, as Gambino was approaching the nineteenth anniversary of his illegal entry into the United States, that he was picked up for the first time as an illegal alien.

Justice moved slowly then as now. Eventually, in December 1941, the plans to put Gambino on a boat and send him back to where he came from had to be scuttled. The Japanese bombed Pearl Harbor, the U.S. declared war against the Axis powers, and Italy was enemy territory.

The outbreak of World War II helped Gambino in several ways.

Not only did he get to stay in America, but he also came up with a method to make big-time money off the war. Of course he did.

Many hoods, like Genovese and Lansky and Luciano, even Anastasia, went to bat for their adopted country and helped in various ways with the American war effort. Gambino wasn't like that. All he could think was *ka-ching*!

After serving his twenty-two months at the U.S. Penitentiary in Lewisburg, Pennsylvania, Gambino quit the bootlegging biz and concentrated his efforts on a racket he invented himself.

America was balls deep into the war. And there was worry that it was more than the United States could handle. It was really two huge wars—fighting the Germans and the Japanese at the same time on opposite sides of the world was all-consuming. It put a strain on the usual supply systems.

A nation used to unlimited consumption—if you had the money—now had to deal with shortages, and a rationing system was set up by the U.S. Office of Price Administration, in which each person was allowed to consume only so much, thus assuring there would be enough gasoline, rubber, sugar, groceries, and clothing for beating the Krauts and Japs.

It is hard for us today to understand just how quickly the entire economy of the United States changed. It happened overnight. We went from every man for himself to all for one, that one being the war effort.

In 1942, the government put a price freeze on sugar, coffee, and other everyday grocery items. Money no longer got you as much food as you wanted. Now, money didn't matter—what the fuck was all that about? Now, you needed fucking stamps.

America discovered recycling at this same time. The baldest, flattest rubber tire was now a wanted commodity, to be melted down and repurposed between a military vehicle and the road.

There was a rubber drive. A scrap-metal drive. Abandoned trestles and rail tracks were dismantled for the steel. Women donated their stockings to be repurposed as parachutes. With so many men overseas, those women left the kitchen and went to work.

To run the rationing system, there were eight thousand rationing boards across the country, which gave jobs to thousands of young women left behind when the young men went off to war.

As is true of just about everything the government does, the rationing system was more complicated than it needed to be by half. Some people struggled with the "fair for everybody" concept and didn't understand why they couldn't buy something if they had enough money to do so.

Most people saw rationing as a system that needed to be endured during tough times. Carlo Gambino, on the other hand, saw it as a system that could be exploited. To placate those who wanted "more than their share" of something, he would supply stamps for a price.

At first, Gambino stole his stamps. Heists were pulled off from safes at the Office of Bulk Administration and, when that got hot, at the Office of Price Administration. Here's an example of Gambino's organizational genius: He knew the best safecrackers in the world. He knew second-story men who turned burglary into an art. And he put his very best specialists on the mission to steal rationing stamps. He made millions.

The government, aware of the thefts, altered the system in an anti-Gambino move, and began to store ration stamps in banks. This didn't deter Gambino for long. There was talk of counterfeiting the stamps, but Gambino felt this unnecessary, and prohibitively risky. Instead, he recruited corrupt OPA officials and bought real stamps at discount.

Gambino wisely invested his stamp money in toilet paper, laundries, butchers, and restaurants and nightclubs. His empire grew. He always remained behind the scenes, with others on paper as the owners and operators of the companies—which further diversified into construction, oil, garments, and waste disposal.

By the time America finished kicking ass in Europe and the Pacific, Gambino was a very rich man—even after kicking up to Mangano.

He'd worked a war-specific racket, made a bundle, and gotten away with it.

The war effort was such that no one was available to investigate or prosecute those clever enough to exploit the government's own rationing system. After V-J Day, when the war ended and the rationing system was dismantled, there was no further interest in finding the thief.

When Gambino's name next appeared in the papers, in December 1945, he was described as one of the nation's top gangsters.

As far as we know, after coming to America on the boat, Carlo Gambino only returned to the old country once. That came in 1948. He and his brother Paul used forged passports and sailed on a freighter to Palermo. (He never flew in an airplane and was afraid to do so. This was the only time Gambino visited Italy, but not the only time he left the U.S. In later years, when the Mob was set up in Cuba, Gambino would boat to Havana for meets.)

Carlo and Paul had an audience with Lucky Luciano and other Mob heavyweights. The subject was importing massive quantities of heroin from Europe into the U.S.

"This is going to make us more money than Prohibition," Luciano said.

CHAPTER 6

The Hatter Clips Mangano

IT SEEMED AS IF GAMBINO'S POWER GREW with each gangland-style rubout, a quick montage of drive-by shootings in a smoky film noir, and many of those strategic hits were carried out by Albert Anastasia himself. It is doubtful if Anastasia worried about Gambino's growing power due to the men he himself was killing. Those kills helped Anastasia, too, and he may have thought no further. Killing was easy. Point Anastasia and shoot. Anastasia could assign his Brownsville, Brooklyn, crew to hit anyone he wanted but often chose to do it himself, because he found killing pleasant.

Mangano was the Boss of the family, Joe Adonis the underboss, but it was his most powerful capo, Anastasia, who conspicuously wielded power. Anastasia was the man who ran the Brooklyn waterfront, skimming off everything that came into or left the country via the Port of Brooklyn. Everybody paid tribute to Mangano, of course, but Mangano never had much of a boots-on-the-ground presence in any of the rackets that buttered his bread.

And Anastasia knew the hotline number to Midnight Rose's back room where the boys from Murder Inc. were playing cards and waiting for a job, much like firemen. The club was elite and there were as many Jews as Italians working there: Kid Twist, Buggsy Goldstein, Tick Tock Tannenbaum, Pittsburgh Phil (who'd never actually been to Pittsburgh), Blue Jaw Magoon. They had strong stomachs, those guys. Instead of putting out fires they made guys disappear. And the Murder Inc. boys couldn't sleep upstairs because Midnight Rose ran a roster of girls up there.

During World War II, while Anastasia was keeping saboteurs and men of questionable allegiance off the docks of New York, Mangano was also doing his part to assist the Allied effort. He had an import-export business and used that framework to become the Army's number one liaison between the American and Italian Mafias.

Gambino, on the other hand, did not consider himself an American patriot. He was mafioso, and to tap off of a big-time pipeline was to live.

Mangano's resilience within the legal system was impressive. He'd been arrested for manslaughter, thuggery, and gun charges, and never broke stride. Within his crime family, though, he wasn't as bulletproof. Among this godfather's children were monsters who would bite the heads off babies. He didn't fear them enough. That was his fatal flaw.

Mangano, to the day he died, gave his address as on President Street, Red Hook, Brooklyn—although for many of those years he resided in a Florida mansion. Then in 1951, Mangano vanished. What happened to him was considered a mystery.

There was no mystery at my house when I was a kid. My dad knew just what happened to Mangano, firsthand information. Anastasia was a man as cold as they come, and capo was never the title he had in mind for himself. Even underboss didn't cut it. There was only one title he cared about: Boss. Anastasia reportedly doctored a tape recording and took it to the Commission to get permission to have Mangano bumped off. The Commission believed Anastasia's evidence to be real and assigned Vincent Squillante to hit Mangano. This was the kind of treachery that the Commission later took into consideration when it was the Mad Hatter's turn.

It happened five years before I was born, but years later, my Uncle Joe told me the story of Mangano's death, one that he'd been an eyewitness to. He said that Albert and Vincent could never get along, argued about everything. Albert heard that Vincent was going to have him killed, and so killed Vincent first.

"Albert did the right thing," Uncle Joe said, "he got the okay from Frank Costello and Lucky Luciano. He had to get word to Lucky in Italy, and Lucky sent back his blessing. Looch said Mangano was not whacking up to him like the old days so fuck him.

"Albert set up a meet with Vincent on Columbia Street at a warehouse." The location was on Red Hook's main drag.

Uncle Joe said, "Vincent was to pick up some gambling money that Albert was whacking up to Vincent. 'That's not the only thing getting whacked,' Albert said."

It was April 18, 1951. Uncle Joe said there was no chitchat, no dramatic dialogue. Albert shot Vincent as soon as he walked into the warehouse. Vincent had a smile on his face and his arms outstretched when Albert shot him.

"He was taken out to sea, gutted, and fitted with concrete shoes. He looked like the fucking mummy," Uncle Joe said.

With Mangano dead, Anastasia became Boss. Gambino became underboss, which he called *substituto*. Now there was only one man between Gambino and a seat at the Commission table: the Mad Hatter, Albert Anastasia.

They never found Vincent Mangano. Not so the body of his brother Philip. At ten o'clock in the morning on April 19, 1951, the day after Anastasia iced Vince, a Brooklyn fishing boat owner and operator named Mrs. Mary Gooch was on her way to work. Running late, she took a shortcut across the Bergen Beach marshes. She feared going that way. During the spring of 1949 she'd discovered a body in those marshes, and on this day her worst nightmare came true. It happened again. Partially hidden in a clump of weeds was the prone body of a man naked from the waist down, bare-ass dead.

Mrs. Gooch didn't stick around. Carrying her shoes in one hand for improved speed, she ran as fast as she could to her marina where she called the police. When cops came, they discovered that the man was wearing a huge diamond ring on his pinky and had three holes in him, one in his neck and two in the face, later determined to have been caused by .45-caliber bullets. (Like Albert Anastasia and his Chicago fedoras, the missing trousers were just theater, to make it look like a sex crime.)

The stiff was ID'd as fifty-one-year-old Philip Mangano, a "laundry-owner." His cover, in addition to folding shirts, was that he was the treasurer for a Brooklyn ship-painting company, a place where he'd never reported to work.

It was big news because he was the brother of the boss, but Philip Mangano was well past his prime and had seen his day. He wasn't a fella, good or otherwise, that people thought about much anymore.

Years earlier, he'd briefly been underboss of his brother's family, but he lacked the right stuff for the role. Still, if Anastasia wanted to ascend to the top, taking out both Mangano brothers was the safest bet.

Back in the old days, Philip had been an enforcer and when Vince told him to hurt people he went out and did it. Now, however, he was a man defined mostly by his weaknesses: women, casinos, the fights, and horses.

Philip liked his women stacked and affectionate. He liked his gambling parlors exotic, airless, and without humor. Basements were best. He frequented those in Lower Manhattan, in particular an after-hours scene out of the wicked Far East beneath a Chinese restaurant on Mott Street.

According to one street snitch, Philip had just come down a staircase lit in only blue light and had been on his way to see his bookie when he was corralled by a couple of guys who led him by the elbows into an impatiently waiting car.

It was a world where getting into trouble was so fucking easy. In addition to his no-show job, he was a card-carrying member of the joint his brother built, the City Democratic Club in Red Hook.

Vince Mangano's degenerate brother had a record of eight arrests including a murder charge—the murder being that of a Manhattan bootlegger in 1923—which was dismissed. Also on Philip's résumé: he worked a hitch as Frankie Yale's bodyguard.

With the Manganos out of the picture, Joe Adonis was boss, Albert Anastasia underboss, and Carlo Gambino had moved up to caporegime, third in command. Movin' on up! The promotion was tempered by health issues, as Gambino at this time was first diagnosed with heart disease.

Gambino was very different from the two men who outranked him. He was brains. They were brawn. They were men of action and deadly dangerous. Adonis liked two things, hurting people and looking in the mirror—which was why he named himself Adonis, an homage to his beauty.

Anastasia only liked hurting people. The mirror, not so much.

Gambino was neither vain nor physically vicious. He was a schemer, and he constructed plots that caused his enemies to eat their own.

As it turned out, Joe Adonis was the only one of Gambino's bosses to die a natural death. He'd taken himself out of the pecking order by moving to New Jersey, and then was removed entirely when the government deported him to Italy in 1956, and everyone moved up another spot, Anastasia as boss and Gambino as underboss.

And that was the way it stayed until one day when Anastasia needed a shave and a haircut.

CHAPTER 7
The Death of Albert Anastasia

WHEN GAMBINO DECIDED that it was time for Anastasia to go, he went about it in the accepted fashion. He took his case to the Commission. He met with Vito Genovese and gave him a list of reasons why the Mad Hatter needed to be taken off:

1) He was moving in on the turf of other families.
2) He allowed Frank Scalise to sell buttons before Scalise's death in 1957.
3) He may have been selling buttons himself.
4) Anastasia wanted to strike back after the shootings of Scalise and Frank Costello, acts that could start an all-out war, a battle of attrition, the kind of war that the Five Family system was designed to prevent.

There was also an incident that troubled the Commission. Anastasia got on the Commission's shit list when he shot a man named Arnold Shuster after Shuster ratted on the legendary bank robber Willie Sutton. The hit was not Commission sanctioned, involved an outsider, and was done purely at Anastasia's whim—he didn't like squealers.

Genovese listened to Gambino's summary of the situation, nodded, and listened some more. It turned out that Genovese had a list of his own why Anastasia needed to go. Albert was trying to move in on the casinos in Havana, Cuba, that were being run by Miami Boss Santo Trafficante. Trafficante had complained about the intrusion to Lucky Luciano, who relayed the message to Genovese, who knew that Gambino would move on up if Anastasia were hit, an eventuality that pleased both men.

Murder Inc. was gone, some of them sizzling in Ol' Sparky, but the idea behind it, that Commission-sanctioned hits should be carried out by gunmen who were not personally involved in the beef, lived on. So, the hit was given to another boss, the Olive Oil King himself, Joseph Profaci. He said he knew a crew that was perfect.

During the early autumn of 1957, the FBI was going after Anastasia with renewed vigor, and the fear was that Albert was in such big trouble that he was a candidate to flip. Even if he didn't flip, the fact that law enforcement seemed on the verge of nabbing him for good was troubling. He was showing up in headlines, which was bad for business.

On October 26, 1957, a special agent of the FBI called Gambino on the phone and asked him to volunteer to be interviewed. Gambino said no. He had other business. Even before Gambino came to the Commission with his reasons to kill Anastasia, the Commission had reportedly urged Anastasia, who was one of them, to make like Costello and retire.

The commissioners were wealthy men, and it seemed that with each scandal Anastasia caused with his impulsiveness, Treasury agents were menacing their accountants, scrutinizing their books, and pretty soon "everybody knows our business."

They were fed up with unwanted headlines and with a man whose name had become in America synonymous with brutal gangland violence. He who lives by the gun dies by the gun.

Profaci assigned the hit to the President Street Boys.

Like all hoods, the Gallo brothers had to start at the bottom and work their way up. Their first assignments were small street crimes. But they were ruthless and efficient, so they were quickly promoted to a more important role as Profaci muscle. They roughed up victims under the regime of Francesco "Frankie Shots" Abbatemarco, who ran the family's million-dollar-a-year numbers racket.

You had to have balls of steel to keep from being eaten alive by the streets during those wild days. Luckily, the Gallo brothers had them. Whoever Profaci wanted hurt, the Gallos hurt. Legs were busted. Heads were busted. Whatever. The Old Man says you should shape up. The Old Man was Profaci, who came to trust the Gallo brothers to be as violent as necessary without fucking up, and that was why he assigned them the hit on Anastasia.

The hit team would consist of Joey and Larry Gallo, a young street hood from Red Hook named Carmine Persico (himself on the passing lane toward the top), and Larry's number one gunman, Joe "Jelly" Gioielli.

The first task was to find out where and when Anastasia would be vulnerable. To accomplish that, the boys grabbed Anastasia's bodyguard and took him to President Street in Red Hook where the situation could be explained to him.

Before I can tell you about how the President Street Boys found out the when and where, I need to tell you about Cleo, the pet lion that lived in the basement of Armando "Mondo" Illiano's club on the block. Mondo's cousin Punchy lived in my mom's building when she was growing up.

Joey Gallo knew a guy named Tony who sold exotic animals—weird animals that normal people didn't keep as pets. The guy liked to play the horses and knew Joey through the bookmaking operation.

The first animal Joey bought from Tony was a monkey. But the monkey threw his shit around. Joey was going to shoot the monkey but ended up calling Tony to take the little shit-thrower back.

"What else you got?" Joey asked.

"A lion cub named Cleo."

Joey's eyes lit up. He had the soul of an extortionist and knew that a lion could be a tremendous persuader. The lion moved into Mondo's basement. It was little at first—but it had big, big paws. She grew and grew and grew.

Everyone today claims to have seen the lion in person. In reality, the only guys who got to see the lion were crew members and the poor jerks who owed them money. One guy who we know saw Cleo in person was Albert Anastasia's bodyguard, Anthony "Coppy" Coppola.

Joey and Larry Gallo snatched Coppy and took him to President Street.

"We need you to do something," Larry said.

The beads of sweat were popping out on his forehead. "Look, Larry, what's this all about?"

They showed the lion to Coppy.

"What the fuck was that?"

"We need to know your boss's schedule."

"The man has a routine," Coppy said.

Coppy was released unharmed, and the boys knew exactly when and where they could find Albert Anastasia.

After giving Coppy a head start, Carmine Persico, Joey and Larry Gallo, and Joe Jelly caught the subway at Carroll Street. It was called the RR train back then, the Broadway local. On the train they stood, held on to a leather strap, and cursed out Walter O'Malley, who'd just announced he was moving the Dodgers out of Brooklyn.

At 10:15 a.m., Friday, October 25, 1957, fifty-three-year-old Albert Anastasia entered Grasso's Barbershop off the lobby of the Park-Sheraton Hotel at Seventh Avenue and Fifty-Fifth Street in the city.

Anastasia had just left the hotel lobby where he'd been chatting with a boxer who was fighting at Madison Square Garden that night. With Anastasia as they entered the barbershop was his godson Vincent Squillante, Long Island trash czar. Owner Arthur Grasso was also head barber, and Grasso himself always made sure to take care of Anastasia.

The Mad Hatter was a creature of habit. When in a bar, he always sat on the same barstool, and when getting a haircut he sat in Grasso's chair number two.

At 10:18 a.m., four men in business suits, each wearing a black glove on their right hand, a scarf, a fedora, and aviator shades arrived at the hotel, which was kitty-corner across the street from Carnegie Hall. Outside, Manhattan was teeming.

One of the men (Larry Gallo) stood near the Fifty-Fifth Street entrance, one stood in the lobby just outside the barbershop, and two entered the shop with guns in their gloved hands. As the hit men entered, they didn't start firing right away. They were too cool for that. Anastasia's face was wrapped in a hot towel. He wasn't going anywhere.

One of the gunmen used the muzzle of his gun to gently push Grasso out of the way. The shooters took up positions on either side of Anastasia's chair.

Anastasia now sensed the interruption, ripped the towel off his face, and reacted. Looking into the mirror, he went out swinging, but at the reflection of the gunmen. He then raised his left hand and two bullets tore through his palm. The shooters got in close. There were powder burns on Anastasia's hand.

The gunmen fired ten shots, each saving one bullet in case it was needed during the getaway. Anastasia was shot three times in the head, once in the hip, and twice in the hands. Four bullets missed their target.

Weighed down by lead, Anastasia dropped to the floor and settled on his back between barber chairs two and three. In chair number three was Squillante, but neither gunman paid any attention to him. The garbage czar was frozen with fear. The barbershop now reeked of a combination of gunpowder and hair tonic. There was a moment of silence as Anastasia lay still. Then the manicurist screamed and slumped over in a faint.

On swift, well-polished shoes, the hit team retreated into the lobby, and then to the street. They were once again a quartet. Three of them hopped eagerly into an American-made car that tore down

West Fifty-Fifth Street at urgent speed. The fourth walked briskly north two blocks and ducked into a nearby subway, the downtown BMT to Brooklyn. We know because he stashed his gun in a garbage can down there.

Virginia Nelson—the redheaded owner of The Red-Headed Woman, a hotel dress shop—was first to call police.

Squillante snapped out of his paralyzing terror and dashed out, vanishing into the Manhattan tumult by the time police arrived.

Next to Grasso's was a flower shop owned by Constantine Alexis, who said he heard about six shots in three flurries: one shot, pause, two shots, pause, three more shots. There were more, of course, but sometimes the gunmen fired simultaneously.

"I ran into the barber shop and saw the body on the floor," the florist recalled.

"Did you recognize the victim?" an investigator asked.

"Oh sure," Alexis said. "I knew him because he used to buy flowers."

Alexis saw a weird scene. Things were still frozen. Those unable to flee, including Arthur Grasso, looked like losers in a game of freeze tag.

"It seemed as if everyone in the shop were unable to do so much as blink," the florist later said.

"How many shooters?"

"I saw five or six men run out of the hotel," he replied. "Some went out the Seventh Avenue exit, and others ran out the Fifty-Fifth Street exit."

Investigators soon realized that not all of the running men were gunmen.

"One of the fleeing men still had shaving cream on his face," the florist said.

Along the same corridor that led to the barbershop was a luggage shop owned by Joseph March, who was entering the hotel and ran into several men running out.

"One running man stumbled and fell to the floor on his back.

While he was down he screamed, 'They're going crazy in there! They're shooting!'" March recalled.

Cops questioned Grasso: "Describe the shooters?"

"Nah, faces covered."

"Anything unusual about them?"

"Yeah, they were both wearing one black glove—on their shooting hand. One five-five, one five-seven."

There were many newspapers in New York back then—morning, afternoon, and evening editions. And competition among them was intense. So, when word of the barbershop assassination hit the wires, there was a rush on the location. Within minutes of the shooting, a crumpled and jabbering pride of press, reporters and photographers, barged into the shop to observe and photograph the body. The photographers' flashbulbs back then were literally explosive and strobe-lit the scene, memorializing the carnage and intensifying the lingering scent of gunpowder.

One detective just arriving said, "Witnesses?"

"Yes, sir," a uniformed cop replied. "Two customers, five barbers, a manicurist, and a couple of bootblacks."

"What did they see?"

"Might as well be blind, sir."

One witness said the shooters might have been Italian men and everyone laughed.

With Anastasia dead as a doornail, Gambino became boss. Because he had done the right thing and had Commission approval before the shooting, he ran unopposed for the top position.

The first thing Gambino did was rename the family after himself: the Gambino crime family—a name by which it still goes today. The family underwent a dramatic change once someone with brains instead of brawn began calling the shots. The Gambinos would now be involved in the infiltration of legitimate business.

"We no longer skim. We control," Gambino said. "We run the company, *capisce*?"

Gambino took to being boss like a fish to water. He loved to hold court and made a point of meeting in person all the new members of the crime family that now bore his name.

He spoke in allegories, especially to young recruits, to whom he dished out wisdom.

"You must be like a lion and a fox," he would say. "The lion frightens the wolves; the fox recognizes traps."

CHAPTER 8
Apalachin

IN THE 1950S, Apalachin, New York, was not a village. It wasn't much of nothing. You could drive through it and never even realize you missed it, a zero-traffic-light town. Two hundred and seventy-seven people lived there, wherever "there" was. There was no downtown—just a dusting of homes in a hilly rural area.

No, it wasn't a village, or a hamlet, or a town. It was technically a "census-designated place" on Route 17 along the Susquehanna River, about fifteen miles east of Binghamton, due south of Syracuse, and not far from the New York State/Pennsylvania border.

The census had designated it totally within the Town of Owego in Tioga County, named after the nearby Apalachin Creek. The word "Apalachin" is Native American for "from where the messenger returned." The area is best known, of course, for that thing that happened there in 1957.

Less than three weeks after Albert Anastasia had his last shave, on November 14, 1957, there came to a 150-acre hilltop estate in Apalachin a big sit-down, a convention of more than a hundred upper echelon wiseguys.

These were not just guys from New York City. Delegates gathered from around the country. Guys were there from Buffalo, Chicago, L.A., Texas, Louisiana, Florida—even from Puerto Rico.

So many black Cadillacs and Lincolns! A few limos chartered

from the city. In that rural area, the hoods looked about as out of place as a bow tie at a biker rally. They wore silk suits and shiny, shiny shoes. They smoked expensive cigars, hand-rolled in Havana. Their struts were menacing.

In sparsely populated areas, cops know every car. The Barbara estate, home of a soft drink mogul, had a reputation as a busy place, with a lot of comings and goings, but the parade of Italian gangsters was glaringly obvious.

The cover story was that there was going to be a "barbecue" in "Mr. Canada Dry" Joseph Barbara's landscaped backyard. Barbara, in addition to being a major bottler, was a capo for Stefano Magaddino in Buffalo, and good friends with Joe Bonanno and the boys from Castellammare.

Vito Genovese was all smiles and puffed-out chest as he headed north to the big meet. He thought that, with Anastasia gone and little Carlo Gambino destined to take his place, his own position on the dais would be strengthened, one step closer to Boss of Bosses, which was Genovese's dream. But that isn't the way it worked out. For one thing, Carlo Gambino's diminutive stature and mild manner were poor indicators of his dangerous nature. For another, the party that Genovese thought was going to be his coronation turned out to be a disaster.

On the way up from Brooklyn, Carlo Gambino rode in the back seat of a limo. There were four others in the car: brother-in-law and first cousin Paul Castellano; soldier Salvatore "Charlie" Chiri; Frank Cucchiara (from Boston, importer of cheese and dope, aka Frank Caruso, Frank Russo, and Frank the Spoon); caporegime Carmine "the Doctor" Lombardozzi; and Joseph "Staten Island Joe" Riccobono, an old-time hood who used to break legs for Louis "Lepke" Buchalter in the garment district back in the day.

There might actually have been a barbecue, but the real purpose of the meet was to evaluate the state of the system as set up by the great Luciano. With Anastasia's elimination, there was fear that chaos would reign—very bad for business. There was also the matter of Anastasia's power and turf—would it stay in his family, as Gambino hoped, or be divvied up, as per the wants of the others.

Genovese, as mentioned, thought he'd be named Boss of Bosses. Gambino expected that he would formally be named Boss of the old Mangano family and be given a chair at the Commission table.

There was also a plan to talk about removing the stigma of selling dope. It was supposed to be forbidden, and was for those who weren't sanctioned sellers, but it was too lucrative. Opening up the nasty business would increase earnings. There were millions to be made selling dope, and as long as the junk wasn't being sold to Italian boys and girls, who really cared about the damage babonia could do to a community?

This was not the first time Barbara's estate was used for a big-time sit-down. There had been a handful of meets at the location, including one just a year earlier. Because of Barbara's standing in the community, the earlier powwows came and went without fuss. Barbara claimed that he had the local cops in his hip pocket. Considering what happened, that must have been an exaggeration. Perhaps he'd forgotten his quarterly donation to the Police Athletic League or something.

The New York State police officer who led the 1957 Apalachin bust, Sergeant Edgar Croswell, later testified how he got wise to what was happening, and it had nothing to do with failure to pay bribes. He said he'd happened to be in the lobby of a local motel when he saw Barbara's son renting three rooms in advance, without knowing exactly who was going to be staying in each room.

The ever-observant Sergeant Croswell had been aware of possible criminal activities at the Barbara estate since the previous year. So, the choice to use the location for a huge Mob convention was a mistake—to say the least.

With the meet now underway, and all of those luxury cars parked on the Barbara grounds, Croswell called for backup. In minutes, cops had the place surrounded. They watched through binoculars and jotted down license plate numbers.

There have been those who've suspected that, considering the number of hoods who didn't show up at Apalachin—Meyer Lansky, Carlos Marcello of New Orleans, Frank Costello, for example—and the perceived omniscience of Carlo Gambino, that the fix was in at Apalachin.

The theory goes that Croswell's stories about being a great detective were bullshit. He hadn't heard shit in the lobby of no motel and was blind to the sudden influx of luxury automobiles on the area's roads.

The theory goes that Gambino tipped off the local cops and then went to the meeting anyway to be arrested, that Gambino was desperate that Vito Genovese not become the Boss of Bosses, as this was the role he eventually saw for himself. So, he shit on the birthday cake.

I don't know.

Why take such a hit, get your name in the papers, get fingerprinted and all of that, in a country that wants to deport you, just to govern the rise of another gangster?

It reminds me of the theory that FDR knew in advance about Pearl Harbor but did nothing so as to give America an excuse to enter World War II. It seems like a stupid way to go about it, and neither FDR nor Gambino were stupid.

In the long run, the thing that tipped the power scale in Gambino's favor wasn't the bust at Apalachin but his superior skills at placing good friends in the upper echelons of the other families.

Cops gathered on Route 17. The road was blocked to prevent getaways. When everyone was in place, they raided the joint.

Picture the scene: All of these tough guys, powerful men, puffing out their chests, then suddenly dropping their drinks on the lawn, chucking their IDs, and hightailing it into the nearby woods, getting mud on their shiny, shiny shoes, tossing their Havana cigars. They ran like escaped prisoners popping out of a tunnel, like degenerates fleeing the busted crap game. That moment has been called the American Mafia's single greatest humiliation.

Luckily for the cops, the hoods couldn't run well or far, and the police had no trouble netting most of them and hauling them into their suddenly overcrowded police station.

Fifty arrests were made. Among those netted in the raid were Joseph Bonanno, Joseph Profaci, Jerry Catena, Vincent Rao, and Vito Genovese. What a haul. Carlo Gambino and Paul Castellano didn't run. They sat quietly and waited to be arrested, another move that fed the rumor mill.

Now, Joe Bonanno is a lying liar and there's not much reason to believe anything he wrote in his memoirs, but he does have an interesting take on the Commission. As no other commissioner has ever publicly talked about that coveted table of men, it's interesting what he has to say. He said that Gambino replacing Anastasia at the table had, like it was the Supreme Court or something, thrown the Commission to the left of center, with Gambino, Lucchese, and Genovese forming the liberal wing of the Commission, while Bonanno, Profaci, and Magaddino were on the conservative side.

I'm not an expert on politics. Nothing the Mob did ever struck me as particularly liberal. I guess this had to do with which crimes the family was willing to commit, drugs and sex work being the most controversial.

And it probably had more to do with the purity of the bloodline. Remember, these guys didn't just feel that only Sicilians mattered, they believed that only Sicilians *from their hometown* mattered. If that was the criteria, then the Gallo crew of President Street, Red Hook, must've been considered ultraradical. The Gallos ran with Greeks and Arabs and even a midget.

Bonanno's view of the Gallos was simple: They were children rebelling against their father and for that they needed to be punished and taught a lesson. The President Street Boys reached out to Gambino for support in their civil war against Profaci, and Gambino pissed Profaci off by giving them an audience.

It was against the rules for one father to take the side of another father's children. That's probably the conservative thinking Bonanno was talking about. Point is, Bonanno claimed to be worried about the political balance of the Commission as he rode to Apalachin. He was but one of several hoods who believed they had a shot at coming out of the conclave on top.

As Gambino was arrested at the Barbara estate, he gazed upon the raiding policemen with kind eyes and a small smile. It was as if he couldn't believe what he was seeing but was amused by it. He allowed himself to be led into a waiting squad car and taken to a place where he was interrogated.

"Name?"

"Carlo Gambino. You will have to excuse my English."

"That's all right. Address."

He gave the address of his Ocean Parkway home.

"Your occupation?"

"I am a labor relations consultant."

"I'm not sure what that is . . ."

"I am a middleman, between labor and management, smoothing wrinkles, preventing what might disrupt business. Excuse me, I cannot speak without my hands."

The smile got a little bigger.

The police investigated Gambino's story—and it checked out. That was exactly what he did on the waterfront. Police found Gambino was also associated with a high-priced law firm headquartered in Midtown.

On November 15, the day after the bust, the New York State Police issued a list of the men who had attended the Apalachin meeting. Gambino, now fifty-five years old, was on the list, his occupation listed as "works in labor relations."

A wire service reporter said that he couldn't vouch for what

Gambino did along the Red Hook piers, but he did learn that years earlier the distinguished-looking little man had been busted both for operating a still and grand larceny.

The scribe also found it interesting that the only other attendee busted at Apalachin who included "labor" in his occupation was James DeLuca, secretary of Local 66, Hotel and Restaurant Workers Union in Buffalo.

The background checks on the Apalachin crew revealed a concentration of interest in the waterfront and in construction. Several of those picked up were already the subject of a Senate or other federal probe.

For law enforcement, the Apalachin raid was a catalyst for interagency cooperation, as it was in everyone's interest to pool their knowledge, so the FBI, the New York State Police, local cops, and the NYPD were all making nice.

Even if they wouldn't be able to hold these guys for long, they took the opportunity to gather information used to fill in the blanks regarding how the Mob worked.

The others picked up at Apalachin were:

- Anthony F. "Guy" Guarnieri, forty-seven years old, dress factory operator
- Pasquale "Patsy" Turrigiano, fifty-one years old, a grocery clerk who'd been arrested in 1950 for operating a still
- Ignatius Cannone, thirty-two, restaurateur
- Bartolo Guccia, sixty-six, operated a small fish store
- Joseph Barbara, Jr., twenty-one, son of the host
- Emmanuel Zicardi, fifty-seven, show worker
- Simone Scozzari, fifty-seven, an illegal alien who listed his home as Palermo, Italy
- Frank Zito, sixty-four, no occupation listed
- Costenze P. Valenti, thirty-one, a wholesale greengrocer from Rochester, New York
- Louis A. LaRasso, thirty-one, construction worker

- Carmine Lombardozzi, aka Alberto, aka King of Wall Street, aka the Italian Meyer Lansky, forty-four, Gambino's "stocks and bonds guy" who maintained "trade offices" in Brooklyn
- Frank Majuri, forty-seven, construction worker
- Michele A. Miranda, sixty-one, auto salesman
- James Osticco, forty-four, transportation manager
- Joseph Cirello, a food and liquor importer from Dallas, Texas
- Frank DeSimone, forty-eight, attorney
- Joseph Bonanno, fifty-two, listed as "retired"
- John Bonventre, fifty-four, salesman from Brooklyn
- James Colletti, sixty
- Charles Chiri, fifty-nine
- Paul C. Castellano, a familiar face listed by the feds as a forty-five-year-old Brooklyn butcher
- Russell Bufalino, fifty-four, "curtain salesman"
- Gerardo V. Catena, fifty-seven, vending sales company owner
- Dominick Olivetto, fifty, from Camden, New Jersey
- Joseph Ida, auto garage owner
- Joseph Profaci, sixty, Brooklyn, owner of an olive oil distributing firm
- Joseph Magliocco, fifty-nine, Long Island
- Salvatore Falcone, of Utica
- Angelo Sciandra, thirty-three, orchestra leader from Pennsylvania
- Patsy Sciortino, forty-two, manufacturer of bleach for dry cleaners
- Rosario Mancuso, fifty, concrete business
- Sal Monachino, sixty-three, beer distributor
- Patsy Monachino, fifty, operates beverage company
- Salvatore Tornabe, sixty-one, beer salesman
- Joseph Rosato, fifty-three
- Louis Santo (real name Santo Trafficante), forty-two, operator of the Sans Souci nightclub in Havana, Cuba
- Anthony P. Riala, sixty-one, New Jersey motel owner

- John Scalish, forty-five, Cleveland cigarette distributor
- John A. DeMarco, fifty-four, real estate
- Frank Cucchiara, sixty-two, cheese manufacturer
- Natale J. Evola, fifty, garment delivery business
- Michael J. Genovese, thirty-eight, operated car wash business
- Gabriel "Kelly" Mannarino, forty-two, owned junkyard
- Vincent Rao, fifty-nine, real estate
- Armand Rava, forty-six, owned restaurant
- Joseph Riccobono, fifty-three
- And lastly. the host of the meeting, Joseph Barbara, Sr., fifty-one, soft drink manufacturer.

Bonanno was found hiding in a cornfield. The onetime kid sent to America to run things there for his old man, to be paterfamilias of a crime organization that would one day bear his name, was deeply embarrassed by the arrest. His ruddy complexion was downright puce, and he was panting like a hound in the heat.

There were probably more, but two men who successfully escaped into the woods were Sam "Momo" Giancana, Chicago boss, and Carmine "Lilo" Galante, who despite having a cigar lit from the time he was thirteen, still had the lungs to dash into the woods and disappear.

Invitees who didn't show up at all included Frank Costello, who only months earlier bought a permanent part in his hair from a bullet fired by Vincent "the Chin" Gigante; Meyer Lansky, the biggest all-time Jewish gangster; and Carlos Marcello, New Orleans and eastern Texas boss.

The stories the hoods told the cops were all over the place. Carmine Lombardozzi told police that he drove Carlo Gambino to the meeting because he and the host, Barbara, shared a heart problem and wanted to discuss surgeries and other treatments.

But most of them agreed on one thing: Their decision to drop in on Joseph Barbara was spontaneous, and they were surprised and delighted to see that there were other guests on hand as well. A few admitted that there was a planned event, a cookout, some drinks, but denied that it had anything to do with business, legitimate or otherwise.

Meeting for a barbecue was not illegal, so cops didn't hold any of the mobsters for very long. What was accomplished, however, was that a roster of the Mob's upper echelon was now written down, a list of names that future U.S. Attorney General Robert F. Kennedy would use as a guideline to fight the Mob. (Plus, when the RICO laws were put in place years later, the knowledge that the gangs worked together and that there was a so-called Commission enabled the Department of Justice to broaden the scope of its conspiracy prosecutions.)

The Bosses of four out of the five New York City families were busted at Apalachin—Gambino, Genovese, Profaci, and Bonanno—but authorities didn't know what they had. Of the five NYC Bosses, only Lucchese, in the hospital at the time, didn't attend.

The feds, of course, desperately wanted an excuse to imprison all the goodfellas at Apalachin, but it wasn't easy. The best they could do was bust guys for "refusing to answer questions." Both Castellano and Lombardozzi were arrested for this. Castellano did a year behind bars for keeping his mouth shut about why he was at Apalachin.

Gambino, on the other hand, walked free. As per his usual style, he clutched his chest and threatened to have a heart attack, and the feds let him go. But he would never again be able to move about without an FBI shadow.

Genovese was hurt most by the Apalachin raid. In his mind, the presumed purpose of the meeting was to abolish the old system and to proclaim himself king of the underworld. And the whole thing had been horribly botched. His stock plummeted.

The damage done to the Mob in Apalachin couldn't be measured in jail time. One of the things the Mob had going for it was that it really was organized, yet law enforcement didn't know how it worked. Now they had a roster, and that would go a long way toward figuring out the infrastructure.

All invitees to the party were Sicilian. Eleven of those picked up in the raid ended up appearing before grand juries. I don't know who did the counting, but it is said that, combined, the hoods testifying for the grand jury hid behind their Fifth Amendment rights 870 times. There would be no self-incrimination.

The guy who drove Gambino to the meeting, Lombardozzi, was the luckiest guy in Apalachin: On the agenda was a vote to determine whether Lombardozzi should live or die. He knew something was up when they asked him to wait in Barbara's garage while his ears burned. The guy had been short on the tribute, but Gambino came to his defense, saying he was an earner, and he had skills that weren't easy to replace. The guy could work Wall Street. He stole stocks, bonds, and securities—much as Don Carlo had stolen ration stamps during World War II. He also earned by selling shares in worthless stocks. Abandoned gold mines were a specialty, allegedly making three million bucks in this manner. When the conversation about Lombardozzi was over, it was decided that his life would be spared, but he was ordered to bump up ten grand. It wasn't the last time Lombardozzi would be on the carpet.

The Apalachin meeting had ramifications close to home—my future home, that is. On President Street, in the Red Hook section of Brooklyn, the Gallo crew plotted their own takeover of the world. When the Commission divvied up Anastasia's rackets, Profaci got his share and gave them to his senior officers. The Gallos, who'd worked their balls off for the old man, got squadoosh. Civil war would ensue, which formed the reason my dad became a President Street Boy. Larry Gallo needed a bodyguard and Ricky DiMatteo was a guy who once decked boxing champ Emile Griffith in a bar fight.

Far from my future home, the feds were now focused. They couldn't jail Gambino, but his presence at Apalachin put Don Carlo in the FBI's crosshairs. Whatever happened to those efforts to deport him years ago? Oh yeah, World War II got in the way. Well, Sicily in the late 1950s was no longer enemy territory, and efforts to deport Gambino resumed.

* * *

With the Apalachin meeting a bust, Vito Genovese scheduled another conclave of the Commission at his Greenwich Village headquarters, and, though not as well attended as the upstate fiasco, the agenda was about the same. There were questions to be answered. With Anastasia croaked, what happened next?

Because of new laws—specifically the Narcotics Control Act—the Mob "ban" on selling narcotics would continue. (It is hard to understand a world in which everyone agreed that selling heroin was forbidden yet everyone did it and made tons of money doing it, but sincerity was never a Mob strongpoint.)

Regarding other topics, the Commission decided that they would crack down on nonunion labor. Workers who were not under the Mob's thumb were to be discouraged.

Genovese explained to those who didn't already know, that Anastasia was killed because he was out of control, and was whacking guys for personal reasons, whacking guys sometimes on a whim. Besides, he had been selling buttons and that was something that needed to be stopped.

It was decided that all "members" who had purchased their buttons were hereby ordered to give the buttons back. The books were closed on new members indefinitely until real-versus-bought buttons were sorted out.

Anastasia, Genovese announced, had also been whacked because he had absolute control over the New York waterfront, a lucrative area that needed to be better shared among the families. (That must've made Gambino's smile twitch.)

Anastasia, Genovese said, was also infringing on the territory of other fathers. His moves in Havana were in direct conflict with Santo Trafficante, the Florida boss. Meyer Lansky was down there and he didn't like Anastasia at all.

It isn't hard to imagine what fifty-seven-year-old Carlo Gambino thought as he listened to all of this. As public policy he agreed with it, but in reality he knew much of it was so much bullshit. There was still talk of the taboo of dealing babonia. But, truth was, heroin was going to be sold, and the new head of what was Anastasia's family—that is, himself—was not going to share the waterfront without a fight. One imagines he listened with his usual calm, but inside, the wheels were turning. These were dangerous and powerful men. His schemes now demanded a new depth, a new sophistication, a new viciousness.

That smile would've broadened only slightly when Genovese got to the final item on the agenda. He nominated Carlo Gambino as the new father of Anastasia's family, a mere formality, and from that point on Gambino would be referred to as Don Carlo.

Gambino was unanimously elected. He looked around the table with satisfaction. He had taken the pledge of omertà thirty-seven years before in Palermo, Sicily, and had—without personally dirtying his hands—moved to the top.

As he looked around the table, he saw that he was surrounded by "friends," and those who didn't already owe him allegiance were weaker than he and would soon join the others in subservience.

Gambino gave a small speech thanking his fellow commissioners for the honor. "I now announce my officers," he said quietly in Sicilian. He said that Joseph "Banty" Biondo would be his underboss, Joseph "Staten Island Joe" Riccobono his consigliere, and his brother Paul Gambino and cousin Paul Castellano would be his top captains. No one voiced an objection.

How did Biondo get to be underboss? He'd executed some sensitive missions in his day, and earned his respect. Joseph "Joe the Blond" Biondo, aka Joe Banty, aka Cunniglieddu, who always had on him one of his well-stamped passports. Over the years, Biondo's regular task was to take an attaché case full of cash to Italy and give it to Lucky Luciano.

Biondo was born in Barcellona Pozzo di Gotto. In America, he was one of the OGs, an original gangster—a racketeer, sometimes alongside Gambino, when the family was run by the Manganos and then Albert Anastasia.

One of Biondo's nicknames meant "Little Rabbit." He was five-four, 130 pounds. One of his aliases, Banty, was short for Bantam, as in bantamweight, a weight class in boxing (115 to 118 pounds), and also because he had that rooster way of strutting with his chest puffed out.

He was a bootlegger during Prohibition. When booze again became legal, he moved in on New York City's taxicab union. A cab strike ensued, and cab owners who wouldn't pay their drivers as per Biondo's demand had their vehicles set on fire. From there, Banty went on to be arrested for extortion, guns, drugs, and murder. The murder charge stemmed from a teenage gang fight in which a member of the other gang was killed.

He grew up to be a trusted friend of Luciano and Dutch Schultz and was in on the whacking of Salvatore Maranzano.

(On the negative side, Biondo had a nasty habit of thinking of himself before the family. By 1965 Gambino'd had it with Biondo and told him his days were through. He didn't whack Biondo, though. Instead Biondo was involuntarily retired and replaced by Aniello Dellacroce. Outside the Mob world, Biondo's health deteriorated quickly. He died in 1966 of natural causes and was buried in Maple Grove Cemetery, in Queens.)

CHAPTER 9
The Late Fifties

MONDAY, TUESDAY, HAPPY DAYS. Elvis, Hula-Hoops, bobby socks, opportunistic fear of communists—ah, good times. For Don Carlo, the fifties were nerve-racking times. He could never completely relax. Hearings began anew to deport him in October 1958. An alphabet soup of government organizations were up his ass.

A Narcotics Bureau supervisor testified before the New York State Joint Legislative Committee on January 9, 1958, that "the Gambinos are reported to exercise control of the narcotics smuggling activities between the Mafia element in Palermo and the United States on behalf of Salvatore Luciano."

The FBI concentrated on investigating the way Gambino had invested millions of dollars acquired through illegal rackets into legitimate businesses, including garment, paper, food, and waste management.

The bureau also knew an annoying amount about Gambino's private life, due to the fact that they planted bugs, shadowed him everywhere, and paid off informants inside his private circle. This didn't help Gambino's already swollen trust issue.

The FBI also poked around Gambino's family tree. Just how incestuous was it? One memo referred to the "resulting imbeciles and morons that come from such close intermarriage." The special agent was relieved to find out that Gambino's offspring were just fine. (It also should be noted that modern generations of Gambinos and Castellanos have welcomed fresh blood into the mix and have remained healthy and strong.)

The Gambinos' poor bloodline came up in conversations caught by FBI surveillance, also. Thomas "Tommy Ryan" Eboli was overheard saying he couldn't stand Don Carlo. He said that the Gambino crime family was full of degenerates. Asked what he meant, he said he heard a Gambino soldier was hit for fucking his mother-in-law. I don't know who that was. I never heard that story.

When Carlo and his wife, Kathryn, went on vacation to Miami Beach, Florida, their suite was well bugged, so the feds learned that Carlo won a lot when he went to the track, and she didn't care for "all the Jews" who "drank too much."

The Gambinos, the bug revealed, did not always get along and when they didn't, Don Carlo had a harsh tongue, calling her a shrew. He said she talked too much, and if she didn't shut up, he'd cut off her tongue. The tapes proved that Gambino could, if he needed to, raise his voice.

The revenuers went after Gambino's assets, which didn't jibe with his stated income. Though he lived a middle-class existence, he had millions in cash, jewels, and other valuables stashed in a series of safety-deposit boxes.

Predictably, when Gambino was called to testify on his own behalf, he collapsed and left the courtroom on a stretcher. They took him to Flower Fifth Avenue Hospital, where he remained free on $10,000 bail.

The FBI had heard a rumor that Gambino owned a converted Coast Guard cutter, but when they looked into it, they found Don Carlo's boat was merely a 1958 fifty-five-foot Wheeler Cabin Cruiser. Nice, but not a warship.

The feds knew where every one of Gambino's safety-deposit boxes were, and they even seemed to know what was in them, reporting on stashed jewels and cash. "We believe he could raise ten million dollars on a moment's notice," some special agent penned in his report.

One conversation FBI surveillance picked up was about the upcoming marriage of son Carl, Jr., to Carmela Zuccarello, reception to be held in Manhattan's ultra-tony Plaza Hotel.

The recording featured Carlo and Kathryn Gambino talking to an event planner. The Gambinos were downright chatty when discussing wedding details but clammed up when asked what they apparently considered personal questions.

For example, they needed to be prodded and probed before revealing the last name of the bride. And they never did give the event planner the precise location of the wedding, saying only "Astoria," which is a large neighborhood in northwest Queens.

It is believed by many that Lucky Luciano, by this time in exile in Naples, was a tremendously wealthy man who had the world of organized crime under his command. Yet there is evidence that Luciano was having money problems. A stupid brothel charge had cost him everything: jail, and then after everything he did to help the U.S. Army take Italy from the Nazis, deportation.

He'd spent millions on lawyers trying to stay in the U.S. and had a plan to earn in a new way. In a eureka moment, Looch announced to his colleagues overseas that he was planning to sell the rights to his life story to Hollywood. Dean Martin would play him in a big movie and the money would flow in.

The idea had barely gotten off the ground when Tommy Eboli showed up in Italy with a message from Luciano's childhood buddy Meyer Lansky—and also from Mafia Bosses Gambino, Lucchese, Genovese, and Bonanno.

The message was, "Cut it out." To turn the story of the American Mob into a Hollywood movie struck them as a bad idea. Why put a spotlight on something that remained in the shadows?

Luciano didn't like the idea of anyone telling him what to do, but, bottom line, the movie never got made. It would be another decade before Francis Ford Coppola would adapt a novel by Mario Puzo and make the game-changing film, *The Godfather*.

* * *

It was true that Albert Anastasia had been a miserable fuck without real friends, and when he hit the floor of Grasso's Barbershop, not many grieved. But there were gunmen out there who remained loyal.

Well, there were at least two guys who remained loyal. The first was John "Johnny Roberts" Robilotto, a mortician by trade and a gunman who had worked his way up to captain under Albert Anastasia. Robilotto's funeral parlor was Tozzi Funeral Home on Washington Avenue in Crown Heights, Brooklyn.

Robilotto had been the gunman who, on October 4, 1951, in Joe's Elbow Room Restaurant in Cliffside Park, New Jersey, killed Guarino "Willie" Moretti after Moretti's mental state deteriorated due to advanced syphilis and he became the only gangster to cooperate with the U.S. Senate Select Committee on Organized Crime. Robilotto was arrested for that murder and admitted that he, too, ate at that restaurant, but knew nothing about the hit.

Robilotto either didn't know or didn't care that Anastasia had been hit with Commission approval. He was overheard saying he was going to take out Gambino—maybe just words, maybe just drunk words, but he said them in front of Valachi, who told Gambino, and Robilotto had minutes to live.

On September 7, 1958, Robilotto's body was found sprawled face up in the gutter of Utica Avenue, about a hundred feet south of the Kings Highway service road in the Flatlands section of Brooklyn. He'd been shot four times with a .38.

Police were tipped to the stiff by a phone call at 3:35 a.m. from a pedestrian who said, "There's a man on the ground."

The caller not only supplied the location of the still man but gave cops the license plate number of a car he had seen leave the scene.

The NYPD sent four radio cars, an emergency truck, and a handful of homicide detectives. Identifying the corpse was harder than they'd hoped because the killer had ripped the labels from the dead man's expensive brown suit, and all pockets had been turned inside out and were empty. All Robilotto had on him in death were a pair of eyeglasses, a religious medal, a set of keys, and thirty-two cents in change.

Once they did ID Robilotto, cops knew it was Mob shit and upward of fifty detectives were put on the case. More than one hundred persons, some of them women, were questioned regarding the hit.

They tried to trace the victim's movements before he was shot. As late as three a.m., Robilotto had been in a bar only a block away from the place where his body was found. The precinct took the phone call thirty-five minutes later, so police knew the killing must've taken place between three and three thirty.

The caller remained anonymous, but the numbers he supplied had value. The plate belonged to a Mrs. Mary Russo, thirty years old, of Little Italy. Cops spoke with her and learned that the car that morning had been driven by her husband, Frank Russo, manager of the Alsid Social Club on Coney Island Avenue.

They found Frank Russo, who said that the sedan they were looking for was parked in front of the club, but he didn't know where it was during that morning's early hours because he lent it to a friend.

Cops then chased down the friend, who turned out to be an ex-con who'd done time for armed robbery. He was picked up and taken to the Bedford Avenue police station. The guy admitted to seeing Robilotto alive in the bar, and then again dead by the side of Utica Avenue. Police learned that Robilotto left the bar first and the unnamed man followed about twenty minutes later.

"I seen Robilotto sprawled on the ground, got out and looked at the body," the witness said.

"Why didn't you summon help?"

"He was dead. What good would it do?"

"That's it?"

"And also, I didn't want to get involved."

"Okay, what did you do next?"

"I got back in the borrowed car and drove away."

Police checked the car in question and found no traces of blood. Police did some research into the victim and found that he'd been living on St. Marks Avenue in Brooklyn, but the superintendent at that address denied knowing him.

Robilotto had an estranged wife named Estelle who lived on Park Avenue in Manhattan, and a brother named Benjamin who lived in Greenwich Village, in an apartment where the mortician sometimes stayed.

Behind closed doors, police suspected that Robilotto may have been hit as residue of the Anastasia hit, which as far as police theories goes was on the money.

Gambino still wasn't quite in the clear. Robilotto wasn't the only gunman who wanted to avenge the hit on Anastasia. The other was one of Robilotto's henchmen, Armand "Tommy" Rava—and he was still out there.

Rava was born in 1911, raised in Bensonhurst, Brooklyn, and in adulthood lived on Sixty-Eighth Street, in Dyker Heights. He was first busted in 1940 for selling bootleg booze in Brooklyn. The stills were in New Jersey, but the booze was sold in New York, Connecticut, and Pennsylvania.

He was next arrested in 1941, for vagrancy, while in the company of Frank Galluccio, the man who gave Al Capone's cheek and neck their scars during a Coney Island altercation.

Rava had been arrested at Apalachin, gave his occupation as "owns restaurant." He wanted to strike back against Gambino as soon as Anastasia hit the barbershop floor. Soon thereafter he disappeared. Gambino never worried that he might come back. In 1959, Rava was named a nonindicted coconspirator, suspected of hindering a federal investigation. But it made no difference. He was gone.

With Rava disappeared, the late Albert Anastasia was out of men willing to avenge his death. And no bullets were fired at Gambino.

It wasn't until 1967 that the FBI got an inkling as to what happened to Rava. An informant known in reports as "NY T-7" told the feds that Tommy Rava was iced by Salvatore "Little Toddo" Avarello, aka Salvatore Aurello, aka Sal Aurella. The Sicilian-born Avarello grew up in Bath Beach, Brooklyn. One of his exploits made the papers in 1934, when he broke into a young woman's SoHo apartment, forced her to strip down to her stockings and high heels, and then robbed her of forty dollars in cash and a hundred-buck wristwatch. The victim seemed cheerful enough as she showed off her legs the next day for a tabloid photog. Avarello defeated the odds again and again and lived to be eighty-eight years old.

In 1958, a Bureau of Narcotics investigative report read, "Investigation was conducted after some thirty odd Sicilian aliens had been smuggled into the United States aboard the SS *Pamorus* at the Port of Philadelphia in May 1948, disclosed that Carlo Gambino was involved in the smuggling of these aliens and that some of the aliens, in turn, had been smuggling substantial quantities of heroin into the United States as payment for being brought into the country."

During the first half of the 1950s, the U.S. government cracked down on narcotics by lengthening the average jail term from two to four years in jail. By 1956, that figure was six years. Minimum sentence for a second conviction increased to ten.

These were pre-RICO days, however, and investigations that disclosed involvement weren't enough. You can bet Gambino was never within miles of heroin.

Gambino had his money in a lot of legit businesses. It was the American way. Now those businesses were catching grief, tainted by fed investigations. On February 12, 1958, the FBI issued a memo stating that Gambino was among those who attended the Apalachin meeting—and also that Gambino owned an interest in the Carol Paper Products Corp. The memo said the books and records of the Carol Corp. had been furnished to investigators "pursuant to a subpoena duces tecum." The records were found to be stored at the offices of Abrams, Merriman and Co. on Madison Avenue, and were brought to the U.S. courthouse at Foley Square in New York City. The estimate was that it would take "nineteen Agent days" to complete the investigation and promised a report on the subject by the first week of March. The man in charge of the investigation was Assistant United States Attorney Stephen K. Kaufman of the Southern District of New York.

On March 5, another memo was issued, this one listing Gambino's known aliases: Carlo Basso, Don Carlo, Carlo Don, Carl Gambino, Carlo Gambriano, Carlo Gambrino, Cambrino T. Goldberg, Mr. O'Conner, Carlo Stone, Carlo Seaman, Harry Stone. (My favorites are Carlo Don, and Carlo Seaman. LOL)

The remainder of the memo had to do with the records of the Carol Corporation. It was released to the public only with details redacted.

The investigation broadened. A second subpoena was drawn up for additional records regarding Carol Paper. Now the FBI was also interested in the books and records for Taste Well Foods, Inc. of Pelham Road in New Rochelle.

Gambino had a seat at the Commission table, but his ambition was still not fulfilled. He wanted to sit at the head of that table, to be the Boss of Bosses. The number one obstacle between Gambino and his dream was Vito Genovese, who also wanted the ultimate job.

Gambino spoke to Lucky Luciano and Meyer Lansky about Genovese. They agreed that Genovese's ambition needed to be stifled. They decided to frame him as a narcotics dealer—an easy fix for Gambino, who could arrange complex conspiracies without even writing down notes.

The plot centered around a Puerto Rican loser by the name of Nelson Cantellops, who would be bribed to testify that Vito Genovese was behind a multimillion-dollar international dope cartel. Cantellops kept holding out, but when the offered bribe got to $100,000, with Lansky himself kicking in some of the dough, the Puerto Rican accepted. In return for testifying that he saw Genovese buying heroin, he was given the money (by the gangsters) and his freedom from Sing Sing (by the government).

Framing Genovese was a ballsy move, because Genovese was second to none in viciousness and would have killed with a smile on his face had he an inkling that he was being set up.

It was all pretty simple, really. The witness was bought. The only other thing to do was to send an anonymous note to the New York Narcotics Bureau saying that an up-the-river inmate named Nelson Cantellops was willing to bring down Genovese while under oath. Since everyone else was too scared to betray Genovese, the authorities leaped at the opportunity—and didn't spend much time thinking about the convenience of it all.

Cantellops was interrogated. He took the oath and recited an affidavit. He told his story to a grand jury. As Gambino read the newspapers each morning, following the progress being made, Genovese was indicted and charged with violation of the newfangled Narcotics Control Act.

In 1959, the feds successfully prosecuted Genovese for conspiracy to import narcotics. Genovese got fifteen years in jail and died behind bars ten years later. Although Genovese continued to give orders from jail, he couldn't be Boss of Bosses while incarcerated.

CHAPTER 10
Yes, We Have No Bonanno

IN 1962, LUCIANO DIED IN NAPLES, ITALY. Minutes after his funeral, police questioned the priest who arranged the services, quizzing him about a slot machine racket in the Mount Vesuvius and Bay of Naples areas. The slot machines, police learned, had been imported to Italy from Germany in boxes labeled TOYS. The priest said he knew nothing.

"He was never in my church when alive," said Father Guido San Martino.

After some unnecessary fuss, Luciano's body was returned to the U.S. and entombed in St. John Cemetery in Middle Village, Queens.

Gambino took charge of the Commission. His crew now had five hundred soldiers and more than a thousand associates. And just about everyone was happy with the new pecking order.

Well, everyone except Joe Bonanno.

Joseph Bonanno, who came to America from Sicily as a man in his twenties to set up operations for his old man, who loved when his men called him "Father," who distinguished power and money, preferring the former.

As Gambino's power grew, to the detriment of others at the table, Bonanno thought the American Mafia was making a mistake. Sure, Gambino was Sicilian born, as was Bonanno, but Bonanno had been a godfather since the beginning, he was a charter boss in the original Five Family system. True, Bonanno was younger than Gambino, but he nonetheless felt that he had seniority over Don Carlo. (What Bonanno didn't consider was that Gambino's current family was far more powerful than his own. In fact, Bonanno's domain was a house of cards, about to be undone by an undercover agent working his way in called Donnie Brasco.)

Bonanno didn't get down and dirty like Genovese, being the son of a godfather in Sicily, but he did see himself as special. To stifle Gambino and accelerate his own power, Bonanno would have to curry favor from the other fathers. When that didn't work, he decided to go about it the old-fashioned way: with a gun.

Not all commissioners were anti-Bonanno. One who saw things Bonanno's way was Giuseppe "Fat Joe" Magliocco, who was a new boss, taking charge of the Profaci family after Profaci died in 1962.

Magliocco, like Profaci before him, believed that the "liberal" team of Gambino and Lucchese was behind his problems with the President Street Boys, that Gambino was committing a sin against his fellow boss by siding with Profaci's "children," i.e., the Gallos.

Joe Bonanno purposefully set about to become Magliocco's best friend. The men played golf together, they went fishing, they sailed on Bonanno's yacht. They sat in steam rooms with towels across their laps.

One day in 1963, Bonanno suggested that Joe Magliocco hit Gambino and Lucchese. With them off the board, Bonanno and Magliocco would get a much bigger piece of the pie.

Magliocco gave the task to Joe Colombo, a rising star in the Profaci family. The plot backfired on Bonanno, and here's why:

One of the very smart things that Gambino always did was, when he encountered a good man who would make a good gangster, he'd place them in one of the other families, rather than within his own. That way, he had friends who owed him a favor in all the families, chips he could cash in if interfamily turbulence erupted. The men Gambino planted served as spies for Gambino, so he often knew what the other bosses were up to. One of those guys was a former longshoreman named Joseph Colombo.

So, when Bonanno told Colombo he wanted Gambino and Lucchese whacked, instead of carrying out the hits, Colombo informed the targets, and the targets brought the issue to the Commission. They even brought in the out-of-town guys since the Mob and the syndicate and the Outfit were all the same fucking thing now.

They called in Sam "Momo" Giancana from Chicago, a very interesting man, a guy who shared a mistress with President Kennedy. He also banged Phyllis McGuire of the McGuire Sisters for a while. Sugartime. Nice work if you can get it.

Also brought in were Angelo Bruno of Philly, John Scalish from Cleveland, John LaRocca of Pittsburgh, and others. They brought Magliocco and Joe Bonanno on the carpet. They scared the shit out of these guys.

After the meeting, which Bonanno survived, he split for California. Magliocco was ordered to retire from the Life, which he did, but not for long. In December 1963, he died of a heart attack (or so it was believed).

Bonanno stayed away from the northeastern section of the country for as long as he could. He thought his whereabouts were secret until a guy walked up to him and subpoenaed him for a federal grand jury in New York. Bonanno came to the city with his lawyer William Power Maloney. Power was his middle name.

The two men were on their way to Maloney's apartment at Park Avenue and Thirty-Fifth Street when Bonanno was snatched.

"Come on, Joe—my boss wants to talk to you," a goon said, and Bonanno was led into a nearby car.

According to Maloney, the guy who grabbed Joe was six feet, two hundred pounds. He wore a black raincoat and black fedora. He had a gun in his hand and he fired a shot in Maloney's general direction when Maloney tried to follow the kidnappers' car, a beige two-door sedan, recent model, unknown make, New York plates. Maloney ceased pursuit.

The lawyer reported the abduction immediately. The NYPD took it seriously. They had five hundred circulars with Bonanno's photo on them, and they went out to the precincts throughout the five boroughs. A cop spokesman said they wanted every cop in the city to have a mental picture of the man "wanted as the victim of an alleged kidnapping."

Police said they were on the lookout for New Jersey hoods Gerald Catena and Thomas Eboli, two of the bigger names outed by big-time rat Joseph Valachi, guys who were boots on the ground for the incarcerated Vito Genovese.

There was debate about whether the kidnapping of Bonanno was real, or just a stunt to avoid testifying for a grand jury.

Nobody could find Bonanno's wife, Fay. She disappeared the same morning that Bonanno was snatched. She told her sister that she was going to see friends in Brooklyn, and that was (allegedly) the last anyone had heard from her.

Also hard to find was Joe's thirty-two-year-old son Salvatore, known as Bill, who'd been functioning as Bonanno consigliere without Commission approval. Nepotism was rampant in the Mob, just as it was in all walks of life, and it was often overlooked—but in this case the move rankled because Bill Bonanno was viewed as a lightweight. Bill was seen a couple of times after his father's kidnapping and then he also vanished.

Joe Bonanno's brother-in-law Frank Labruzzo disappeared from his home in Bellerose, Queens, a couple of days after the kidnapping. Other Bonanno soldiers who couldn't be found included John Joseph "Johnny Burns" Morales, Joseph "Little Joe" Notaro, and Frank Mari.

The papers speculated that Bonanno was whacked. But truth was, Bonanno was alive and held captive somewhere deep in the Catskills. The kidnappers, like Bonanno himself, valued power over money, and there was no cash ransom.

"You retire from the Life and give up all your rackets and you live," he was told. "Otherwise, not so much."

As Mario Puzo would soon put it, it was an offer that the man from Castellammare could not refuse. So, in December 1964, Bonanno was banished from the Mafia. He went to the American Southwest, twiddled his thumbs, and counted cacti.

With Bonanno gone, a meeting was held in January 1965 at the

Villa Capri in Cedarhurst, Long Island, one of the well-to-do "Five Towns" just east of JFK airport. The meeting was to decide who would take over the Bonanno crime family. In attendance were Gambino, Lucchese, Colombo, Magaddino, and Philadelphia's Angelo Bruno. The Genovese family was repped by underboss Eboli.

Magaddino suggested that the chair be filled by the Sicilian-born Gaspare DiGregorio, a Brooklyn clothing manufacturer whose role in Mob activities was not well known. It seemed that the strongest item on DiGregorio's résumé was the fact that he was best man at Joe Bonanno's wedding and was godfather to Bonanno's eldest son, Bill. DiGregorio had never been convicted of a crime, although he was once arrested for murder.

The others approved of DiGregorio, but only after shrinking the Bonanno family's turf and increasing their own. After the meeting, Jersey Boss Sam "the Plumber" DeCavalcante told an associate that the Five Family system, as set up by Lucky Luciano and Meyer Lansky, was now a three-family system, with the only remaining bosses of note being Gambino, Lucchese, and Magaddino. There might be other "bosses" sitting at the Commission table, but, according to DeCavalcante, their votes didn't matter.

We know about the meeting at the Villa Capri because the FBI was all over it. The feds listened in and immediately gave details to the *Daily News*, so the hoods could read what they said in the morning paper.

For the same reason, we know about a meeting soon thereafter in a Little Italy eatery. With the feds listening in, Carlo Gambino and Sam DeCavalcante seemed to know that there was a bug in the room. They spoke only of their biological families. After eating, Gambino went to the men's room. DeCavalcante followed him moments later. The men turned on the faucets in the sink, and then conducted business in whispers that the FBI could not hear.

We get a clue as to what was discussed in that Little Italy men's room from DeCavalcante, who talked about the meeting with Don Carlo when back in New Jersey, unaware that the feds had a bug in his office.

Sam said, “Carlo and I straightened it out.” He outlined the plan: Bonanno’s lieutenants would all join the Gambino family, or the DeCavalcante family with Gambino’s approval. He said that Magliocco had planned to bump off Gambino and Lucchese but didn’t survive to do it.

The most controversial statement on the recording was that Magliocco did not die of a heart attack as everyone thought, but had been killed by Gambino with a poison pill.

That last statement got the feds all excited. They disinterred Magliocco and re-autopsied the body—but no trace of poison was found.

Sam the Plumber had his phone tapped for five years, so they already knew a lot about him. One of the best conversations police listened in on was DeCavalcante, Anthony Boiardo, and Angelo “the Gyp” DeCarlo, talking with disgust about the messy fashion in which Willie Moretti had been blown away in an East Bergen restaurant. There were so many more dignified ways to kill, the three men agreed. You could just overdose the guy with dope and shove him behind the wheel of a car.

When DeCavalcante wanted his secretary to call Gambino about something, he always asked her to contact “Uncle Harry.” Gambino would get on the phone and whisper something in code, “seven fishes in a rising tide” or something, which meant the location of an upcoming meet.

After Magliocco died—heart attack, poisoned, whatever—Colombo’s loyalty to Gambino was rewarded, as he became the Commission-approved head of what was now the Colombo family.

CHAPTER 11

That Day in Dallas

FROM THE MOMENT GAMBINO assumed his role as Boss of Bosses, one of the biggest thorns in his side was the fucking Kennedy brothers, John and Robert. They were ambitious Irishmen, sons of a billionaire bootlegger, dripping charisma and wildly popular, and part of their public stance was they would destroy the Mob should they be put in control.

In 1960, John was elected president in a squeaker over Richard Nixon, and Robert became attorney general. The brothers delivered on their promise to go to war with the Mob, and during the first year of their brief reign, the Kennedys saw 121 mobsters indicted and seventy-three convicted of crimes.

This was bad enough, but it got worse. JFK had made a deal with Chicago Boss Sam Giancana—with whom, as we know, he shared a mistress—to lay off the Outfit if Giancana would rig the election and win him Illinois. Giancana stuffed ballot boxes, Kennedy won, and then reneged on his promise, allowing his wolverine of a younger brother to gnaw relentlessly at the Outfit's ankles. The Commission—and that meant Gambino—had no choice but to give JFK the thumbs-down.

And so, JFK was whacked in Dallas. Allegedly by a cockeyed ex-marine turned communist, Lee Harvey Oswald, whose uncle worked for Carlos Marcello, the New Orleans don. Oswald was then whacked by a nightclub operator named Jacob "Sparky" Rubenstein, aka Jack Ruby, who ran errands for Al Capone as a kid, ran guns for Santo Trafficante as a grown-up, and at the time of the assassination was operating a dank strip club and running drugs and women in Dallas. The Kennedys were out, Lyndon Johnson was in, and the war against organized crime ground to a halt.

In 1968, when Robert Kennedy looked like he was going to grab the power for himself, he, too, was taken out.

The JFK assassination took place on November 22, 1963. JFK was whacked by a cross fire of snipers. Texas governor John Connelly was also severely wounded. Both men had their wives with them, and the women were uninjured. The assassins were world-class snipers. The genius of the conspiracy was that it implicated everyone who otherwise would be in charge of investigating it.

Everybody covered their own asses: the FBI (Director J. Edgar Hoover was friends with Frank Costello and famous for saying "there's no such thing as the Mafia"); the CIA (counterintelligence hotshot Cord Meyer was married to one of JFK's mistresses, which must've been damn humiliating); Dallas police (who allowed the patsy to be slain on national TV), et cetera. Big Oil in Texas ran "security" organizations with bigger budgets than the CIA. A lot of spooky guys freelanced. Plus, deep in the heart of Texas, those of a like mind had ways of getting together outside of work, sometimes in right-wing clubs like the John Birch Society, sometimes while wearing hoods.

To be honest, the plot couldn't have been handled by Mob guys alone. But the overall structure feels like a Gambino plan. Having Mob guys and spy guys working together wasn't even unusual in 1963, as the two groups shared a common enemy in Cuba, that being Fidel Castro, who kicked the Mob out of Havana and turned the island nation communist.

Despite the fact that there had been an obvious cross fire in Dealey Plaza that day, everyone got together, all three branches of the government, and the FBI, and convicted the dead patsy of being a lone-wolf assassin. They convinced a large chunk of the public that the assassin's assassin also acted alone, according to the "official version" of events, despite the fact that the Dallas nightclub owner had to kick up to the same man who employed Oswald's uncle: Carlos Marcello.

And so, JFK was dead, his brains blown out all over Elm Street, his widow splattered with blood and guts. They named an airport after him, and Gambino turned that airport into a gold mine. It was a win-win, the only kind of game Gambino knew.

(A famous man, who everyone is looking at, is blown away in front of a crowd, and the whole scene is designed to look like something it ain't. Change the name and it describes the attack on Joe Colombo, which you'll read about in chapter 16.)

It was only weeks before the assassination in Dallas that Joseph Valachi famously flipped and, in exchange for his life, blabbed on TV and radio what he knew about the organization he called *Cosa Nostra*. Luckily for the Five Families, Valachi was not in the upper echelon of organized crime and thus didn't know some of the bigger secrets. But he knew a lot more than the U.S. public, and when he testified before Arkansas senator John L. McClellan's Permanent Subcommittee on Investigations, he told America about a lot of things they'd never heard of before. Omertà. Soldiers, capos, consigliere, underbosses, and bosses. The way tribute kicked up the line and guys got iced if too much stuck to their fingers. He spilled the beans about the families and the Committee.

Valachi's singing resulted in not a single prosecution, but it had a cultural effect. Mr. and Mrs. Middle America suddenly knew about meets, and scores, and contracts, how the common rackets worked, and the difference between button men and associates.

And, to some, that was the beginning of the end for the American chapter of *la Mafia*. With an organizational chart and a partial cast of characters, law enforcement was no longer quite so mystified by Mob activity.

CHAPTER 12
Gambino's Babonia Team

IN 1964, THE CHIEF INSPECTOR of the NYPD's Central Intelligence Bureau, John Shanley, testified before a Senate crime investigations committee, and the subject of Gambino's crew came up.

"On average, men working under Carlo Gambino have been arrested six times. One of every five men has been arrested for homicide. Three out of four have been arrested at least once for possession of a weapon. One of three has been arrested for narcotics. Two of five have been arrested for felonious assault," Shanley said.

The narcotics division of the Gambino family was run by underboss Joseph Biondo. He was the liaison between the American Mob and the bosses of the international heroin trade.

As we've learned, Gambino only returned to Europe once after coming over on the boat, and that was in 1948 for a meeting with Lucky Luciano and others about importing heroin into the U.S. After that, Gambino sent Biondo overseas for such meetings, usually delivering attaché cases of cash to Luciano.

We know this to be true because federal narcotics agents followed Biondo during a 1951 trip. He had dinner with Lucky Luciano and then partied at night in Rome with dope dealers Francesco "Chick 99" Callace, Dominick Petrillo, and Giuseppe Pici.

Chick 99 was born in Corleone in 1900, came to New York on the boat when he was thirteen, and became a member of the bootlegging 107th Street Gang of Harlem. Chick was a made man by the

1920s and was involved in importing heroin since about 1937. He was arrested in 1943 for narcotics trafficking. He served a few years in jail, was released, and was deported to Italy. He moved to Palermo and continued to be a cog in the heroin-importing chain.

After Biondo returned to New York City, Callace was arrested in the Rome airport with three kilos of H. While out on bail Callace snuck back into New York City, but it was a mistake. He hadn't been there long when he was murdered.

On November 13, 1954, Callace's body was found behind the wheel of a 1951 sedan parked in front of a home on Crosby Avenue in the Bronx. There were two bullet holes in his head. Police never found the murder weapon, but it wasn't for lack of trying. Sanitation and sewer workers joined the NYPD in the unsuccessful search.

Giuseppe Pici was another guy who'd been deported out of the U.S. (following a human trafficking conviction) and went to Italy to work closely with Luciano. During the summer of 1951, authorities didn't know where Pici was, but they found out when he was married in a Milan church and used his real name when he signed the register. Known as Joe Pici, his days as a heroin mover ended in 1959 when he sold heroin to a U.S. undercover agent.

The Gambino heroin squad consisted of at least eight capos and other button guys. The known officers were:

"Fourteenth Street" Steve Armone, aka Frank Pizzo, aka Joe Marinello, aka Frank Charmonte. Born in Sicily somewhere around the turn of the twentieth century. Older brother of Piney (see below)—older by a lot, eighteen years older. Came to America when he was six and lived in Queens. Although Fourteenth Street is a major thoroughfare in Manhattan, Armone was named after the one in Long Island City, Queens. Considered his neighborhood's top tough guy as a teenager, Armone was a lifelong criminal, arrested for narcotics, burglary, and assault with intent to kill. This last charge came in 1919, at a time when he was going by Charmonte, and he served three years inside Eastern State Penitentiary. He skipped bail on drug charges in 1931 and was a fugitive for three years, caught in 1934 for recklessly driving his speedboat. He ended up doing another threespot for the drug charges. In 1944, Armone was popped again for drugs, he and fifteen other hoods caught moving the babonia from the Caribbean through Miami and into New York City, transported in small boats. He died in 1960 of natural causes.

Joseph "Piney" Armone, aka Shorty Armone. Baby brother of Steve. Got his nickname "Piney" during the Great Depression by working a protection scheme over street vendors selling Christmas trees. Old enough to have been a member of the Mangano family, the Anastasia family, and the Gambino family. Young enough that he was still on his way up when Don Carlo passed, and he ended up being underboss and consigliere for the Gambino family in the late 1980s. Piney married Mob, his wife being a relative of Genovese capo Dominick DiQuarto. Piney, by all accounts, took after Don Carlo as a devoted family man. The Federal Bureau of Narcotics developed a thick file on him and reported that he ruled over a heroin operation out of two restaurants and a bar in Manhattan's East Village. Armone was caught when he himself was recorded schmoozing with an informant he thought was a delivery boy.

"Hundred pounds of pure shit. Don't fuck up," he was recorded as saying.

In January 1964, Piney was in the Reno Bar at Twelfth Street and Second Avenue in Manhattan when a lone gunman shot him five times but failed to kill him. Spent months recovering in the hospital and when he got out, was indicted in the French Connection case. An influential man during the early days of the John Gotti era, right up until 1988 when RICO nailed his ass. He died in prison in 1992. He's buried in the Cemetery of the Resurrection on Staten Island.

Vincent James "Jimmy" Squillante, aka Jimmy Jerome. Five-two, one-twenty. He's probably best known as the guy getting a haircut one barber chair over when Anastasia was whacked. Born in 1917, Squillante was Anastasia's godson but made the transition smoothly into the Gambino era. As a young man he ran with a crew in the Bronx with Frank Scalise as his boss. Scalise, whose name is also on this list, was Squillante's sponsor when he was straightened out.

Squillante had a clean record until the 1950s, when he went down for tax evasion, extortion, and narcotics. The only beef that brought him time was the tax bullshit. The Federal Bureau of Narcotics had him identified as a top mover of babonia in the Gambino ranks, but they could never nail him on charges. He also had the waste management industry on Long Island sewed up. He had things so well sewed up that almost all the money he made was legit.

It wasn't until someone tried to disrupt his monopoly that he had to resort to tough-guy tactics. Squillante was one of the guys who was grilled by Attorney General Robert F. Kennedy on TV. Squillante put his hand over the microphone and consulted with his mouthpiece before admitting he was Squillante.

When the media began to scrutinize his humongous fleet of garbage trucks, Gambino saw a public relations mess on the horizon. The mess didn't happen because on or about September 30, 1960, Squillante disappeared off the face of the earth.

Michelle Giacomo "Jack" Scarpulla. Sicilian-born, from Palermo—which meant he spoke Gambino's language. Busted for bootlegging in 1939, long after Prohibition was repealed. Arrested in 1943, during World War II, for gouging at his meat market. At a time when Americans were counting their rationing stamps, Scarpulla sold black-market lamb for exorbitant prices.

We can see right there that he had things in common with Gambino, who also sold bootlegged booze to evade taxes and manipulated the system of food distribution during World War II to his advantage.

During the 1960s, Scarpulla's name came up repeatedly during a government investigation into global heroin trafficking, which is how he got on this list. A rat told the law that Scarpulla was "neck-deep" in importing heroin.

Frank "Wacky" Scalise. One of several underbosses to Anastasia. Scalise and Anastasia went way back, doing hits together as early as 1930. On August 15, 1930, Scalise, Anastasia, and a third guy known as "Buster from Chicago" murdered Giuseppi "Peter" Morello, a guy who'd been boss twenty years earlier. The hit went down in East Harlem where the target was "collecting receipts."

When police questioned Scalise, he said he was a contractor. Scalise was made by Salvatore D'Aquila as a capo. D'Aquila was replaced by Alfredo "Al Mineo" Manfredi who, as we saw, was on the losing side of the Castellammarese War and got whacked. Joe the Boss got whacked and Scalise was briefly the head of one of the original five families (1930–31) and known to his underlings as Don Ciccio (most often pronounced Don Cheech).

He went on to be one of the first hoods to develop Vegas, helping to open the Flamingo Hotel and Casino, working under Bugsy Siegel, and by 1957 he was back in the Bronx.

Through all of it, police couldn't touch him. His record was a short one: burglary 1920, and vagrancy 1922. Other than that, clean as a whistle, despite his reputation as a lifelong mobster, and an upper echelon guy at that.

He lived on Kirby Street on City Island (which is technically the Bronx but pokes up out of Long Island Sound between the mainland and Nassau County), although a police tail once reported that he didn't seem to be there much.

He was the subject of several dope-trafficking investigations and in 1955 he testified before a Senate committee investigating narcotics. He probably thought he was Anastasia's friend, but he forgot one thing: Anastasia was never anyone's friend. And sure enough, Anastasia turned on Scalise. During the first week of June 1957, Anastasia sent a message to Italy: He wanted to take out Scalise for failure to pay proper tribute. A sit-down was held between Luciano and Adonis, who approved the hit.

On a hot June afternoon, Scalise had just finished an ordeal. Bronx County Assistant District Attorney Albert Binder had quizzed him for hours about several murders. Wacky had a disorderly mind. He had guys who didn't properly respect him for the things he'd done in the past. Don Cheech. He was fucking Don Cheech. He also had a reputation as a guy who'd sell a button for fifty grand, very bad form, and when a recent shipment of babonia was seized by police, he didn't reimburse his partners. That could mean nothing but trouble.

Although it was technically still springtime in the Belmont section of the Bronx, the direct sun of the approaching solstice baked the teeming tenements and pavement, and rising humidity created an out-of-season dog-day steaminess. It was just after one thirty in the afternoon and Wacky was purchasing ninety cents' worth of fruit at Mazzaro's Fruit and Vegetable Store on Arthur Avenue, just north of East 186th Street.

Now *there* was a guy who showed Don Cheech the proper respect: Enrico Mazzaro, who'd had the same fruit and vegetable store, same location, for generations. Mazzaro put the fruit in a brown paper bag. Scalise paid with a dollar, and Mazzaro fished a dime change out of his right front pocket. The men said their goodbyes and Scalise was putting the dime in his own pants pocket, stepping away from the stand. The proprietor walked in front of Wacky outside to straighten up his sidewalk displays.

Two men brushed by Mazzaro. He heard some shots and looked around. These two men were hurrying by him again. They weren't wearing coats and they had their sleeves rolled up.

The shooters got into an old black sedan and headed north on Arthur Avenue. They'd done a professional job and Don Cheech was still on the sidewalk. Here we have a case of one man on the list icing another guy on the list. Scalise was killed by Vincent Squillante.

Rocco "Rogie" Mazzie. A heroin-trafficking gunman who, in Cleveland during the early 1950s, was arrested for selling dope, but the case never went to trial because the government's star witness got murdered.

There was a time there in 1958 when Mazzie couldn't exhale

without a cop throwing cuffs on him. In January, he was busted while in possession of seventeen ounces of heroin. He was released on $15,000 bail.

In June, Mazzie was arrested again as the culmination of a long federal probe into how narcotics got into American cities. Mazzie was one of eighteen persons to be caught in that trap. A warrant was issued for his arrest but Mazzie, accompanied by his attorney, Irving Rader, gave himself up. The next day, when he appeared in court, he tried to tell the judge that his only source of income was the forty-five dollars a week he got from unemployment insurance. This caused more than a ripple of laughter in the gallery.

The Law took Mazzie off the streets. He was convicted of narcotics charges on September 1, 1959, and was sentenced to twelve years in the fed pen.

Joseph "Jojo" Manfredi. Another guy who lost to the Law. He was busted by the feds for running a "wholesale narcotics ring" that earned $25 million per year. The ring ran H from the French Connection to inner-city U.S. streets from coast to coast. It was Manfredi's bust that brought the feds the last piece of the puzzle. They could now trace heroin all the way from Marseille to New Orleans to New York City to Jojo's factory.

During the trial, the U.S. attorney wanted the judge to admit into evidence a statement the defendant had made soon after his first drug bust the previous winter. Manfredi reportedly said, "I'm a dead man."

Manfredi's defense attorney wanted the statement kept out because it could be construed by the jury as a confession. On November 3, 1972, Judge Harold Tyler called Jojo "the source and center of this conspiracy" and the "top lieutenant of crime czar Carlo Gambino." After that, the judge said he found Manfredi's crimes "terrifying" and sentenced him to thirty years.

The whole ordeal had been excruciating for Manfredi in a number of ways. Not only was he kissing his own tomorrow goodbye, he'd said goodbye to Philip J. and Philip D. Manfredi, two cousins, both his nephews, who were offed about a week before his conspiracy trial began. The nephews were twenty-four and twenty-two years old. One lived in Long Island City, Queens, and the other in Lodi, New Jersey.

But the two Philips' bodies were found together on August 10, 1972, by two beat cops in a dark parking lot in the Clason Point section of the Bronx. One was sitting in the front passenger seat of a 1971 Olds listed as belonging to a woman in Long Beach, Long Island. The other was found twenty-five feet from the car, apparently gunned down while trying to flee.

Both were shot twice in the back of the head. According to eyewitnesses, a black guy whacked the cousins. The first thought was that this was retaliation for the murders of a few black and Puerto Rican junk dealers who were trying to deal junk on Gambino turf. But the race of the shooter hardly lets Gambino off the hook. Gambino had gunmen in Harlem.

And **Andrew Alberti**, born 1920, an active Gambino soldier during the 1950s and the first four years of the '60s. He was a nepotism boy, having inherited many of his rackets from his cab-driving dad.

Andrew's cover was that he owned and operated a wholesale bakery with his brother James on East 137th Street in the South Bronx. He was also, for a time, a prizefight manager, with an up-and-comer lightweight named Johnny Busso in his stable. In 1947, he was arrested for receiving stolen goods, but a grand jury felt there was insufficient evidence to indict. In 1953, he was busted on federal drug charges. He was an important cog in the heroin-importing racket, that was for sure, the American contact for Mr. French Connection, Jean David (dah-VEED), aka the Silver Fox.

According to the official story—which might be true—Alberti took his own life in 1964 on the eve of his scheduled appearance before a grand jury. The timing struck some as familiar, as Joseph Bonanno had been kidnapped only hours before he was supposed to give grand jury testimony.

Alberti, who was expected to tell what he knew about an $88,000 jewelry swindle, was found on the patio of his home in Riverdale, the Bronx, by his wife, his head a pulpy blob from a single shotgun blast. The shotgun was lying nearby.

Medical examiner Dr. Sanford Edberg called it suicide.

The heroin operation was wildly successful. For obvious reasons, customers kept coming back for more, even if they had to steal to afford it. When law enforcement "cracked down," they only put the tiniest of dents in the bottom line.

For example, during the autumn of 1960, the NYPD "cracked down." On October 3, they raided a building on East Seventy-Sixth Street in the city. Arrested was Nicholas Calamaras, a Gambino man, who was placing bags of heroin in the trunk of a taxi when nabbed.

This case got more complicated when it was discovered that the heroin had been brought into the U.S. by Dr. Mauricio Rosal Broz, the Guatemalan ambassador to the Netherlands. The bags in the cab's trunk turned out to weigh 115 pounds, uncut smack, street value twenty million clams. (Broz and Calamaras were convicted of moving and selling wholesale narcotics. Each got fifteen years in prison. Broz, though a diplomat, lacked diplomatic status in the United States.)

The NYPD struck again five days later, again chipping away at the Gambino system, this time perhaps one step closer to street level. They broke into a Harlem apartment and seized a pound and a half of uncut heroin, 125 bags of cut heroin ready for street sale, and twenty-five hypodermic needles. Arrested were five men and a woman.

There were big headlines.

Politicians boasted.

Then it stopped and the babonia biz continued unimpeded.

Everybody has seen *The Godfather*, and the movie's incredible opening sequence on the day Don Vito Corleone's daughter is married. While the party is going on, the Boss is in a dark room with a queue of men waiting to pay their regards, kiss his ring, and in some cases ask favors. Not the wedding, but the lineup of everyone wanting to touch the great man—that was Gambino.

Despite the horrible things that Don Carlo had his minions do on his behalf, he never publicly showed anger. Perhaps he was worried about the Gates of Heaven. He would listen to a poor mother on her knees begging for help because her juvenile delinquent son was addicted to heroin and getting his drugs out of a storefront on Brooklyn's Myrtle Avenue. He would pat her head, stroke her face tenderly, and promise that he would take care of it, and the next day the guy who ran that storefront was gone and the place was padlocked. Instant favor from the big man to the pathetic woman, all done without the slightest inkling that it was Gambino himself who most profited from the heroin sold on Myrtle Avenue, or in Red Hook, or at Lexington and 125th Street in the city, or in one of the other boroughs, or in the whole country.

What was going through Gambino's head when he did these things? Who the fuck knows? Maybe he loved the money that came from addicting America's youth but hated it when someone put a face on it. Maybe his public hatred for dope peddling was simply an act, a strategy by a deep player, designed to make the whacking of rogue dope peddlers seem benevolent. And of course, doing favors for the residents of the communities he "served" was the moral justification for his organization. A bit of hypocrisy perhaps, just for public relations purposes.

CHAPTER 13
A Bug at the Big S

IN THE WEE HOURS OF THE MORNING, on March 22, 1963, NYPD picked a lock at the Big S Service Center on Coney Island Avenue, just south of Prospect Park in Brooklyn, and planted electronic surveillance devices, bugs, in the office of Gambino soldier Michael "Mike Scandi" Scandifia.

The detectives who did the B&E job on the garage had in their pocket an authorization from Judge Mitchell Schweitzer. The judge was told that the guys in that garage were suspects in a $75,000 jewelry heist in Manhattan.

While listening in on the men, police learned a lot, most of it having nothing to do with jewelry. They uncovered a plan, attributed to Carlo Gambino, to take over Local 47 of the Mason Tenders Union (MTU).

The State Investigation Committee later reported that, on the surface, Local 47 appeared completely legit. They duly elected officials and had properly filled out their paperwork. "However," the committee wrote, Local 47 was "racketeer dominated." Gambino's man-in-charge of skimming Local 47 was Accursio "Swifty" Marinelli. Swifty, the committee added, spoke to Don Carlo every day.

About six weeks after the bug was planted on Coney Island Avenue, Marinelli went to the Big S Service Center, where he met with Gambino capo Peter Joseph "Petey Pumps" Ferrara.

As authorities listened in, Marinelli told Ferrara to make sure that MTU member Thomas Cucciara was made an officer of Local 47.

"He is the only man for the job, dig?" Swifty said.

"Where do these orders come from?" Marinelli asked.

Swifty explained that the decision came out of a meeting attended by Don Carlo, Joe Riccobono, Joe Biondo, and Carmine Lombardozzi.

Lombardozzi was, as we've seen, called "the Doctor" because he operated on the investment markets to the Mob's advantage. He had been arrested twenty-five times, and convicted a dozen. He was a stone killer and a ladies' man. He was perpetually tanned, wore gold chains, and often had one too many buttons undone on his shirt. The Doctor was reportedly made in 1951 and worked only a couple of years as a soldier before he was promoted to capo.

Gambino didn't like the fact that the Doctor couldn't keep it in his pants, but he looked the other way because Lombardozzi knew how to do something no one else in the organization could do. He was to the world of stocks and bonds what a card-counter was to a game of twenty-one. Lombardozzi had been living on the edge for some time. He was the guy who waited in the garage at Apalachin while the Commission decided whether to feed him to the fishes.

The men referred to this group—Gambino, Riccobono, Biondo, and Lombardozzi—as "the administration." The need for a new officer for Local 47 didn't exist yet, but the old officer was scheduled to die, so an opening was anticipated. That officer, Frank Stratico, had failed to obey an order from the administration. As it turned out, Stratico stepped down voluntarily, said the right things, and was allowed to live.

The guys at the Big S were so certain no one was listening, they talked about murders and named names. One murder discussed was the whacking of Alfred "Freddie the Sicilian" Sanantonio, a florist with a shop called Flowers by Charm at Avenue T and Ocean Parkway, just around the corner from Gambino's home.

Sanantonio was said to "run with the Mob" and had allegedly flapped his gums about big-time heroin sales and counterfeiting with a federal agent in the room. Such indiscretions were always fatal.

Sanantonio had recently been sentenced to eight years in prison for stealing more than $1 million in U.S. savings bonds. He'd been in prison before, serving time in the early 1950s for narcotics possession.

It was quarter to one in the afternoon on July 11, 1963, when two black cars—a 1962 Olds and a '63 Caddy, both with New York plates—drove by the shop, packed to the gills with killers.

Six gunmen were involved. One of them had thick white makeup on his face, a look so weird that, when asked later what the men looked like, witnesses could remember nothing else.

One of the men said, "This is a stickup," although it was hard to tell why as they immediately started shooting, leaving Sanantonio face down on the floor.

At the time of the shooting, Sanantonio had been talking to a friend who was not shot, and who later told police he only saw guns and no faces. The shooters calmly returned to their cars and drove away.

Only hours after the shooting was done, the hit was discussed in the Big S. The leader of the hit squad was identified as Gambino capo Pumps Ferrara, who in 1964 was indicted by a grand jury and charged with first-degree murder.

So, the bug was doing its job. Then there was a complication. . .

Not long after the hit on Sanantonio, the electronic bug listened in as a caller on the phone talked to Mike Scandifia.

"I can get you dum-dum bullets. These fuckers could blow a hole in a man's head you could put a fist through," the voice said. Those bullets could be used to dispose of "informers," especially "federal stool pigeons." New York cops, the caller said, loved it when federal stool pigeons were offed.

The guy with the bullets, police were shocked to learn, was one of their own, forty-year-old Leonard Grossman, a cop for thirteen years. Grossman came to the garage in person a few weeks later and was taped again.

Grossman was arrested on July 25, 1963. Two stolen guns were found in his car, but the wisdom of the arrest was questioned, as it put an end to the effective surveillance of the garage. The argument was that Grossman was busted to save his life from the hoods who would have eventually turned on him.

Grossman, along with Pumps and Scandifia, was also charged with murder. Pumps went into hiding and was eventually found in a Staten Island hospital where he was being treated for a heart ailment under an assumed name. Nurses didn't know who Pumps was, but they suspected he was somebody, based on the ill-mannered goons who came to visit.

The arrests didn't stick, however, because the court order to install the bug at the Big S was specific to the jewelry theft, so no evidence gathered by the bug regarding other crimes could be used in court.

The dirty cop never squealed and was eventually (in 1968) dismissed from the NYPD for "conduct unbecoming a police officer." Getting fired was not Grossman's biggest problem, as he spent the rest of his life expecting to be shot by gangsters the next time he turned a corner. He disappeared for a time and was eventually found in Israel with a new, hot wife.

Regarding the jewelry theft, Scandifia and John Lombardozzi, Carmine's brother, were arrested for that crime. Scandifia disappeared in 1968. He left his home in Hillsdale, New Jersey, at ten p.m. on December 5, saying to his wife that he was going to an all-night drug store to have a prescription filled, and she never saw him again. Scandifia's car was found a week later, abandoned on an upstate New York country road.

The bug at the Big S may not have resulted in as many convictions as the Law would have liked, but it did its job, throwing havoc into Carlo Gambino's orderly operations, and resulting in the arrest of sixty hoods, all members of the Gambino family. The bug had verified that Gambino was the man in charge.

* * *

One day during the summer of 1964, Carlo Gambino was holding court. There was a long line of people there to pay respects and ask favors. Sabato “Sammy Mintz” Muro, a Gambino soldier, kissed Don Carlo’s ring and told him a story. He had a beautiful young daughter named Arlene who had remained chaste for marriage.

Don Carlo nodded his approval.

But her maidenhood had been taken from her. She was seduced and outraged by Carmine “the Doctor” Lombardozzi. He was the Gambino captain who had accompanied Don Carlo to the Apalachin meeting in 1957, and who often took Mob profits and laundered the money, with a profit, through Wall Street investments.

“What do you want?” Gambino asked.

“I want the Doctor to do right by my daughter”—that is, marry her—“or I will take care of matters myself,” Muro said.

Gambino promised to take care of it. He ordered Lombardozzi to report to him and when he did, told him that he was to divorce his wife, Mary, of twenty-seven years, and marry the young girl whose cherry he’d popped.

“Mary will understand,” Gambino said, referring to Lombardozzi’s wife. “Of course, you must continue to provide for both your old and new families. Your wife must be allowed to continue living the lifestyle to which she is accustomed.”

Lombardozzi would have been gone years earlier if he hadn’t been such a skillful earner. Gambino had a guy at JFK watching incoming mail from overseas. Gambino had a guy at JFK watching over everything, but this guy provided a lucrative task. He went through the mail and stole all the envelopes that looked like they might contain stocks, bonds, or securities. Those envelopes would go to the Doctor, who knew how to convert them into cash. So, he was sloppy with his sex life. The penalty wasn’t going to be death. It was going to be a quick order to zip up his fly and do the right thing.

Lombardozzi did as he was told. Up to a point. He divorced Mary, married Arlene, and immediately took up with a new young *goomada* named Marie. To further complicate Lombardozzi’s life, cops were after him, investigating him for extorting New Jersey restaurants and hotels.

The Doctor was having a cocktail with Marie in the lounge of a Jersey motel when swaggering cops rolled in and told him he was under arrest. The scene that followed was pure comedy. The Doctor decided to have a fistfight with the cops, and the new girlfriend jumped on a policeman's back and began to beat him on top of the head. The police arrested them both for felonious assault. The story made the papers.

Steam came out of Gambino's ears when he read it. The brawl made everyone look bad. Lombardozzi needed punishment. Again, Gambino allowed him to live but he was demoted back to soldier.

Lombardozzi had bigger problems with the feds, and he was soon thereafter indicted for tax evasion regarding winning tickets at Roosevelt Raceway, a Long Island standardbred track. Harness racing was a sport with a reputation for the fix being in. Sometimes boxing the three longshots in the last race of the night could pay off big. It was always the last race because a lot of guys had left and there were fewer people to boo if the fix was blundered and stunk up the joint.

The feds offered Lombardozzi a deal: sing about Apalachin in exchange for immunity from prosecution. He told them to fuck off and went away. He was out and about, however, in 1969 when it was discovered that he had kidney cancer. He had a kidney removed, which saved his life, but he was never healthy after that. He lived until 1992. His heart did him in, not his kidneys, and he was buried in St. John Cemetery in Middle Village, Queens.

In 1965, Gambino built his dream house, precisely to his specifications on Club Drive, mailing address Massapequa, on a South Oyster Bay inlet. It was not a sprawling mansion, but a sensibly sized yellow-brick structure with a two-car garage, pruned hedges for privacy, and small trees in the front yard, and an eight-foot wall on the property line in back.

Inside those imposing walls were Gambino's gardens—one

flower, one vegetable—where he loved to sit and charge up his faulty heart for the stresses of his business.

Closer to the house was a patio and a barbecue pit. All the way in back, docked at the solidly built pier, was his cabin cruiser, which was used for everything from fishing to parties to transportation.

Gambino's next-door neighbor in South Oyster Bay was Tony Russo, a Gambino captain born as Ettore Zappi. His legit biz was mattresses. He was also one of Gambino's many cousins.

Tony Russo was (supposedly) born on the Fourth of July in 1904, in Naples. Carlo brought him over and gave him a job in his crew. When Gambino became Boss, Russo was given multiple businesses to run: loan-sharking and sports book for starters, later porn and "gentlemen's clubs."

As was true of just about every pie Gambino had his thumb in, porn was very lucrative. He got together with L.A. hood Aladena "Jimmy the Weasel" Fratianno. They worked porn like it was just another big-business black market and made a mint.

Carlo had a piece of *Deep Throat*, which changed the game. Guys who'd never seen a dirty movie outside a stag party were suddenly going to theaters in cities across America to see Linda Lovelace, whose problem was that her clit was in her throat. Oh my, what *will* she do??

According to FBI electronic surveillance planted in the offices of Sam "the Plumber" DeCavalcante, guys were getting rubbed out, but only after Gambino was consulted and his approval given.

On these recordings, speakers were more careful than those at the Big S on Coney Island Avenue. When discussing crimes, details were never mentioned, and the conversation was in the sort of vague language mobsters use when making plans: "Go to the place to see a guy and do the thing."

The most interesting thing about the tape was that the Jersey Boys referred to Gambino as "Carl."

The FBI eventually figured out that one of the murder victims being discussed was Joseph "Joey Surprise" Feola, who bucked all kinds of odds to still be alive in 1965. Feola killed a cop, Sgt. Timothy Murphy, in 1931, was scheduled for the electric chair in 1939, got a new trial, pleaded guilty to manslaughter, was paroled in 1948, and went into waste management with Vincent Squillante.

Joey Surprise disappeared for good on April 19, 1965. Rumor has it that he was cubed by one of his own garbage-compacting machines.

CHAPTER 14
The Meeting at La Stella

ON SEPTEMBER 22, 1966, Gambino was part of a big dope-dealing meeting in the basement of an Italian restaurant called La Stella on Queens Boulevard in Forest Hills, Queens. Back then, the neighborhood was known for the U.S. Open tennis tournament, but there were great restaurants like La Stella, too.

Also at the La Stella meeting were Gambino's new underboss, Aniello Dellacroce (for bio info, see chapter 23), Joseph N. Gallo (no relation to the President Street Boys), Joe Colombo, Tommy "Tommy Ryan" Eboli, Carlos Marcello (N'Orlins), Santo Trafficante (Miami), and seven others.

The subject of the meeting was divvying up the rackets of Gambino's childhood friend, Tommy Lucchese, who was terminally ill with a brain tumor. As the meeting took place, Lucchese was near death, connected to an assortment of tubes in a bed at Columbia-Presbyterian Medical Center.

But, just as happened at Apalachin, the meet drew heat. The NYPD raided the conference and dragged everybody to the old 112th Precinct in Maspeth, Queens. The men were strip-searched and fingerprinted.

Police charged all thirteen hoods with consorting with known criminals, they being each other. The meeting was immediately tagged as "Little Apalachin."

* * *

According to a police source, the meeting was called "to give the formal nod" to the man already chosen by those in a position to do the picking. The new kingpin of the Lucchese family was Vincent John Rao, who lived in Westchester County, just north of New York City, and operated out of a headquarters in East Harlem.

He, police said, was a longtime upper-echelon member of the Luccheses and a key advisor to the dying boss. A tabloid the next day offered Rao's résumé, saying that Rao had frequently been mentioned in FBI documents regarding Mob rule. His turf was said to stretch up and down the Eastern Seaboard. He'd been associated with gambling, shylock loans, labor rackets, extortion, and whacking guys who'd failed to do the right thing.

One of the things about the La Stella bust that impressed experts was the intercity nature of those who attended. As had been the case at Apalachin, Mob control was not limited to the three major U.S. cities—New York, Chicago, and L.A.—but had spread to the rest of the country as well, with guys from Florida and Louisiana joining in. It would have been presumptuous to say that guys like Marcello and Trafficante were getting a voice in what was to be done, but at least they were considered important enough to be present when those decisions were made. (If the three, Gambino, Trafficante, and Marcello, had conspired to hit JFK, that would serve as a lifelong bond.)

It was unknown if the official proclamation making Rao a boss had been made at the meeting before the raid came, but the announcement would have been no more than a formality, and the disruption would not make a difference in the Mob's future plans.

All thirteen big-time gangsters were taken to the Civil Jail on West Thirty-Seventh Street in the city and held on $100,000 bail. All were made to spend the night in jail. Nothing but Sicilian was spoken. The guards had no clue what was being said. Some guys shouted. Some guys whispered. Gambino didn't say anything at all.

First thing in the morning, the men were marched into a pair of police vans and driven back over the East River to the Queens Criminal Court building in Kew Gardens.

The La Stella Thirteen—Gambino easy to pick out because he was the little guy—were handcuffed as they stepped from the police vans and marched single file into the courthouse. There were close to a hundred onlookers as the men went from the van to the courthouse, but those curiosity seekers were kept behind police barricades.

Once inside, the gangsters were unceremoniously pushed in front of a grand jury. Police said that the boys were hauled in for consorting or as material witnesses or something, but none were officially booked on any charges at all.

The entire baker's dozen developed laryngitis the instant they heard the words "grand jury," and eventually lawyers found them and got them released on bail, a total of $1.3 million. The police put investigators on the task of finding out where all of that bail money came from.

During the grand jury hearing, which was set up to help figure out how "La Cosa Nostra" worked, only one witness was actually questioned, and he was an employee of the restaurant who said he didn't know who those guys were or why they were having dinner at La Stella.

Despite the lack of actual information learned, Queens District Attorney Nat Hentel, a politician who enjoyed hearing himself talk, held a loooong press conference, during which he called the La Stella meeting "bigger than Apalachin." Which it wasn't. It wasn't even close. Using many words, the DA didn't say much, but he teasingly fingered a stack of manila folders as he spoke.

"We believe," Hentel said, "these men under arrest have knowledge of specific major crimes committed in Queens. The Mob empire has changed over the last few years. New [crime] families have sprung up, like in New Jersey, and new facts must be elicited and brought out."

Good luck with that.

"Which specific and major crimes are these?" a reporter scribbling in a tiny notebook asked.

"For one thing, we are seeking info on the September 20 murder of Joseph Cannistraci near the Long Island Expressway near Lake Success," the DA said.

Cannistraci had been thirty-two years old when whacked and had clearly never missed a meal—his stiff weighed 348 pounds. Cannistraci had been scheduled to be questioned by the rackets bureau of the Queens District Attorney's Office, but he failed to show up on account of being iced.

Hentel told the press that Cannistraci had made land and stock dealings that reeked of corruption and illegality, and he was interested in knowing what the Mob bigs under arrest knew about them.

As it turned out, none of the arrested men had anything to say about Cannistraci. The thing that was troubling Gambino was that someone had dropped a dime on the La Stella meet, telling the NYPD where and when. That was the rat that needed to be taken care of first.

The conference was supposed to be super secret. If no one ratted, the only other possibility was that one of the guys attending the meeting had been tailed. Gambino suspected that wasn't the case, as he and his bodyguards had developed a sixth sense regarding shadows.

Hentel said things he probably should've held in. He said maybe he would call Joseph Valachi to testify before his grand jury. There was a guy who you could rely on to blab about something. The problem with that idea was that Valachi was in solitary confinement in an Illinois federal penitentiary and was probably not the expert on current events that he'd once been.

"I have sent my assistant DA, Albert Perante, to Tioga County, site of the Apalachin conclave, to get all available info on that meeting. We are in touch with the local authorities up there to see if there is a link between the meeting in Queens and that one nine years ago," the DA said.

Hentel said that this investigation involved multiple jurisdictions and different law enforcement agencies, which were working together. These included NYPD, FBI, Treasury agents, and U.S.

Marshals. They were also in touch with law enforcement in the out-of-town locations repped by the La Stella gangsters.

"I am in contact with officials in Louisiana, Florida, New Jersey, and other locations. We feel that the mobsters we nabbed here were superior to those arrested in Apalachin."

It was hard to tell where that last comment came from. It wasn't a competition. The DA was just trying to make himself seem big.

A reporter asked the DA, "What was the La Stella meeting all about?"

"They were discussing what to do about top hoods who were in trouble with the law," Hentel said. When a hood was in too much trouble with the law, he was often murdered to secure his silence, Hentel explained.

Another reporter asked if he had any names, and he said yes, he believed that the fate of Sonny Franzese was discussed; Franzese was a prominent Long Island gangster who was under federal indictment for running a bank-robbery operation.

The bottom line was that they had nothing to hold any of the arrested men, and life went on. Hentel, the long-winded district attorney, was defeated in a landslide in the next election.

CHAPTER 15
Swinging Sixties

AFTER ALBERT ANASTASIA DIED, Gambino inherited the waterfront. There was a surprisingly smooth transition, considering that the guy actually on the docks ruling with an iron fist was the dead man's brother, Tough Tony Anastasio, who must've known who whacked Albert.

When the Mad Hatter was hit in the barbershop, Tony had to go to work for Gambino. It had to have been hell on him. But there was nothing he could do about it. He would either take orders from Gambino or join Albert in eternity.

As it turned out, "natural causes" felled Tough Tony, and he only outlived his more-famous brother by six years. Anastasio's funeral was held on March 5, 1963, on a gray, misty morning. Every member of the International Longshoremen's Association was there. Forty-eight cars were in the funeral procession, which toured Red Hook, Brooklyn, along the piers, at pedestrian speed. The funeral was held in St. Stephen's Church, the Mass celebrated by Tough Tony's priest brother, Sal Anastasio.

Tough Tony was buried in Holy Cross Cemetery, in East Flatbush, and a portly gravedigger was still patting a mound of dirt with the back of his shovel when the dead man's union post was taken by his twenty-eight-year-old son-in-law "Young" Tony Scotto.

Young Tony was a big man—six-two, two hundred, physically

intimidating—yet could work the legit side to Gambino's best advantage. Young Tony could schmooze with politicians, he could sweet-talk the press.

In 1966, efforts began yet again by the Immigration and Naturalization Service (INS) to kick Gambino out of the country. Gambino immediately checked into a hospital with heart trouble.

So, when the INS held its first hearing on the Gambino case, they were forced to do it in Gambino's room, in the U.S. Public Health Service Hospital on Staten Island, New York City's most remote borough.

A federal prosecutor gave a little speech while Gambino lay motionless in bed. He said that Gambino had been arrested sixteen times and convicted six times. "His activities include gambling, shylocking, labor racketeering, extortion, and alcohol tax violations. He is also suspected of being active in narcotics," the prosecutor said.

Gambino's eyes stayed closed, not even a flicker.

Gently, Don Carlo was alerted to the fact that he was about to be quizzed. He was questioned by a federal prosecutor briefly, answering questions in a voice so soft that it was barely audible.

Gambino answered two or three questions and then clutched his chest and said, "I have a pain."

While the feds looked at each other with smirks on their faces, the nurses fussed over Gambino. A doctor came running in and put an oxygen mask over Don Carlo's face.

There would be no more questions.

The feds made one of the doctors take the oath and testify as to what was wrong with the Boss.

"He has arteriosclerotic heart disease," the doctor testified.

One fed swore in another fed and there was testimony to the effect that maybe Gambino was too sick to answer a few questions regarding his illegal entry into the country, but he wasn't too sick to go to business meetings, get a haircut, have meals in restaurants, or attend family events.

* * *

On December 30, 1966, the INS ordered Gambino's deportation on the grounds that he had illegally entered the U.S. from Sicily as a nineteen-year-old stowaway on a ship that docked in Norfolk, Virginia, in 1921.

"I love this country," Gambino said. "It would break my heart to leave." Again, he gingerly touched his own chest.

For five years, Gambino's lawyer, Edward Ennis, appealed the deportation order to the Board of Immigration Appeals in Washington, D.C., always using a note from Gambino's doctor saying that a trip across the Atlantic would almost certainly kill the old man—who was only sixty-four.

Also in 1966, Joe Bonanno's problems managed to get even worse. He'd been shunned by his partners in crime and scrutinized by U.S. authorities. Now his troubles were compounded by Sicilian Law.

Investigating Magistrate Aldo Vigneri flew to the U.S. during the first week of 1966 and announced that he had filed eight thousand typewritten pages of evidence with judicial authorities in Palermo and was seeking indictment of twenty-one persons, including Joe Bonanno. The list included Carmine "Lilo" Galante. Almost everyone on the list was involved in heroin trafficking.

On January 28, 1966, Bonanno's son Salvatore, upset at the downsizing of his dad's crime family by Carlo Gambino and Sam the Plumber, planned to retake some of dad's old turf.

Sal's war erupted in May 1966. A massive gunfight between the Sal Bonanno crew and Gaspare DiGregorio's gunmen. The pitched battle took place on Troutman Street in the Bushwick section of Brooklyn. A peaceful meet had been planned. The two sides, it was hoped, would iron out a truce. But when Bonanno and crew arrived, gunmen up and down the block, stretched out on fire escapes and perched behind windows, began shooting.

Bonanno's men dropped behind a car and returned fire. More than one hundred shots were fired. No one was hit. There wasn't even a graze wound. The gunfight, though bloodless, was precisely the sort of thing that the Five Family system was designed to prevent. Gambino, his power immense, simply told Gaspare DiGregorio that he wasn't boss anymore.

"You retire now," Don Carlo said. Gambino named a new head of the Bonanno clan, Paul Sciacca—a guy no one had heard of. So, Sciacca was boss, but of what? The "family" he took charge of was even weaker than the one DiGregorio had led. The fact that a boss could be fired as easily as Gambino fired DiGregorio raised the question, was he really a boss at all?

As this was going on, Tommy Lucchese was very sick, although he didn't die until July 1967. During his last days he was released from the hospital and allowed to die at home in his Lido Beach mansion. Don Carlo's oldest friend was gone.

Gambino now voted at the table for himself and for the Lucchese family. Two votes.

In May 1966, Joe Bonanno, tired of sitting alone in the desert watching buzzards circle, returned to New York to see if he could salvage any of his previous power. He stayed at his son's house, a fortresslike structure in East Meadow, Long Island.

To help him get his power back, Bonanno brought in a roly-poly international killer, Gaspare Magaddino. The guy had an awesome résumé: fifty notches on his gun, hits on three continents and Latin America.

Gaspare Magaddino, on Friday, November 10, 1967, shot up the Cypress Gardens on Cypress Avenue near Starr Street, killing three of Sciacca's men: fifty-five-year-old Thomas "Smitty" DiAngelo; his brother, fifty-eight-year-old James DiAngelo; and forty-three-year-old Frank "Frankie Five Hundred" Telleri. The killer used a .45-caliber submachine gun. The total number of bullets fired is unknown. What is known is that twenty-two slugs hit flesh. (The Cypress Gardens is now a very cool bar known as The Keep. The bullet holes are still in the wall.)

According to the police, this was not the first time Gaspare

Magaddino had been summoned to New York to do a job. He was the prime suspect in the October 7, 1964, hit on cement worker and degenerate gambler Alvery Galente. Magaddino was also wanted in Sicily in connection with a series of bombings.

The Cypress Gardens killings started an all-out war within the Bonanno family. Upward of twenty guys got whacked, mostly those still loyal to Joe Bonanno. The man who came to New York from Sicily to run the Castellammarese faction for his father in America returned to Tucson, Arizona, exiled, this time for good.

Again, Gambino was safe from rogue hoods from New York's Five Families. All of the remaining bosses were his friends. His remaining worries had to do with a group he had less control of: non-Italian mobsters.

There was a gang working out of Harlem that called themselves Kidnap, Inc. They kidnapped hoods and collected ransom. They did this without Gambino's Good Housekeeping seal of approval.

Kidnap, Inc. had black guys, Irish guys, Puerto Rican guys, even a few Italian guys. Their MO was always the same: They wore badges so that the men they apprehended thought they were being arrested.

One victim of Kidnap, Inc. was thirty-six-year-old Frank "Whitey Marsh" Angelo, a heroin dealer snatched off a Harlem street on June 11, 1966. These guys didn't bluff. They abused Angelo while he was in captivity, demanded sixty grand from Angelo's drug-dealing partner Rudy DeLuca.

DeLuca tried to talk the kidnappers down to thirty thousand, so the kidnappers offed Whitey, cut his body into pieces, and dumped them into the Hudson River.

Another flashy kidnapping by the group came on April 24, 1967, when Mike Luongo was snatched just outside a Harlem nightclub.

The Kidnap, Inc. boys are important to our story because some of the estimated half a million dollars they raked in came from ransoms that Carlo Gambino paid. Gambino, sick of this business, put out the word: fifty thousand bucks for one name of the kidnap gang.

Soon thereafter another rumor made the rounds, that the kidnappers were planning to kidnap Gambino himself and ransom him for a cool million.

Gambino was never kidnapped, but someone did come forward with a kidnapper's name—two names, in fact—and presumably collected the reward. Those names were: forty-nine-year-old Clarence Eugene Christian and twenty-eight-year-old Walter Allen "Butch" Hooker.

On December 23, 1968, Patrolman James Clinton of the Pelham Manor police was cruising through his community, which sits along the northern border of the Bronx, just off the Pelham Bay golf course. The cop spotted a parked panel truck with what appeared to be a sleeping man behind the steering wheel. The officer got out of his car and approached the truck. The man wasn't asleep but rather had a bullet hole in his temple.

Clinton then opened the rear compartment of the truck and found a second body, also with a single bullet wound to the temple. They were, of course, Christian, a Bronx native, and Hooker, who came from Norfolk, Virginia. Christian had one arrest on his record, for dealing narcotics. Hooker had a clean record but was also reputedly involved in selling heroin.

Cops looking into the backgrounds of the victims found that the two men had been bragging about "grabbing Mafia guys" and flashing wads of cash to choke a horse.

The dead men in the truck were only two of five murders that night, all within a five-mile radius. All with connections to the drug trade. The most noteworthy of the other victims was twenty-seven-year-old Joseph Gernie, Jr., a guy from Bensonhurst who was free on bail after being caught in possession of $5,000 worth of babonia and was an actor who'd had a bit part in the movie *The Detective*, alongside Frank Sinatra.

That was the beginning of the end for Kidnap, Inc. But they weren't through yet. In April 1969, they nabbed a guy named Richard Lawrence, a former heroin dealer with few friends and not a dime to his name. He griped that no one would be willing to pay his ransom.

"I'm nobody," Lawrence said.

The kidnappers realized their mistake and said they'd let Lawrence go free if he coughed up the names of some guys who might be worthy of ransom. Lawrence said sure, and the instant he was free he went to the police.

The NYPD set up a trap. On May 13, 1969, Detective Lieutenant Pasquale Intrieri and Detective Delmar Watson impersonated a pair of well-to-do hoods at the Bronx-Whitestone Motel on the Hutchinson River Parkway. Lawrence gave the kidnappers the name of the hotel and sure enough, Kidnap, Inc. was quickly on the scene to do their thing.

The kidnappers were forty-year-old Stanley Tuttle and thirty-nine-year-old Frank Rivetti. With them was a tiny man, no more than five-two, one-twenty soaking wet, the boss of Kidnap, Inc., forty-three-year-old Anthony "Tony the Shrimp" LaSorsca. The Shrimp was a head case, compensating for his shortcomings. He felt that the Italian Mob had rejected him because of his size, and he was going to show them what a big man he could be.

The Kidnap, Inc. trio snatched the undercover cops, put them in a car, and drove—unaware that police were on their tail. The kidnappers drove smack into a roadblock.

Rivetti and Tuttle stopped the car and came out with guns blazing, but they were no match for the cops—Rivetti was killed and Tuttle wounded. The Shrimp ran off, got away from the roadblock, and hijacked a car back to Harlem.

The terrified persons in the hijacked car later identified LaSorsca from photos. LaSorsca's name was in the papers, and that was all Gambino needed. He immediately sent out hunters—an open hit, they called it.

Neither of the undercover policemen was injured. Tuttle gave up the Shrimp during interrogation. The Shrimp was terrified by his new notoriety, and he saw Gambino gunmen around every corner,

While the rest of the Mob was playing checkers, Carlo Gambino played chess. His was a deep game, replete with multitiered schemes that allowed him to accrue power like a black hole sucking in planets. *New York Police Department/ Wikimedia Commons*

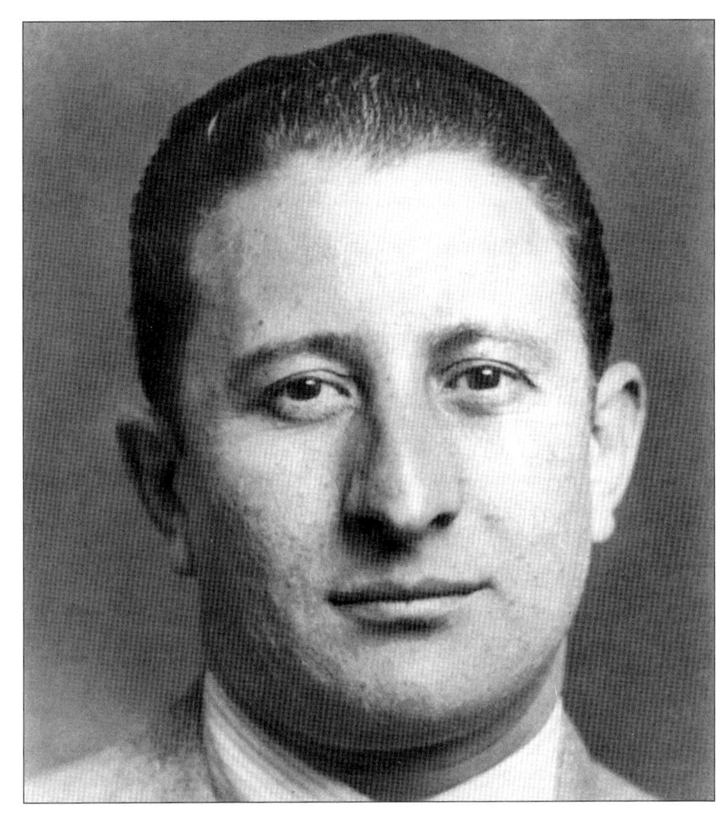

ank DiMatteo's biological d, "Funzi" Milone, ught under the name l Milone. This is a poster vertising his fight at e Paterson Armory in aterson, New Jersey, ainst Stefan Redl, May 4, 957. He lost by TKO at night. *uthor's collection*

REPEAT OF ANOTHER
ZALE-GRAZIANO SLUGFEST
PATERSON ARMORY
SAT. 8:30 P.M.
MAY 4
- 475 MARKET ST., PATERSON, N. J. -
MAIN EVENT 10 ROUNDS
STEFAN REDL
STEFAN REDL
AL ROCKY MILONE
Al "Rocky" Milone
PRICES $5 - $4 - $3 - $2 taxes incl ed
Phone Reservations, ARmory 4-0058

Carlo Gambino grew up to be a man in Palermo—a made man, in fact. He was from a Mafia family and was all buttoned-up before he came over on the boat to work the rackets in America.
Xerones/ Wikimedia Commons.

Palermo street scene from 191
when Carlo Gambino was eight years o
Library of Congre

As kids running the streets, Gambino and Lucchese idolized that era's Sicilian Boss of Bosses, Don Vito Cascio Ferro, shown here in a 1902 mug shot. Don Vito had gone to America as a boy (actually fled, as he was wanted for murder), became an original Black Hand terrorist, made a mint, and returned to Sicily dripping power.
Author's collection

Don Vito's legend crossed paths with Detective Joseph Petrosino, a New York City cop who was relentlessly battling the Black Hand. Petrosino traveled to Sicily in 1909 to lay waste to the underworld but lasted only hours and was quickly assassinated on a Palermo street. Don Vito himself hit Petrosino. The whacking of Petrosino was greeted with shouts of joy by the boys of Palermo, including Carlo Gambino. Carlo wanted to be just like Don Vito when he grew up.
Author's collection

Gambino's first godfather in America was Giuseppe Masseria—Joe the Boss. Like all of Gambino's godfathers in America, Masseria was whacked, on April 15, 1931, at Gerardo Scarpato's Nuova Villa Tammaro in Coney Island. The Masseria hit, and its violent aftermath, proved to be a pivotal moment in Mob history. It helped to put into place the Mob leadership that would remain for most of the remainder of the century. I know this because my uncle Joe Schipani was a driver for Lucky Luciano and told me so. *Wikimedia Commons*

The beautiful but surprisingly humble home of Carlo and Kathryn Gambino for close to forty years. Even after he built his summer place on Long Island, this house on Ocean Parkway in the Midwood section of Brooklyn remained home base when Don Carlo was working in the city. *Author's collection*

Our Lady of Grace Church in Brooklyn. On December 5, 1926, Gambino was wed here to Kathryn. Just shy of fifty years later, the same church was the scene of both their funerals.
Author's collection

At the start of December 1936, Gambino and his cousin Paul Castellano opened a new business venture, The Independent Meat Market on Quentin Road. This is what the location looks like today. Back then, however, the joint was equipped with several grinders and could make hamburger of any kind of meat.
Author's collection

Vincenzo Giovanni Mangano, aka Vincent Mangano, aka the Executioner, was boss until April 18, 1951 when he was clipped by the man who would take his position, Albert Anastasia.

Gambino's first underboss was Joseph "Banty" Biondo. One of Biondo's primary tasks in that role was to take attaché cases full of cash to Italy and give them to Lucky Luciano. Biondo kept his job until 1965, when Gambino forced him into retirement and replaced him with Aniello Dellacroce. Biondo died of natural causes a year later and was buried in Maple Grove Cemetery in Kew Gardens, Queens.
Author's collection

Photograph taken on April 11, 1976, at the 3,500-seat Westchester Premier Theater in Tarrytown, New York, after Sinatra's performance. The back row consisted of Paul Castellano, Gregory DePalma, Sinatra, Frank Marson, Carlo Gambino (with eyes closed), and Jimmy "the Weasel" Fratianno. In front were the godfather's brother Joseph Gambino and Richard "Nerves" Fusco.
Wikimedia Commons

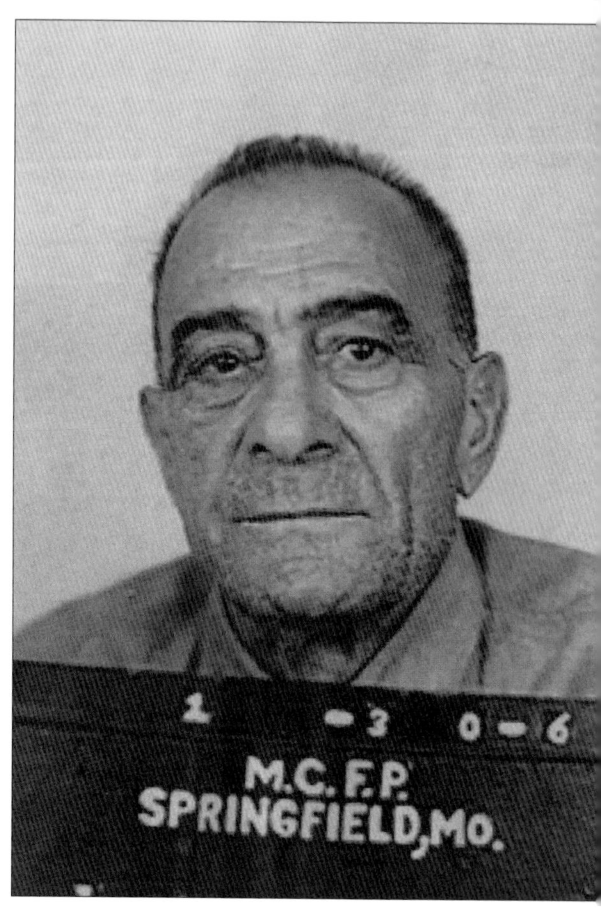

Bad things happened to guys who posed a threat to Gambino's rise to the top. Some guys were just erased. Vito Genovese (shown here) was set up for a major drug bust and forced to spend his remaining years in prison. This mug shot was taken near the end of his life, after he became an inmate at the Medical Center Federal Penitentiary, a jail for the terminally ill.
U.S. Department of Corrections

Former bootlegger Armand "Tommy" Rava was arrested at Apalachin. After that, he didn't travel much. On the rare occasion when he left Bensonhurst, he only got as far as Dyker Heights. He wanted to strike back at Gambino after the Anastasia hit, but soon thereafter disappeared, reportedly iced by Salvatore "Little Toddo" Avarello.
Author's collection

Genovese underboss Thomas "Tommy Ryan" Eboli was overheard saying he couldn't stand Don Carlo. He said that the Gambino crime family was full of degenerates. Eboli got about as far as a hood could get without being Carlo Gambino's friend. In July 1972, his body with its ruined head was discovered on a sidewalk in front of this building on Lefferts Avenue near New York Avenue at one o'clock in the morning.
Author's collection

Vincent "the Chin" Gigante was a boss for a quarter century. My mom, Dee, says she only met him twice, but on one occasion she mentioned to him that there was only one kind of champagne she liked, and from then on, every Easter the Chin would send her a case of Taittinger champagne. To others, he wasn't as nice.
US Department of Justice

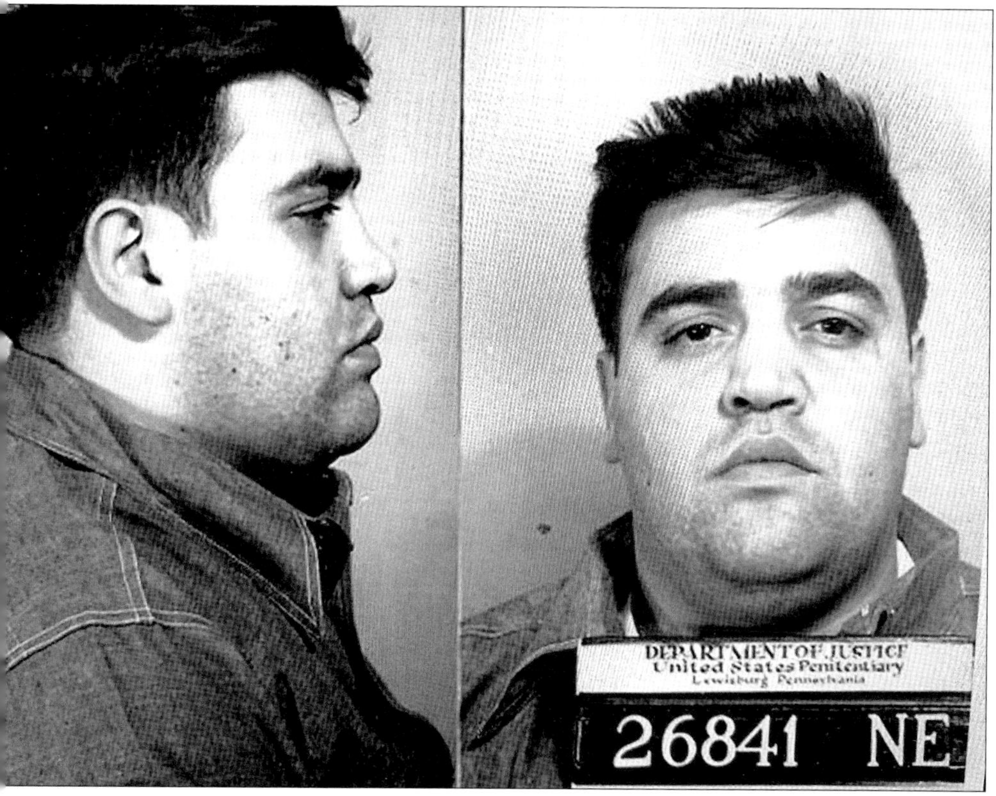

"Big" Paul Castellano was both Gambino's first cousin and brother-in-law. He was untouchable as long as Don Carlo was alive. Once Gambino was dead, however, Castellano's protection dropped and he ended up dead in the middle of a Manhattan street, making way for the John Gotti era.
Wikimedia Commons

The deadliest operation under t auspices of the Gambino crime fami was a massive auto-theft ring run b Roy DeMeo out of a Brooklyn b called the Gemini Lounge, built o a corner lot on Flatlands Aven with a slaughterhouse back roo where scores of victims were off and dismembere
F.

Roy DeMeo, the Gambinos' most prolific killer, died just as you'd expect, whacked by members of his own crew. He's buried in St. John Cemetery in Middle Village, Queens.
Author's collection

Site of the Gemini Lounge, built on a corner lot on Flatlands Avenue. Today, as seen here, the old blood-and-guts saloon is a church.
Author's collection

Gambino porn king Robert DiBernard
was a friend of my dad and was a
his house for breakfast twice a month
DB made his bones with the DeCavalcant
crew from New Jersey, and later becam
caporegime in the Gambino family
DB's fatal flaw was he was a loner
He came and went on his own, no posse
no entourage. He paid his tribute
but he had his own mind
Author's collectio

The DeMeo crew was the deadliest of the Gambino crews. They snatched guys, offed them in the Gemini Lounge, disassembled them in Joseph "Dracula" Guglielmo's apartment, then bagged them up and dumped them here, in Jamaica Bay off the Canarsie Pier.
Author's collection

My mom on the left, DB on the right, and DB's wife in the middle, in a detail from a group shot taken at my wedding.
Author's collection

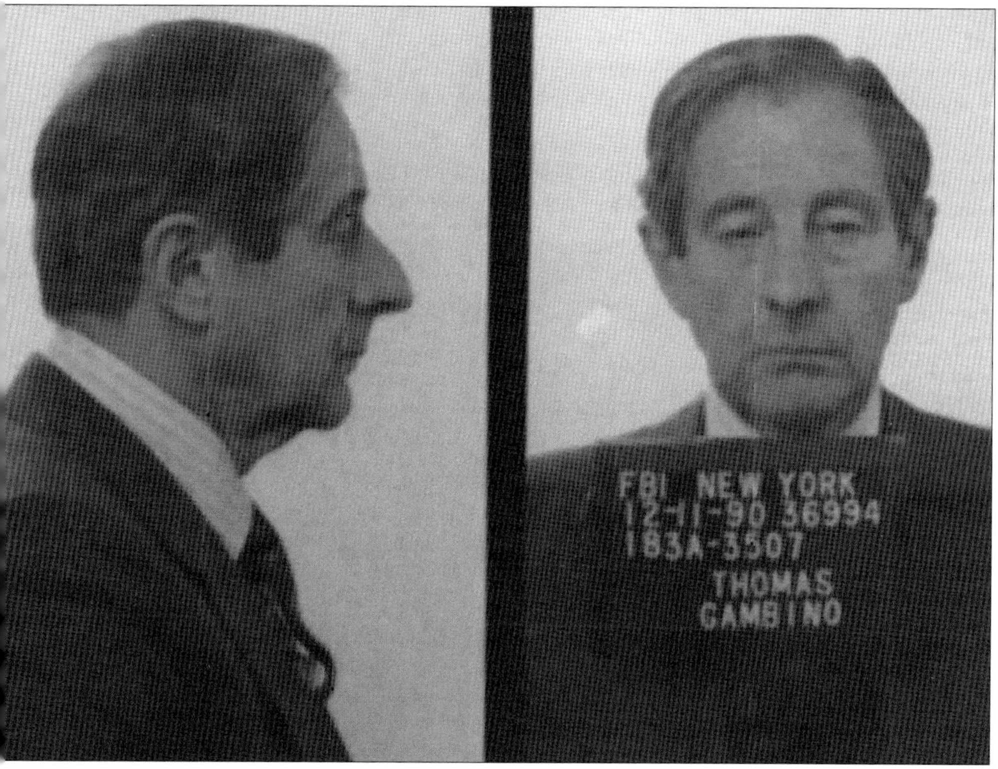

Carlo's son Thomas Francis Gambino was born on August 23, 1929. With Don Carlo as his dad and Big Paulie as his uncle, it should surprise no one that he went into the Life, became a made man in the family that bore his father's name, and did all right for himself. There was power in his last name, and he knew it. In 1995, the feds put him behind bars for five years for racketeering.
FBI

Seventy years ago, Aniello Dellacroce bought and set up shop at the Ravenite Social Club in Little Italy. Here's the way the joint looks today, a long time since it was a clubhouse.
Author's collection.

THE CARLO GAMBINO FAMILY

X MEMBERS CONVICTED AS RESULT OF U.S. BUREAU OF NARCOTICS INVESTIGATIONS

KEY TO ACTIVITY CODE

1A. CURRENTLY IN JAIL FOR NARCOTICS
1B. AWAITING TRIAL FOR NARCOTICS
1C. PREVIOUS CONVICTION FOR NARCOTICS
1D. SUSPECTED OF BEING ACTIVE IN NARCOTICS
2. GAMBLING
3. SHYLOCKING
4. LABOR RACKETEERING
5. VENDING MACHINES AND/OR JUKE BOXES
6. EXTORTION, STRONG ARM AND MURDER
7. COUNTERFEITING
8. CRIMINALLY RECEIVING
9. ALCOHOL TAX VIOLATIONS
* IDENTIFIED BY JOSEPH VALACHI

BOSS

CARLO GAMBINO
ALIAS
"DON CARLO"
FBI #834-460
N.Y.C.P.D.-B#128760

Successor to:

ALBERT ANASTASIA
VINCENT MANGANO
PHILIP MANGANO

UNDERBOSS

JOSEPH BIONDO
ALIAS
"JOE BANTY", "CUNNIGLIEDDU"

Successor to:

FRANK SCALICE
ALIAS
"DON CHEECH"

CONSIGLIERE

JOSEPH RICCOBONO
ALIAS
"STATEN ISLAND JOE"

CAPOREGIME

PRESENT

PAUL CASTELLANO — "CONSTANTINE"
ANTHONY ZANGARRA — "CHARLIE BRUSH"
CARMINE LOMBARDOZZI — "THE DOCTOR"
PAOLO GAMBINO — "DON PAOLO"
JOSEPH COLAZZO — "GUS"
ARTHUR LEO — "CHINK"
ANIELLO DELLACROCE — "O'NEIL"
ETTORE ZAPPI
ROCCO MAZZIE — "ROGIE"
CHARLES DONGARRO — "ROSARIO"
ANTHONY SEDOTTO — "TONY THE GEEP"
PETER FERRARA — "PETEY PUMPS"

FORMER

JOHN ROBILOTTO — "JOHNNY ROBERTS"
FRANK CASTELLANO
ARMAND RAVA — "TOMMY RAVA"
VINCENT SQUILLANTE — "JIMMY JEROME"
GIUSEPPE TRAINA
ANTHONY ANASTASIA — "TOUGH TONY"
STEVEN ARMONE

SOLDIERS – BUTTONS

ANDREW ALBERTI
SEBASTIANO BELLANCA — "BALD HEAD," "BENNY THE BUM"
MIKE D'ALLESIO — "MIKEY DEE"
ANTHONY GRANZA — "SKUNGE"
JOSEPH MANFREDI — "JOJO"
ANTHONY PLATE — "TONY PLATE"
AL SERU
GERMAIO ANACLERIO — "JERRY"
SALVATORE BONFRISCO
CHARLES DeLUTRO — "CHARLIE WEST"
FRANK GUGLIELMINI
JAMES MASSI — "JIMMY WARD"
GIACOMO (JOHN) SCALICI
JAMES STASSI
MICHAEL BOVE — "MICKEY BONE"
NICHOLAS DiBENE — "BENNY"
SALLY GUGLIELMINI
FRANK MOCCARDI — "FRANK THE BOSS"
JOSEPH SCALICI
JOSEPH STASSI — "JOE ROGERS" "HOBOKEN JOE"
JOSEPH ARMONE
ANTHONY CARMINATI — "LITTLE TONY"
ALEX DeBRIZZI
JOSEPH INDELICATO — "JOE SCOOTCH"
SABATO MURO — "SAMMY MINTZ"
SALVATORE SCALICI
FELICE TETI
EDUARDO ARONICA
JAMES CASABLANCA — "VINCENT CASABLANCA," "JAMES COSSIA"
CHARLES GAGLIODOTTO
GIUSEPPE LoPICCOLO — "JOSEPH"
FRANK PASQUA — "BIG FRANK"
GIACOMO SCARPULLA — "JACK"
ARTHUR TORTORELLA
PETER BARATTA — "BULL," "PETE BARATO"
FRANK GAGLIARDI — "FRANK THE WOP"
FRANK LUCIANO — "FRANK MILLER"
MICHAEL PECORARO — "SKINNY MIKE"
MIKE SCANDIFIA — "MIKE SCANDI"
PETER TORTORELLA
CHARLES BARCELLONA — "CHARLIE THE WOP," "SLEEPY"
MATTHEW CUOMO — "JOE CUOMO"
MICHAEL GALGANO — "BLACKIE," "BLACK MIKE"
ANIELLO MANCUSO — "WAHOO"
DOMINICK PETITO — "JOE PITTS"
FRANK BARRANCA
ALEX D'ALLESIO — "POPE"
PASQUALE GENESE — "PATSY JEROME"
GENARO MANCUSO Alias "JERRY"
LARRY PISTONE
PAUL ZACCARIA
ERNESTO BARESE — "FRANK MARTIN"
JOHN D'ALLESIO — "JOHNNY DEE"
HUGO ROSSI

This is the chart prepared for the McClellan Committee hearings in 1963.

FBI surveillance photo of John Gotti.

Gambino's body was placed on view in a $7,000 bronze casket, beginning at two in the afternoon on October 16, 1976, at Cusimano & Russo funeral chapel on West Sixth Street in Gravesend, Brooklyn, twelve blocks west of Gambino's Brooklyn home. *Author's collection*

The Gambino tomb in St. John Cemetery, in Middle Village, Queens. Don Carlo rests below his daughter Phyllis and over his wife Kathryn. *Author's collection*

lurking in every shadow. So, he turned himself in to police, and Kidnap, Inc. officially ceased to exist.

LaSorsca was arrested at a prearranged spot along deserted Waterbury Avenue, off East Tremont Road, near Saint Raymond's Cemetery. It's unclear if any of the principals knew it, but this was the precise location of an attempted ransom drop after the Lindbergh baby was kidnapped in 1932.

In the long run, all members of Kidnap, Inc. were either killed or sent to jail. For all the Shrimp's efforts, he never even put a dent in the Mob he felt had rejected him.

Back during the spring of 1953, the New York State Crime Commission, with help from the New Jersey Law Enforcement Council, had climaxed an eighteen-month investigation with a report saying that the only way to clean up the docks was for the state to control the waterfront and drive the corruption out.

On paper, the idea sounded very tough and effective.

Fifteen years later, the commission was still hearing sworn testimony from witnesses about the same old corruption that had been on those piers ever since there were piers.

In 1968, the commission listened to the testimony of Salvatore Passalacqua, who said that Tough Tony Anastasio hired him back in 1959, and that he had paid Anastasio thirty bucks a week for the rest of Tough Tony's life.

That was same old, same old, but Passalacqua's testimony got more interesting. During the summer of 1965, his pier boss, Gaspar Romano, told him his presence was requested at a meeting in the union office. When he got there he found Don Carlo, Young Tony, and Joe Colozzo.

According to Passalacqua's sworn testimony: "[Colozzo] told me the reason for the meeting was to introduce me to the boss, Carlo Gambino, because if there was anyone who deserved to become a member of the honorable family, then Don Carlo should know about it so that he could, after following the tradition of the laws, and if I was willing to accept an invitation, they were ready to take me into the family as one of their peers.

"I told them that I was not ready to give an answer on the spot, because that was not the reason I had gone to the meeting in the first place. Young Tony asked why I needed time, why I couldn't give an answer right then. Then Carlo Gambino said, 'Give him time so he can think about it.' And then he said to me, 'When you leave this room don't say anything to anybody, so that what we speak about here is just between us.' And then he told me that if I agreed to join them, I would get my orders from Young Tony and that I would have to submit to his orders at the risk of my life.

"Ten days later there was another attempt to persuade me to join and I stalled for more time. Scotto told me that he'd gone to Don Carlo and had gotten down on a knee to pray for you. I told Mr. Scotto that Mr. Gambino was a scoundrel. He said, 'Don't let anyone hear you say that. You are the scoundrel for having insulted him.'"

Scotto, when asked in 1970 by the New York State Joint Legislative Committee on Crime, denied ever attending any meeting with Passalacqua. He was also asked if it was true that Carlo Gambino and his wife attended Scotto's wedding to Marion Anastasio, Tough Tony's daughter, and the reception afterward on New Year's Day 1957 at the Plaza Hotel in the city. He said it was. During that same interrogation, Scotto was asked if he was a member of the Mafia. Scotto took advantage of his Fifth Amendment right to avoid self-incrimination.

Colozzo and Gambino had in common a method of dealing with the Law. Like Don Carlo, Colozzo's heart ailment always grew much worse when he found himself in a courtroom. He was indicted by a federal grand jury in 1962 for submitting false union reports, but the case was never tried because of multiple delays related to Colozzo's health.

And, like Gambino, Colozzo's heart troubles were not totally imaginary and eventually did him in, but he was a free man at the time of his death (1971), and on holiday in Italy. Even during his last days, according to FBI surveillance, Colozzo was a regular guest at Gambino's Oyster Bay home, often in the company of Dominick "Joe Pip" Petito, a Gambino soldier.

Petito, like Colozzo, was a familiar face on the piers, relaying messages from Gambino to union leaders in Red Hook.

Always looking to expand his empire, Gambino in 1963 decided to take the moneymaking systems he had in place—on the docks and on the roads—and use them to tap into construction on Long Island, specifically the Nassau-Suffolk Buildings Trade Council. The idea was: nothing gets built on Long Island without Gambino getting a piece. He assigned two waterfront veterans, Colozzo and Petito, to supervise the start-up.

At one point, the Nassau County district attorney hauled Petito in and grilled him about his trips to the Gambinos' home. He said he didn't know nothing from nothing, he was just the driver. He took Colozzo to the meetings in his Cadillac and waited in the car.

Shadows knew everyone's routine. Colozzo and Petito didn't just have meetings with the Boss, they were known to meet regularly with Joe and Paul Gambino, and with first cousin Thomas Masotto, who according to law enforcement files was strictly legit.

Masotto (who was not strictly legit) had only once been in trouble, back in 1959, when he purchased a gun to keep behind the counter at his meat market that turned out to be one of forty-five guns stolen from a shipment coming into town via a Manhattan pier. (Another of the guns that fell off that same boat was used to bump off Frankie Shots in 1959, a hit that greatly affected the President Street Boys.) Masotto lost his pistol license in the deal but was not arrested. In fact, he'd never been arrested.

Masotto was born in Italy in 1907, and came to New York as a small boy. One of his sisters, Yolanda, was murdered in Highland, New York, on July 29, 1942. She was thirty-five years old at the time and ran a pastry store on Avenue U in Brooklyn. She was vacationing upstate when she received an unsigned telegram and went out. Six and a half hours later, her body was found with fourteen stab wounds, lying at the side of a road. Interestingly, she'd been stabbed with two weapons, an ice pick and a knife.

Masotto was always true to Cousin Carlo, but he knew no finesse. He was the sort of guy who used sledgehammers to handle jobs that only needed a screwdriver. He once was the subject of FBI electronic surveillance. His Freeport, New York, home was bugged up and down. The house soon thereafter burned to the ground. That's one way to get rid of the electronic surveillance. Trouble was, Masotto went away for arson.

Yolanda's wasn't the only murder in the Masotto family. Yolanda and Tom's brother Constantino "Jerry" Masotto, of Seventh Street, Brooklyn, was stabbed to death in New Orleans during the summer of 1943, found buried in a shallow grave approximately three months later. He'd told his wife he was going out to buy a newspaper and never returned. Jerry, a bigamist living under the name Gene Mano, had been the one to drive his sister upstate for her vacation and was considered a "key witness" in her murder. Carlo Gambino's cousins Yolanda and Jerry, both stabbed to death within a year of each other, were the only members of his biological family to be hit until nephew Manny was taken many years later.

Cousin Tom owned a series of meat markets and hadn't shown up on FBI radar. The first inkling that he wasn't legit came when they learned Masotto was often responsible for relaying personal, top-secret messages from Don Carlo to the top echelon of the other families. Instead of throwing slabs of meat on a scale, he was known to hang out on the Red Hook piers and was observed strutting about as if he owned the place. When the feds put a sharper focus on Masotto, they learned some uncomfortable truths, one being that there were New York City judges who considered themselves good friends of Cousin Tom. Masotto realized after a time that he was being tailed by feds, and his visits with his pals on the bench ended.

Throughout the late sixties, the feds tailed Don Carlo wherever he went. One day they followed him to a meeting at a Midtown Manhattan Chinese restaurant where he met with Joe Colombo, accompanied by Vincent Aloi, Angelo Bruno, and John Scimone.

Aloi, at six-two, two-twenty, towered over Gambino. There were few men who Don Carlo trusted more. Vinnie, as Gambino called him, was the thirty-five-year-old son of Sebastiano "Buster" Aloi, a friend from the old days running the streets. Gambino was Vinnie's godfather, not just as boss but by baptism as well. Vinnie ran a banquet hall for elegant weddings in Queens.

In an impulsive move, NYPD detectives swept in (with or without knowledge that an FBI op was underway) and busted the men for loitering, a terrible idea that took the men off the streets for exactly two hours before a judge set them free.

The men merely returned to the restaurant and continued their meeting—and their meal.

The next time this group got together it was at Gambino's Oyster Bay house, with a friend of Cousin Tom providing one hundred pounds of lobster. The feds had to stay outside. (According to the fish-market owner who sent the lobsters, Don Carlo complained about their quality and Cousin Tom was reimbursed for the cost.)

In 1969, the U.S. Justice Department compiled a chart of the top echelon of gangsters in the U.S. According to the feds, Gambino's underboss was Dellacroce, his consigliere was Joseph Riccobono, and the capos were (in alphabetical order with a few biographical highpoints):

- David Amodeo, head of the Gambinos' largest crew in the Bronx;
- Domenico "Mike" Arcuri, worked out of the city but also had rackets in Connecticut;
- Paul Castellano, who we know, Gambino's cousin and brother-in-law;
- Joseph "Gus" Colozzo, another Anastasia boy, known as "Iron Claw" on the docks. Not a big man but had a knack

for scaring the shit out of guys, busted in 1951 for holding a gun on a representative of the International Longshoremen's Association;

- Frank Corbi, who went on to be Boss of Baltimore, Maryland, reported to Joseph N. Gallo;
- Joseph "Joe Butch" Corrao, son and nephew of Gambino members; operated out of Little Italy;
- Pasquale "Patsy" Conte, born 1925, died 2017, age ninety-two, indicted in 1987 for the murder of Pietro Alfano in Greenwich Village, busted at JFK Airport trying to flee the country but charges dropped without explanation; retired from the Life because of Alzheimer's;
- Charles Dongarra, controlled a large crew, told his boys in 1962 that Gambino forbid rackets involving bombs, kidnappings, or drugs;
- James Eppolito, capo probably best known as the blood uncle of the bad cop, Louis Eppolito;
- James "Jimmy Brown" Failla, born 1919, died 1999; ran a crew out of Brooklyn, but his turf also included parts of Staten Island, Manhattan, and New Jersey; raised in Bensonhurst, for thirty years controlled the Trade Waste Association of Greater New York; in 1989 participated in the murder of Gambino soldier Thomas Spinelli; later served as Don Carlo's driver/bodyguard;
- Pumps Ferrara, once overheard on electronic surveillance in a Coney Island gas station talking about his part in the murder of Alfredo Santonio;
- Joseph Gambino, the Boss's brother;
- Olympio Garofalo, capo, small crew of ten, but good earners;
- Anthony "Tony Naps" Napolitano, born 1926, died 2010, charter member of the 107th Street Mob, moved dope on a city-to-city level, spent seventeen years in prison on drug conspiracy charges;
- Joseph Dominic Paterno, became capo at a very young age, worked out of New Jersey;

- Frank Perrone, New Jersey capo, and the sort of guy whose bachelor party made the papers;
- Gaetano "Guy" Russo, born in 1891, Palermo-made; the Mob's undertaker, most in the straight world thought him legit; operated a big-time funeral parlor, Cusimano & Russo; already old when Anastasia was bumped but became a trusted and respected elder member of Gambino's braintrust; died in 1970;
- Anthony Scotto, Young Tony, much discussed;
- Anthony Sedotto, aka Tony the Geep, former member of Vincent Squillante's crew;
- Joseph Silesi, caporegime of Gambino's Miami crew;
- Giuseppe Traina, aka the Peasant, from San Giuseppe Jaco, Sicily, future underboss;
- Mario Traina, capo, Giuseppe's son, who lived to be old;
- Ettori Zappi, aka Tony Russo, capo, Gambino's Long Island neighbor, ran porn;
- Joseph Zingaro, a smart guy who some wanted to be consigliere instead of Joseph N. Gallo. It took RICO to take him down.

In 1969, Vito Genovese died of a heart attack in a federal penitentiary, creating another vacuum that Gambino quickly filled. To use Valachi's language, with Genovese and Lucchese gone, it was no longer *La Cosa Nostra*, it was *La Cosa Gambino.*

When Tommy Lucchese died, Gambino lost one of his oldest friends, one of the few guys still around who knew Gambino back in Palermo. To soften the loss, Gambino took control of the JFK Airport rackets.

Gambino bled John F. Kennedy International Airport in a way that greatly resembled the waterfront operation in Red Hook, Brooklyn. The docks and the airport were lucrative in the same way. Power with a capital *P* came with controlling what comes in and goes out of New York City at the point of entry and exit.

For Don Carlo, things didn't just fall off the truck, they fell off planes as well. And there were a lot of planes. Some of them jumbo cargo jets. Back in Gambino's day, an estimated $10 billion worth of stuff passed through JFK a year, and that was when $10B was real money.

To bleed that cargo, teams of operatives were set up, spotters to single out the valuable shit, and hijack teams to make away with some of it. The other way to tap into that money was to exploit the airport workers the same way they had the stevedores and longshoremen, by controlling the unions.

The most important union at JFK was Teamsters Local 295, which controlled the loading and unloading of freight. The second most important was the National Association for Air Freight, which represented the truck drivers who drove all of that stuff to and from the airport.

When a young John Gotti wanted to be a Gambino associate, he was tasked with hijacking trucks at JFK. When he got good at that he moved on to bigger and better things.

Truth was Tommy Lucchese laid the groundwork and had wormed his agents—Anthony "Tony Ducks" Corallo and John "Johnny Dio" Dioguardi—into the two key unions before the Gambino takeover. But, as was true when the Italians drove the Irish out of power on the piers of Brooklyn, Lucchese's operation was simplistic compared to Gambino's network.

In 1971, a fed grand jury indicted the director of both Teamsters Local 295 and the National Association for Air Freight. The feds claimed the Teamsters and Air Freight unions were run by "ex-cons and racketeers."

According to legend, the Gambino guy inside Local 295 was Harry "Little Gangy" Davidoff, secretary/treasurer. Growing up in Brooklyn, the Davidoff brothers—there were three—were all shot at least once. Little Gangy and one brother were shot in 1943 in a Brooklyn bar, while the third brother, Bummy, an ex-pugilist, was killed in 1945 during a saloon stickup. In a way, Harry was the

"Tough Tony" of JFK. If a trucking company didn't do what it was told, the whole fleet's headlights might be smashed by morning.

Gambino milked airport workers in several ways. There were those who were degenerate gamblers and were given easy outlets for their addiction. When the slobs inevitably ran into debt, they were steered to a shylock, where they could get a ridiculous loan that they'd never be able to pay back. Those that fell behind in their payments were hurt, rarely killed (dead men never pay the bill), and sometimes a deal was made—forgiveness of debt in exchange for a lifetime of servitude—and the poor guy would become a poorly paid non-button employee of Carlo Gambino.

As the 1970s dawned, the decade that would turn out to be Gambino's last, there was trouble. After trailing him and listening to his conversations for decades, the feds finally busted Gambino. It happened during the spring of 1970. Carlo and Kathryn were walking along Ocean Parkway near their home when the NYPD pulled up and slapped some bracelets on Don Carlo.

"What did I do?" he asked, still smiling, though the handcuffs hurt.

They didn't tell him, but they told his lawyer and his lawyer told him. He was being charged with plotting to steal $30 million from an armored truck in the Bronx. The hijackers were caught and one of them dropped Gambino's name.

The case got far enough that Gambino was indicted, but there would never be a trial. Beside the say-so of the street crook in custody, police had nothing to connect Gambino with the crime. Manhattan Federal Judge Marvin Frankel ruled that Gambino wasn't healthy enough to survive a trial and stayed the case indefinitely.

We've talked about Gambino being a wise man who planted guys who owed him a favor in other families. He was always socially and professionally situated to be untouchable. It might've been true love, I guess, but even romance seemed on Gambino's side. His oldest son,

Thomas, married Tommy Lucchese's daughter, and when Lucchese died in 1967, Gambino's son inherited his garment district holdings.

Tommy Lucchese had formed an alliance with a Jewish mobster, Louis "Lepke" Buchalter. Together they controlled New York's garment district. In the mid-1940s, Buchalter was sent to the electric chair for murder. Soon thereafter, Lucchese had the garment district locked down. Gambino had some of the garment district at that point, but only a small piece.

The rest belonged to James "Jimmy Doyle" Plumeri, a vicious and iron-fisted Lucchese capo shaped like a johnny pump. Plumeri was a Mob veteran, past his prime. Plumeri had first been arrested when he was twelve. He'd been shot and almost killed during the summer of 1933, already in a war over trucks. His first major conviction came in 1936, extortion. And he did a stint in the fed pen in 1965 for tax bullshit.

How did Gambino take over?

One truckload at a time.

There began in 1969 a crime wave of hijacked trucks. Over a twelve-month period, an estimated $50 million worth of garments were stolen. Oddly, none of the hijacked trucks belonged to Gambino. All of them belonged to Plumeri.

Gambino goons went to Plumeri and told him that, in exchange for a major chunk of the garment district, they would do their best to protect the Plumeri trucks from future hijackings.

Gambino only had to apply a portion of the pressure. The insurance companies helped by informing Plumeri's interests that their premiums were going to go sky high if the hijackings didn't cease.

A big chunk of the pressure on Plumeri was supplied by law enforcement. In the spring of 1971, he pleaded guilty to seven counts, which included tax evasion and conspiracy to skim union pensions. Plumeri had been to trial and sentenced by a fed judge to two years in jail and a $1,500 fine for each count.

And the final thing on Plumeri's mind—keeping him up at night, as Gambino set sights on his garment empire—was his health. It was so bad that his lawyer argued that the two years in jail would shorten his life, and the judge listened. So, stressed to the max, Plumeri didn't have to go to jail after all.

Gambino's next salvo was both informative and instructional. Key figures in the garment district received a visitor who had a little chat with them. If they switched to using Gambino trucks, the chances of their stuff getting snatched was nil.

And Gambino's final move was the removal from the earth of Plumeri himself. At about seven a.m. on September 17, 1971, Plumeri's body was found by a New York cop who was on his way to work, in front of a home on Fifty-Fourth Avenue in Maspeth, Queens.

The body was sprawled face down next to the curb, wearing a finely tailored gray suit, a white shirt, black socks, and black shoes. His silk necktie was tied tightly around his throat where it had been used as a garrote to strangle him. His wallet was missing, so he had to be identified through fingerprints.

Detectives didn't like the looks of it. The trend in 1971 was to disassemble dead hoods and dispose of them in a way that they would never be found. Gangsters vanished. But this body was by the road like the fucking Black Dahlia, for all to see. The display, police understood, had meaning.

"It is a very unusual rubout," said NYPD Detective John O'Connell. Eventually O'Connell would figure it out. This was Gambino demonstrating that in the garment district, all along so-called "Needle Alley," he was Boss now.

So, control of the garment district had gone from Lucchese to Plumeri to Gambino in about four years.

The garment district's volatile nature may have been interpreted as weakness by some members of law enforcement. NYPD Deputy Commissioner Kellerman decided, to make a point that the garment district was run by crooks, he would launch a nuisance campaign: If you can't beat 'em, annoy 'em. The police offensive took the form of thousands of traffic tickets.

For generations, trucks being loaded in the garment district ignored parking rules and police ignored these violations. Now, during the autumn of 1972, every truck parked illegally, and that meant every truck received a ticket.

To further harass Gambino, Kellerman went to the newspapers, and the TV news, and talked about the crooks who ran the garment district.

"This is the beginning of an offensive against organized crime," Kellerman said, with microphones shoved in his face. "We are going to run the gangsters out of town."

Kellerman's plan depended on the Mob's grip on the garment district being unstable. He completely underestimated the well-oiled machine that was the massive Gambino crime family. Don Carlo fought back.

When Kellerman identified Consolidated Carrier Corporation as a Mob trucking company, because Gambino's sons Thomas and Joseph were listed as officers, the corporation sued the City of New York for harassment, to the tune of $1 million. The case never made it to court, but there weren't any more parking tickets, either.

CHAPTER 16
Who Vegetabled Colombo?

IN THE BIG PICTURE, this is a story about Carlo Gambino, the clever way he had of getting things done, removing enemies and competitors until he was a monopoly. He doesn't appear until the end of the story, but bear with me. . .

I was a little kid when Joey Gallo went away for extortion, and when he got out ten years later—on March 11, 1971—I was a teenager, and already on the President Street block hanging with my dad and the crew, driving for guys. I was underage but tall.

When Joey got out of jail and came to the club on President Street, he pulled up in a black Caddy. Driving was Bobby Boriello, a friend of my family. Bobby would stick *fugazi* credit cards in my mom's apron pocket. "Go out and use them now," he'd say with a laugh. That was the kind of guy he was. If he was doing well, his friends were going to be doing well too. We stayed close to Bobby until the day he was killed, April 13, 1991, at age forty-seven. His death was a big loss to the family, and if you knew Bobby, you'd know why. The day Joey got out of jail, it was Bobby behind the wheel of the Caddy.

Also in the car was Peter "Pete the Greek" Diapoulas. The Greek could carry his weight, but he had no personality. Pete was Larry Gallo's friend from the time they were kids. Pete worked the gambling operations in Brooklyn's Greek neighborhoods. Today, organized crime is more cross-cultural than it was back in the day. The

Gallos were progressives when it came to pushing their operations into non-Italian neighborhoods. Point is, nobody liked Pete. There was nothing to like. He was all muscle and dull to the extreme when he wasn't hurting someone.

But Bobby and Pete all but faded out of sight when the other passenger got out of the Caddy. It was Joey Gallo. *Click.* There is a snapshot of that moment in my head. He looked frail. His eyes were sunken into his head, I was standing out in front of the club and watching with wide eyes. I was amazed (and thrilled) when Joey looked at me and said, "Hey, you're Ricky's kid." I didn't say anything. I nodded a little.

We were all a little troubled by the change in his appearance. It looked like Joey had been on a decade-long hunger strike. His clothes were hanging on him. His face seemed to be wrapped tightly around his skull. Joey had been off his feed, and eventually he got around to telling his inner circle why. In prison everything is color-coded—white guys and black guys, with no mingling—and Joey had sided with the wrong color. To express their displeasure, Aryan Nation assholes were putting shit in Joey's food—that is, actual feces.

The concern over Joey's starvation eased up some the second Joey opened his mouth and began to pinch cheeks. Same old Joey. He might have been pencil-thin, but he still had his spirit. His brother Albert, aka Kid Blast, greeted him with open arms and they all went into the club. In the club was most of his crew. It was the first time Joey had been there since Larry died of throat cancer in 1968. Some of the guys that were there, Joey had never met. They came in while he was in jail.

My friend Goombi and me went into the club to serve coffee and drinks and food. Goombi lived on the block and I was Ricky's kid, but we were at the bottom of the totem pole and did as we were told.

The men spent four hours talking around a table, while Goombi and I stayed out of the way. Sometimes the men laughed. Sometimes they were angry, but I couldn't hear any specific words to tell what the subjects were. That is, not until Joey got up to leave.

As he was leaving, he said, "Fuck Joe Colombo, and don't give him or anyone in his family anything, and I'm not kidding."

Now that Joey was back, the Gallos were their own thing and didn't kick up to nobody. It was a declaration of war. There had been war when Joey was young, peace while he was in prison, and now that he was out, the winds of war were again blowing down the block.

The next week, Colombo sent a capo, Rocco "Rocky" Miraglia, to speak to Joey. Miraglia was in his late forties at the time. The choice to send Miraglia was calculated. He'd gotten along with Joey back in the day. He was also a cousin of my godfather, Robert "Bobby Darrow" Bongiovi.

Maybe, Colombo thought, Joey would listen to him. Well, it didn't work out that way. Joey wasn't in the mood. He had brooded for a whole decade behind bars and now that he was out, he wanted to grab all the power and money in the world, and he wanted to grab it now, yesterday.

Miraglia was there to make friends. He brought an envelope and gave it to Joey, who threw it back at him.

"Hey, Rocky, you go back and tell Colombo to go fuck himself!"

Rocky stayed nice. He said, "Joey, I care about you, and I gotta tell you, you're making a mistake."

With that, Miraglia left. The door had just shut behind Rocky when Joey announced, "Go get guns. Get ready to go to war."

Joey said from now on no one in the crew was to go to Colombo for nothing. The crew was not to take any money to Joe. No scores. We were not to do our drinking in any Colombo bars and we were not to partner up with any of Colombo's crew in any of our operations.

And so, just as had happened years before when the President Street Boys went to war with Profaci, the mattresses went up and the block became a fortress. Joey might've been impulsive and hardheaded, but he was sharp as a tack, and he knew if he was going to sustain his crew as its own thing, he was going to need support from the other bosses. Within a few months, Joey was going to Sullivan

Street in the city and speaking to Frank "Funzi" Tieri and Vincent "Chin" Gigante. These meetings were held in Chin's club. I wasn't privy to the moves Joey made, but I know firsthand about some of it. The break from Colombo was in the works.

Me and Goombi were taking turns driving Joey to Sullivan Street. Usually, Joey was accompanied by Pete the Greek. He had a series of sit-downs with the bigs, I stayed in the car, and not long after that, we noticed something new on President Street.

Black guys.

Joey found prison to be two factions at war that needed to be separated or else there was trouble. The whites tended to be intolerant meatheads and the blacks lost souls. Joey sided with the black guys. I mentioned the shit in Joey's food. Hanging with the Black Muslims over the neo-Nazis was a dangerous yet fantastic business move. There were lots of black people in Brooklyn with money to spend; neo-Nazis were harder to find. Still, it couldn't have been a relaxing way to do his time.

So, when we saw the first black guys on the block, well, we noticed. But we didn't think anything was wrong. It was the natural order of things. The crew had always been mixed. The Gallos didn't care where your people came from. Joey had a hippy liberal side, a sensitive sense of fairness . . . on occasion.

Besides, Goombi and I were used to seeing black guys. One of our jobs was to go to a black joint called the Caribbean Lounge in the hood every Friday night to pick up the number slips.

So, brothers were on the block. We just shrugged it off. But I kept an eye on them, and I noticed that the black guys always came to the block with a bag full of money and they left with a small suitcase full of money. That kind of thing also didn't strike me as all that unusual.

A few months after Joey came out of jail and had words with Joe Colombo, Colombo held his second annual Italian-American Civil Rights League Rally in Columbus Circle. We'd all been to the first.

Colombo was a hypocrite, railing against society's tendency to think all Italians are hoods when he himself was a major hood. The first rally went great. Sinatra was there. The second rally, not so much.

In 1971, the President Street crew got their instructions. Joey said do *not* go to Colombo's fucking rally. Stay away. All of South Brooklyn got the word. Don't go to the rally. Don't close up your shops out of respect for the rally.

Joey told us to go out and whenever we saw a posted bill advertising Colombo's rally, we should rip it down and rip it up. He told us to piss on them, but we ignored that part.

What us younger guys didn't know was that Joey wasn't alone in his boycott of Colombo's Unity Day at Columbus Circle. Carlo Gambino had given the rally the thumbs-down also—looking back on it, probably not a coincidence. Don Carlo had his own group of juvenile delinquents out tearing down pro-rally posters.

Young Tony Scotto, who'd closed the piers so his workers could attend the rally the year before, announced that the piers were staying open this time, and everyone should report to work.

Now this Gallo crew doctrine—"Don't go to the rally"—became very important, because things didn't go well for Joe Colombo at that rally. Attendance and enthusiasm were way down from the year before, but Colombo was still in his glory.

He had Columbus Circle decked out for a party, and many people were wearing T-shirts with the rally's slogans on them: "WE'RE NUMBER ONE" and "ITALIAN POWER!"

There was nothing about the preparation that said this rally was going to be anything other than bigger and better than the first. The red, white, and green banners Colombo had printed up by the thousands, the colors of the Italian flag, were going up on every bare wall in the city. Colombo didn't limit the papering to Italian neighbors as he did in 1970. He put up the posters in Chinese and Polish and Jewish neighborhoods, for these people were the Italian-Americans' brothers and they, too, understood the sting of prejudice. Colombo had invited a rabbi to speak.

"Monday is a day for the ordinary people to show their pride in their heritage and love of their country. Tens of thousands of Italian shops will be closed in honor of the day," Colombo said, brimming with confidence. "We pray that the powers that be leave us alone. We hope the FBI stays away and hope to God there is no trouble."

Plenty of people heard this and steam came out of their ears. Colombo had a huge public platform, and he was clearly out of his mind. He was no longer a godfather, he thought he was the Second Coming.

Colombo stayed all smiles during his second rally, even though attendance was way down—from maybe fifty thousand the year before to five thousand this time. If Colombo was disappointed that he didn't get his million people representing all of the oppressed cultures in the world, he didn't let on. And he was grinning from ear to ear as he walked to the podium to give his speech.

That was when the day went sour. A twenty-four-year-old Harlem street hustler named Jerome Johnson approached, wearing League press credentials and disguised as a photojournalist with a Bolex movie camera on a strap hanging around his neck.

Johnson pulled a 7.65-millimeter automatic and, from a distance of about one yard, pumped three shots into Colombo's head. Colombo fell to the walk on his side and slowly rolled onto his back.

Colombo's son and another guy wrestled Johnson to the ground. An NYPD officer, Robert Krisch, grabbed the shooter by the ankles. Johnson was continuing to shoot. One bullet went between Officer Krisch's legs and burned the leg of his trousers.

At that moment, another man (never identified) stepped forward, pulled a .38-caliber Smith & Wesson revolver from a black attaché case, and shot Johnson twice in the back, killing him instantly.

By the time two more uniformed cops arrived at the scene to jump on the shooter and pin him down, Johnson was dead. The second shooter escaped into the chaos. His identity remains unknown.

Two rally officials jumped up on the stage and grabbed the live mic. "Keep cool, keep cool," they yelled over and over again, afraid that a riot might break out.

Medical attendants loaded Colombo onto a gurney and then into an ambulance. They didn't have to wait for an ambulance to arrive. There were six already at the scene on standby in case of emergency.

After Colombo was whisked away, there was a half-hearted attempt to continue the show, but the crowd had pretty much dispersed.

Colombo didn't die, not right away anyway. He was taken by ambulance to Roosevelt Hospital where a priest administered the Last Rites. A team of doctors operated on his brain for four and a half hours, managing to remove only two of the three bullets. Brain dead, tubes in every hole. Joe Colombo had been vegetabled.

It's been said that, after being shot, Colombo never moved again. That was almost true. While 99.9 percent of him was paralyzed, two fingers on his right hand retained movement and twitched uncomfortably for seven years before his body joined his brain in death.

Colombo was given the Last Rites a second time after the surgery. This time the ceremony was performed by the Rev. Louis Gigante, the Chin's brother and the chaplain of Colombo's Italian-American Civil Rights League.

Police tried to find a connection between Johnson and the President Street Boys. Johnson didn't know any mobsters well, and those he did know were with the Gambinos.

FBI investigators learned that Johnson had been a regular at an after-hours joint called Christopher's End, which was inside the Christopher Hotel on Christopher Street in New York's West Village. The place was run by a Gambino associate named Paul DiBella.

Johnson was also friends with a Gambino porn peddler named Michael Umbers, who during his life had made a complete tour of New York State's correctional facilities. Both Johnson and Umbers, witnesses said, were into freaky sex scenes.

The only thing most noticed about the shooter was that he was a soul brother, and everyone knew Joey Gallo loved the brothers.

Someone asked Colombo's son Anthony if he thought maybe Gambino might've had something to do with his dad's shooting.

"That's ridiculous," Anthony said. "Mr. Gambino is a dear friend. Crazy Joey did it, and I want revenge."

Joey swore up and down that it wasn't him that hit Colombo, but whoever the fuck did it sure wanted it to look like it was Joey.

Police said they'd received warnings in advance of the rally that non-friendly factions might be represented, but nothing to indicate that the host of the party was to be gunned down.

One morning at 11:30 a.m., the *Daily News* received a phone call from someone identifying himself as a member of the Black Revolutionary Attack Team. The initials spelled BRAT.

"We're the ones that assassinated Colombo," the voice said. "This is only the beginning. One of our brothers was killed today. The racist society will pay for what they're doing to our black brothers."

This was the only time authorities ever received a communication from BRAT. Suspicion today is that the call was a red herring, diverting suspicion away from the actual sponsor of the hit.

Not that many people in the world were smart enough to set up a hit that appeared to be one thing but was actually another. The hit on Colombo was more like a political assassination than a Mob whacking.

There were elements of subterfuge, sleight of hand, distractions galore, and all carried out right out in the open where everyone could see. It ain't easy hitting a guy and leaving a false signature—and that signature sure looked to be Joey Gallo's.

Expecting incoming, we hit the mattresses right away. After a few weeks, Joey and Blast got the call to go to Chin's Sullivan Street club to meet with Chin and Funzi.

Chin was Boss Vincent "the Chin" Gigante and Funzi was Francesco Alphonse "Funzi" Tieri.

Funzi's legit setup was as owner of several garment manufacturing plants and a trucking company that moved TV dinners. His not-so-legit business involved controlling the Jersey docks, bookmaking, and shylocking.

Together, Chin and Funzi were the upper echelon of the Genovese family. The Chin would be Boss for a quarter century. My mom, Dee, says she only met the Chin twice, but on one occasion she mentioned to him that there was only one kind of champagne she liked and from then on, every Easter, the Chin would send her a case of Taittinger champagne.

To others, he wasn't as nice. (He's also in the Malingerers Hall of Fame, pretending for years that he was senile even as he ran a crime family, wandering around New York's Greenwich Village with a blank expression on his face and wearing a rumpled bathrobe.)

I drove Ricky, Blast, and Bobby Boriello to the meet at Chin's club on Sullivan Street. Goombi drove Joey, Pete the Greek, Steven Cirello, and Tony Bernardo. As we drove, the guys seemed relaxed. No one was worried about walking into a trap. Nobody worried about getting whacked. I didn't think about it at the time, but the feeling was that the fix was in, and everything was going to work out fine.

This was not the first time we'd gone to a Sullivan Street meet. Previously, there had always been a backup plan in case of trouble. A gun somewhere. An instruction, "If we're not out in a few minutes, come in shooting." Whatever it was.

We parked down the block on Sullivan Street. My dad's last words for me were, "If we're going to run long, I'll come out and tell you guys, so you don't worry."

"Sure thing, Pop," I said.

Me and Goombi worried anyway. We stayed near the cars. We couldn't go in anyway because we were carrying pistols and would not have been allowed in.

I said, "What the fuck will we do if they don't come out?"

"Yeah, and how long should we wait before we make a move?" Goombi said.

"Maybe we should just kill everyone," I said. (I'm fifteen years old.)

"We're fucked either way," Goombi said.

"Yeah, let's just sweat it out," I said.

Just about then, we saw a car pull up. Four more guys got out of the car. *Click*, another snapshot. The last guy who got out was Don Carlo Gambino. Me and Goombi looked at each other with our mouths open.

"How the fuck are we going to go in now?" I said.

Goombi flashed me his goofy dum-dum look and we started laughing.

The sign we were looking for was Ricky to come out and tell us everything was going well. And he did come out, bringing us coffee because we were outside for a while. As he handed us the cardboard cups he said with a smile, "We're OK, boys. You look like you seen a ghost."

"No, we're good, Pops," I said.

"We'll be out soon," he said and went back in.

And they were. Everyone got into the cars and we drove directly to President Street. No one said a word. They all went into the club.

We got our instructions: "Boys, go over to Roy Roy's club and tell him and the rest of the crew that we're here."

We did that and, suddenly alone in Roy Roy's club, we poured a few Dewars. Mine with water, Goombi's with club soda. We sat there and after a couple of drinks, I said, "That was fucked up."

Goombi laughed. "Fuck them all, we should've gone in like cowboys."

Then we cracked up laughing. A couple of drinks and I could feel the nerves in my neck relaxing. Reality had a nice glaze, and I didn't think about it that day. But after a while, it hit me. The only way Joey walked out of that meet alive was if there was someone there who knew Joey didn't hit Colombo. Orrrr that somebody knew he did hit Colombo, but everyone was cool with it.

The next day we were told what Goombi and I had already figured out: Joey got cleared from the Joe Colombo hit by Don Carlo and Chin.

The whole hit on Joe Colombo was weird. I'm not sure I ever believed that Joey had *nothing* to do with it. He may not have ordered it. He may have arranged it as a favor to a friend. New friend, old friend, who knows? Maybe it could just be coincidence: seeing black guys leaving President Street with suitcases of money, Don Carlo going to Chin's club, the boys getting the pass, and Joey giving out buttons.

After that meeting with Gambino and Gigante, the rumors started that we were getting released from the Colombos and transferred to the Genovese family. I wish I could be more specific. I wish I was a little older at the time, but I was just coming up in the crew. I was on a need-to-know basis, and I hardly ever needed to know.

So, the President Street Boys were expected to be separated from the Colombo family, from whom they'd already declared independence, and come back in under Chin. Chin went so far as to give Joey fifteen buttons to give out, at a time when the ranks were supposed to be closed, and we were all straightened out. But no one told the remaining Colombos, in particular Carmine "the Snake" Persico, and his friends, and the war between the Colombos and the President Street Boys went on, deadly on both sides.

Why would Gambino have Colombo whacked? When the heads of the Profacis kept dying of natural causes, Gambino pretty much hand-picked Colombo to take over, a move that didn't please everybody. Gambino chose Colombo because he was faithful to Gambino, but his critics had some solid points, so solid that Gambino eventually listened to them. Colombo was almost completely unknown outside of Brooklyn when he took a seat at the commissioners' table, and he was, even without being a boss, a very rich man. His loan-sharking ops were so strong that at any given moment, he had millions of dollars out there in the pockets of degenerates, pockets with holes in them.

According to some guys, Colombo wasn't terribly bright. He sometimes walked around with things in his pockets that he didn't want found if he happened to be searched. In December 1970, for example, Colombo and his bodyguard Rocco Miraglia—same guy who once came to President Street with an envelope—rode in a gold Buick station wagon, pulled behind the State Supreme Court building, and parked the vehicle in a spot reserved for a judge. One of the things Colombo shouldn't have been caught with was Miraglia, who was wanted for perjury. A couple of FBI agents saw the hoods park and immediately approached to arrest Miraglia, who was carrying an attaché case. One fed went to grab the case and Colombo stepped in.

"Uhhh, that's mine," he said.

It was a smart thing to say. If the case was Miraglia's, who was under arrest, they could open it and see what was inside. Colombo, however, wasn't wanted for anything so they couldn't search his case. Surprise, feds said that Miraglia was carrying the case, it was his, and back at FBI HQ they opened the case up and found lists of names and money figures, a complete layout of the money flow in the Colombo crime family. Among those listed as receivers of tribute was "CARL," who was slated to get thirty grand. Uh-oh. There were a bunch of Gambino guys mentioned in there, as well. The attaché case had provided the government with another roster they could use to figure out how the organization they called LCN worked. To be able to connect Don Carlo with actual crimes was like a dream come true for the feds.

Was any of that involved in why he was vegetabled? Maybe. My theory is that it was Colombo's hypocrisy that did him in. Holding rallies to keep Italians from being mislabeled as gangsters was a fine project unless you, yourself, were a gangster, in which case it left a bad taste. The thing that triggered Colombo to want to hold a pro-Italian-American rally in the first place was that the feds had been investigating his son. The first Columbus Circle rally was a great success—big crowd, Sinatra—but after that first rally there was a protest march to FBI headquarters in Manhattan. There were hoods with anti-FBI picket signs.

Gambino saw this on TV and had to blink to believe it was real. This behavior was so far from anything that might happen in Palermo that Don Carlo had to have it explained to him.

What could possibly be accomplished by starting a war—a war of words, anyway—with the FBI? This flew in the face of one of

Gambino's first rules of behavior: Do NOT unnecessarily piss off authorities.

Colombo organized another protest, this one of a Staten Island newspaper. Colombo's beef was that the paper was using the word *Mafia*. As a result of the protest, more people than ever were using the word, another thorn in Gambino's side.

A huge banquet was held, and Joe Colombo was named the Long Island Man of the Year. Gambino could've cared less. All this posturing wasn't making money, and Gambino was hearing complaints that Colombo was spending so much time trying to convince the masses that he wasn't a crook, that it was hurting business.

Colombo invited reporters from the New York tabloids to his business office, and there he griped about the way the FBI was treating him.

"Here, look out the window. See the window with the white curtains? That's where they are. Listening. Want to wave to them?"

"Do you ever see them?"

"At night, when they light cigarettes," Colombo said.

"They are listening to us right now?"

"Yes. They have everything bugged. They are listening in my bedroom. Tell your readers this: my bedroom today, yours tomorrow."

Later, he added, "If they are out to get you, they are out to get you. I am appealing a conviction now. Do you know what I did? I filled out an application wrong. Made a mistake. I'm human. They say it is perjury and tell me I have to go to jail for two and a half years."

"How much of that have you served?"

"Twelve days, now I'm out for the appeal."

"You must have a great lawyer."

"I credit God for keeping me out of jail. I visited the Bishop of Toms River and he prayed with me. My league is under God's protection. Anybody who goes against my league will feel His sting."

Colombo switched the subject to the great things his league did. "We're helping with the expenses of an Italian boy who's arriving here today, en route to Texas for open-heart surgery." He finished the interview by bragging about his upcoming rally in Columbus Circle. "We expect a million people to attend. Nothing can stop us because God is on our side."

Gambino read this shit in the paper and did a slow burn. For a moment, the twinkle went from his eyes.

A man who was willing to battle the U.S. government and the daily newspapers and Hollywood, who was too stupid not to get caught with revealing documents, a man who ran expensive campaigns because he felt his family had been disrespected, well, that was not a man who should be sitting beside Don Carlo at the commissioners' table.

How did the Colombo family react to the shooting? According to Joseph "Joe Pesh" Luparelli, mere hours after Colombo was vegetabled, Joseph "Joe Yack" Yacovelli set about getting permission from the Commission to have Crazy Joey whacked. Pesh said he was in Monticello, New York, where the harness races were held, when he heard about the shooting at the rally. He immediately drove back to the city and went to the Gambino family hangout on Mulberry Street in Little Italy, the Ravenite, where he found Yack in conference with Carmine "Junior" Persico. Also, there was another Colombo guy, Joe Notch, who was Colombo's driver and bodyguard and as such felt he was in charge of payback.

"Let me go," Notch begged. "Let me go to President Street and shoot that fuck."

"Forget it," Yack said at first, but then, "All right, go. It's your suicide."

Carmine "Sonny Pinto" DiBiase came in. According to Pesh, Pinto told Pesh to take Yack to his home to hide out until things cooled. Pesh took Yack to his place on Twentieth Lane in southernmost Bath Beach, Brooklyn. His orders were to stay with Yack, guard him, and drive him if he needed to go someplace.

Yack stayed with Luparelli for a few days and moved to a

three-bedroom apartment in Nyack, New York, with a nice Hudson River view. The guy who owned the place had a boat docked outside. Again, Pesh accompanied him.

While there, Pesh drove Yack to a meeting in the city. Yack met Gambino underboss Aniello Dellacroce at the Market Diner in downtown Manhattan, on the West Side near the vegetable markets. Pesh had two guns on him—his own, and Yack's. Yack never carried his own gun so he'd be clean if arrested. Dellacroce and Yack sat in a booth in the diner, leaning forward, talking low. After that, Yack only had one more guy to speak with, Carlo Gambino, who was sick in bed. Yack told Pesh, "I want you to do everything right because I don't want nothing to go wrong. Of all things, I don't want no tail." Pesh promised he'd have his eyes glued to the rearview as they went to see Gambino. Once the commissioners had been consulted, Yack announced it was OK to "smash" the President Street Boys. The Colombo-Gallo war went on. Gambino's game was both deep . . . and ice cold.

How cold was Carlo Gambino? His allegiance was pure, and it was to the brotherhood he had pledged to serve so many years ago in Palermo. His world order involved a setup that didn't include Colombo, and it didn't matter that Gambino was the godfather of Colombo's young daughter, it didn't matter that Colombo once foiled an assassination attempt on Gambino, perhaps saving his life. When you gots to go, you gots to go.

One thing we do know: Gambino didn't get to enjoy the removal of Colombo. His life at that time was blanketed with sadness.

For years, Carlo Gambino had hosted a huge Fourth of July celebration in Oyster Bay, with fireworks and lots and lots of free food. So, it was an ominous sign when the celebration in 1971 was canceled because of Kathryn Gambino's failing health.

A month later, Kathryn passed away following a long illness. She was laid out at Cusimano & Russo funeral chapel in Bensonhurst.

Her funeral was celebrated by Father Dominic Sclafani, who described her as "a very good churchgoing woman who went to Mass regularly."

Her funeral was held at Our Lady of Grace Church, her parish around the corner from her home, where the priest celebrated the Mass of resurrection. It was the same church where she and Carlo had been married.

As usually happens at "Mob funerals," the Law was all over the neighborhood, photographing everyone who went into the church for the funeral and jotting down license plate numbers outside. At Carlo Gambino's orders, the perimeter around the church could be maintained by NYPD. The FBI, he ordered, was to be kept at a distance with the other curiosity seekers—and that was how it was. Whether inside the perimeter or out, the photographers were disappointed. Although hundreds attended Kathryn's funeral, they didn't get a single photo of anyone they found interesting. Don Carlo's most powerful friends had stayed away.

With Kathryn gone, her sister Providencia and husband Phil Villano moved into the downstairs apartment on Ocean Parkway and took over Kathryn's role of hosting Don Carlo's many and varied visitors.

Carlo Gambino had been a widower for three months when the efforts to deport him revved up again. Gambino's lawyer had used up all appeals. Now the feds encountered a new problem they hadn't counted on: Italy didn't want Gambino.

The feds went so far as to buy a plane ticket, Trans World Airlines, to Rome. In case Don Carlo missed his flight, they also purchased for him a stateroom on the passenger ship *Cristoforo Colombo.*

The authorities had a couple of reasons to think Gambino wasn't going to be on the TWA plane when it took off: one, didn't want to go, two, afraid of heights.

As it turned out, Gambino boarded neither the plane nor the ship. Two days before his scheduled departure, Gambino checked into Victory Memorial Hospital in Dyker Heights, Brooklyn, where he rested in a room overlooking a golf course. Simultaneous to his checking in, his lawyer made a public statement that the recent death of Gambino's wife had aggravated his heart condition.

Again, the feds sent government cardiologists, from the U.S. Public Health Service, to check on Gambino's weary chest. They reported back that Gambino's heart condition was real. They described it as "permanent, deteriorating, and cannot improve."

The bottom line was that Gambino was never going to be well enough to fly or sail across the Atlantic. Given no other choice, the Immigration and Naturalization Service ended forever its deportation efforts.

After that, Gambino was rarely seen in public. More and more frequently, his business associates went to him, and meets were held in his upstairs apartment in his longtime home on Ocean Parkway.

He was infirm and a lift had been installed so he didn't have to do any stairs. He lived upstairs while the main floor was occupied by his wife's sister and her husband, who doubled as his caretakers.

No one was ever allowed upstairs without careful screening. Not only was Gambino safe from attack but he was fairly certain that no feds had bugged his place. As those same FBI agents were still watching his house twenty-four seven, they knew who his most frequent visitors were: brothers Joe and Paul, Big Paul Castellano, and Joe N. Gallo. They were relaying Gambino's orders to the troops.

The FBI reported that Gambino's family came to visit him every day, because they didn't know which day would be his last. His kids, both brothers, usually some cousins. He held court in a comfortable nest.

When plans were put in place to have the President Street Boys reenter the Five Family system, this time under Chin, we assumed that meant that the war with the Colombos would be over. But no.

Joey was living life like he didn't have long to live. In the year he'd been out of jail, he'd gotten rid of his old wife and gotten a new one. He became a city guy, hanging out not with other gangsters but with showbiz and intellectual types. He stayed in the city a lot. He had a place on Fourteenth Street. He resisted tight security.

On the morning after his forty-third birthday, the final morning of his life, he was in public without a thought of what was about to happen. All Joey Gallo had was his old childhood buddy Pete the Greek. If you want the complete story on the Joey Gallo hit, read my book *Mafia Hit Man*, about Carmine DiBiase, the guy who really killed Joey.

With Joey lying dead in the middle of a Little Italy street, the Colombo-Gallo war erupted full scale. Gambino sold guns and ammunition to both sides and then sat back and counted the corpses.

By the time the war was over, the Gallo crew was a lot easier to deal with. Blast was the only remaining Gallo brother, and he lacked the ambition and inclination to keep the crew a viable entity. It was complicated and fucked up. Shifting allegiances and the consequences for those shifts made me reevaluate everything I'd ever thought. The crew split up and was reabsorbed into the system. In one way or another now, everyone worked for Don Carlo.

CHAPTER 17
Clipping Eboli

THOMAS EBOLI WAS BORN in Naples, Italy, in 1911 and became a naturalized American citizen as a child running around the teeming narrow streets of Greenwich Village. By 1918, while the First World War raged in Europe and the Spanish Flu was killing thousands a day in America, Eboli was earning tip money doing favors for gangsters.

As a young man, the five-seven, one-fifty-pound Eboli boxed in prizefights under the name Tommy Ryan. Irish fighters put more butts in the seats than Italian boxers, so Tommy Ryan he was. And the name stuck.

He was a neighbor in Little Italy of Vito Genovese, friends just about from the day they arrived in America. He attended the 1932 wedding of future super-rat Joseph Valachi.

Eboli was arrested nine times between 1933 and 1969, which isn't a lot if you look at it in terms of arrests per year. The charges ranged from vagrancy to assault, but he always had a top-notch lawyer. He was convicted twice and never went to jail.

The convictions were for disorderly conduct in 1945 (fined five dollars), and for assault in 1955. The assault beef came when, during a boxing melee in Madison Square Garden, he punched a ref and a promoter. That bought him a hefty fine and ended his career in boxing. Like many pugilists before and since, he morphed from a fighter into a gangster seamlessly. Both occupations needed tough guys.

He did as he was told and rose in the ranks. He worked the docks on the west side of Manhattan. He supervised the scams and skims on his old stomping grounds in the Village, south of Fourteenth Street and north of Houston.

He got as far as being acting boss of the Genovese family after Tony Bender was disappeared by a couple of guys from Jersey. This was the dawn of the seventies. It was the era of weirdo sex joints—you could smell them from the sidewalk, usually in downtown Manhattan, but sometimes midtown—where people of oddball desires got together and whatevered.

Eboli had a piece of most of those joints.

Eboli got about as far as a hood could get without being Carlo Gambino's friend. Although the two knew each other—they both were among those arrested in the La Stella raid—by 1972, Eboli was one of the last obstacles between Carlo Gambino and continued domination.

Eboli was acting with a foolish confidence. At this time, Gambino was very sick with heart trouble, and Eboli believed he wouldn't have to worry about Don Carlo much longer.

It was noon on a Saturday, September 30, 1972. An ambulance pulled up quietly to the Gambino home on Ocean Parkway. Two bulky men wearing white entered the home carrying a stretcher, and came out carrying Carlo Gambino, covered to his chin with blankets. He appeared tiny and barely alive.

This time the ambulance was no gimmick. The feds noted that the heart attack, if that was what it was, didn't coincide with any grand jury hearings, Senate investigations, or deportation hearings.

He was taken to Columbus Hospital in the city—later known as the Cabrini Medical Center. Posted in the lobby was a family spokesperson, unidentified, who answered all queries the same way: "Mr. Gambino is suffering from a severe heart condition. He is allowed no visitors or phone calls. That's all the info I can give you. Goodbye."

There was a flurry of gangsters being subpoenaed while Gambino was in the hospital, and some cynics thought maybe that was the thing the hospital stay was helping him avoid. But most knew the truth, and it was dire.

Despite the grimness of that moment, Gambino would survive. Eboli would not.

On July 15, 1972, a Saturday night, Eboli put on his sharpest suit, shoved a fat roll of cash in his pocket, and climbed into the back of his '72 Caddy. The next thing anyone knew for sure was that his body with its ruined head was discovered dead on a sidewalk at Lefferts Avenue and New York Avenue at one o'clock in the morning.

Exactly how the killing was done was a mystery, but the sponsor and motive for the killing were obvious. Eboli had represented the last vestiges of opposition to Carlo Gambino.

Eboli's domain was New Jersey and Lower Manhattan. He controlled bars, a vending machine company (partnered with Vito Genovese's brother, Mike), a record company, and unions along the Jersey docks from Newark to Monmouth.

Now most of that would be Gambino's—like everything else.

Like many of Gambino's deep moves, the hit on Eboli was multilayered. Not only was Tommy Eboli an obstacle that Gambino needed removed, but he happened to be in the middle of a $3 million heroin deal that cost Don Carlo a shitload of cash.

Eboli's key contact in the smuggling system was Louis Cirillo, who owned a bagel shop in the Bronx. Cirillo'd been popped by the feds and was in deep shit. Cirillo ended up getting twenty-five years.

A judge said Cirillo was responsible for importing one-sixth of all the babonia coming into the country. So, what happened was, Gambino gave Eboli $3 million to purchase heroin from the tons Cirillo was bringing in.

But Cirillo was arrested with Gambino's money still in his pocket. Gambino blamed Eboli. So, that was another reason why Don Carlo wanted the old prizefighter they called Tommy Ryan off the board.

* * *

Talking to the press only hours after Eboli's body was discovered, one cop said, "We think he was suckered by someone close to him."

There were other clues that Eboli had been set up for the kill. Only a few hundred yards from the spot where the body was found, police discovered a panel truck with New Jersey plates, parked with motor running. In the truck cops found a .45-caliber machine gun with a jerry-rigged silencer.

At first, it was unknown if this was the murder weapon—or even if the gun had been recently fired. (Later, it would be theorized that the machine gun was in the vicinity just in case the initial barrage failed to finish the job.)

An FBI spokesman threw in his two cents saying, "The machine gun is particularly significant. Eboli's crime family had an assassination squad that specialized in supplying silencer-equipped machine guns. They are the only group that makes silencers like that."

The spokesman told a Long Island reporter that the New Jersey assassin squad had previously supplied silenced machine guns to Boston hoods and, much closer to home, to the President Street Boys during the war against Profaci.

Even though the murder reeked of being a Mob hit, police still went through the formality of ruling out robbery as a motive. Eboli was wearing a blue jumpsuit and a blue-and-white-checkered shirt. He still had more than two grand in cash on him, plus he was wearing a three-stone diamond ring, a Lucien Piccard watch, and a gold crucifix. Whoever riddled his body with bullets didn't care about any of that.

The medical examiner showed up at the scene and started counting holes, a process that could not be completed properly until he had the stiff up on his table. But he could tell immediately that Eboli had been shot at least five times in the head. The holes were small. Looked like a pocket gun. Probably a .32.

Around his body, scattered in shards, were pieces of bloodstained glass from a car windshield.

* * *

Most significantly, police had eyewitnesses. One of those observers saw a car "near Eboli" at the time of the murder. The car, the witness said, contained six white males. Another witness said he saw a flash of light near a panel truck at the time of the shooting, and he heard a man's voice call out, "Let's get out of here."

The NYPD went at the crime scene hard, determined to miss nothing. This was the highest profile Mob hit since Colombo, a little more than a year earlier. The New York cops received full cooperation from the Jersey cops in Fort Lee, where Eboli lived in a luxury apartment on Horizon Road.

Eboli had spent the bulk of his career under the assumption that one day he would rise to godfather. His ambitions, however, were hindered by his health. He had a heart attack in 1969 and was scratched off the list of contenders by the Commission.

To make it worse, Eboli had his heart attack in public, while testifying at a New Jersey State Investigations Commission hearing into organized crime's infiltration into legitimate businesses. While Eboli was sputtering in anger on the witness stand, his ticker hemorrhaged and there was a big fuss.

"I'm a sick man!" he yelled as he clutched his chest and slumped in his chair.

All Eboli was doing was invoking the Fifth Amendment again and again, but as he did so the veins in his temples began to throb. Beads of sweat popped out across his furrowed forehead. Then he wheezed, yelled, clutched, and slumped. It was embarrassing. He was carried out on a stretcher with his shirt open, gold crucifix resting on a jiggly man tit.

Some suspected malingering.

"Give him an Oscar," one witness said.

Police knew his heart trouble was real but raised an eyebrow over the convenient timing of his attack.

Eboli survived his cardiac arrest but was thereafter considered by the Commission as damaged goods. When the job of boss of the Genovese family came open, Eboli would have gotten the position had he been considered robust. Gerardo Catena got the job instead.

Catena went down for three years for refusing to answer questions from the Jersey investigations commission. With Catena in jail, Eboli was acting boss—the highest post he would achieve.

Now, with Eboli croaked, the job went to Mike Miranda, the consigliere, a fellow that Gambino did not fear.

In death, the authorities and the press conspired to chip away at Eboli's legacy. His street nickname, they said, was "Tommy No-Guts." They said that for a guy of his prestige he wasn't much of an earner, and there had been a problem of his guys defecting to the Gambinos.

At first, cops found the logistics of Eboli's shooting hard to figure. Eboli owned a brand-new Caddy, but it was nowhere to be found. How had Eboli gotten to the scene of his death?

Then their answer walked in a precinct door: Eboli's "longtime partner," fifty-three-year-old Joseph Sternfeld, accompanied by a mouthpiece.

"Who are you?" a cop asked.

"I drove Eboli to Crown Heights, and . . ."

"And what?"

"And I witnessed the murder. You can stop looking for Eboli's Caddy in Brooklyn," he said. "I returned it to the garage at Tommy's house on Elaine Terrace, Fair Lawn, New Jersey."

Detectives asked him questions while a stenographer took it down.

"It was midnight Saturday. I drove Eboli to Crown Heights and dropped him off on Lefferts Avenue, between Nostrand and New York Avenues. I returned fifty minutes later to pick him up, parked in front of a certain house on Lefferts. I saw Eboli walking toward the car—but he never made it. A red and yellow truck rolled up and gunmen opened up on him. I watched until a bullet hit the left, front window of the Caddy. At that, I threw it into gear and booked."

"Did you recognize any of the occupants of the drive-by truck?"

Sternfeld shook his head.

Sternfeld, whose address was in Cliffside Park, New Jersey, was held as a material witness in a murder. Bail was $250,000. Sternfeld got in a police van and took a ride to Rikers.

Police were suspicious of Sternfeld. He claimed to make a living with the GI Joe Frankfurter Service, selling dirty-water dogs under an umbrella on a sidewalk in the Village. But he was more, an enemy of the Law who once picketed the offices of the Nassau County district attorney because the DA subpoenaed Tina Franzese in an attempt to get her to talk about her imprisoned husband, Sonny. Sternfeld felt that grilling wives crossed a line.

Police went to the garage in New Jersey and confiscated Eboli's Caddy. It was transported to Canarsie, where it was given a thorough once-over by crime-scene specialists.

The car did not back up Sternfeld's story. It had many bullet holes. There was blood and broken glass inside the car. Since Sternfeld had not been wounded, that blood had to belong to Eboli, who apparently was shot while inside the car, not outside on the sidewalk.

Cops gave Sternfeld the third degree about who hit Eboli, but the driver said he didn't know. They asked him why Eboli had to go to Crown Heights, who was he there to meet? Again, he shrugged.

"I'm just the driver. Nobody tells me nothing."

In charge of the investigation into Eboli's murder were Inspectors Timothy Dowd and James O'Brien, and Chief of Detectives Louis Cottell. The major thrust of the legwork was a thorough canvassing of Eboli's favorite places, most in Greenwich Village, where he had an apartment for when he was in the city.

Some of Eboli's friends were well known, or they became well known later on. One was the Chin, Vincent Gigante, who hit guys on Eboli's orders and in 1957 put a permanent although nonlethal part in Frank Costello's hair. Gigante was arrested and charged with the attack on Costello but was acquitted by a jury that knew what was good for it.

Some said Eboli was the driver on the night of the attempted hit on Costello. Gigante would eventually go to jail at the same time as Genovese, convicted on drug-smuggling charges. While Genovese died in prison, Gigante got out and ran the Genovese tribe while maintaining the public persona of a senile old man wandering in his bathrobe.

Another of Eboli's friends that investigators wanted to talk to was Francesco Alphonse "Funzi" Tieri, a Genovese gangster from the old days. How good of a friend was Funzi? That was a matter of conjecture. Tieri's standing was greatly improved with Eboli dead. Plus, he was friends with Aniello Dellacroce, Gambino's right-hand man. Tieri, with Gambino's sanctioning, was free to expand his ops—betting, lending, and threatening—into Manhattan and Jersey.

Another possibility was that Eboli was hit because he was about to be in a legal jam that might make yapping seem appealing. Fed agents were on his ass. He'd been called the first target in a concentrated attack on organized crime. So maybe he was stiffened before he could sing.

I heard Eboli was anti-babonia and stepped on the toes of guys selling dope out of bars. These guys were supposed to work for Eboli but had gone into business for themselves. Maybe.

The most telling stat, I think, is the $3 million Eboli borrowed from Gambino to start up a junk business, a business that tanked because cops rolled it up the second he laid out the welcome mat.

Eboli's bullet-torn body was taken to the Romanelli funeral home, at Eighty-Ninth Street and Rockaway Boulevard in Ozone Park, Queens. His funeral was on July 19, 1972.

Authorities kept leaning on Sternfeld. Kings County DA Eugene Gold hauled Sternfeld out of Rikers and into his office with the door shut for hours on end. Three straight days. About two-thirds of the way through the process, an investigator came out of the DA's office with armpit stains and shirtsleeves rolled up.

"He's starting to break," he said to an underfed scribe in the hallway. “He’s telling us more than he did before but there’s still a lot that he knows that he isn’t telling.”

“What have you learned?”

“We now know why he took Eboli to Crown Heights. We know who Eboli met there before the murder.”

Another source revealed that Sternfeld had referred to a series of meetings in Crown Heights, and he’d mentioned the names of some tough guys who were at those meetings. True or not, that’s a hell of a rumor to go public. Sternfeld must’ve felt like toast.

The feds entered the investigation and began to round up anyone they could find who’d ever been in the same room with Eboli. They scoured Manhattan, Brooklyn, and Jersey for witnesses. To excuse their involvement, the feds said that Eboli might have been lured across state lines to his death. All the victim had to do to get the feds involved was cross the Hudson.

Despite the FBI being on the case, Eboli’s murder went unsolved.

CHAPTER 18

The "Kidnapping" of Manny Gambino

A WHILE BACK, we took a look at a group called Kidnap, Inc., run by Tony the Shrimp. They nabbed Mob guys and held them for ransom. Kidnap, Inc. had a plan in the works to snatch Don Carlo himself. As it turned out, just snatching friends of Carlo Gambino was prohibitively dangerous.

The gang was wiped out, but there were desperadoes out there in the urban wilderness who thought it could have worked if it had been handled properly. One of these copycats who decided to go the kidnapping route was Robert Senter, a Gambino and Colombo associate, and proprietor of the Canarsie Recycling Company located on Foster Avenue in Canarsie.

His first victim, Senter figured, would kill two birds with one stone. He would bring big ransom, plus the guy was Senter's bookie, Senter's shylock. He could collect ransom and erase an arm-and-a-leg debt with one snatch.

Robert Senter was born in 1936 in Sea Girt, New Jersey. In 1972, he had long hair and a formidable mustache that looked stolen off the lip of a porn star. Robert's company removed debris and collected garbage. He was also into things that had nothing to do with garbage or recycling, things like union racketeering.

On May 18, 1972, with the help of two accomplices, Senter stole his first human being. The reason this is so important to our story is the victim wasn't just anybody. He was Carlo Gambino's nephew, Joe's son, twenty-nine-year-old Emanuel "Manny" Gambino.

Among Senter's jobs was collecting for Manny's loan-sharking business. Manny was snatched outside Henry Hill's supper club, The Suite (aka Spartan Lounge, aka Lido Cabaret), on Grand Avenue in Maspeth, Queens, purchased with heist money.

Senter was known, for reasons now unclear, as smarter than the average hood. He reportedly attended Fordham University in the Bronx, and Georgetown University in Washington, D.C. But none of his formal education moved him to join the legitimate world. He had a flimflam heart and a reputation as a fast-talker, and was a guy with confidence-game skills. He might've been a good trial lawyer if the urge to be bad hadn't been so overwhelming.

Senter lived in the south end of Asbury Park, New Jersey, in a small white house fifty yards from the Atlantic Ocean. On the short term, snatching Manny Gambino was a questionable business move for Senter. On the long term, it was a complete disaster.

Senter apparently decided to exploit recent history, which included the kidnapping for ransom of Frankie "the Wop" Manzo by James McBratney, Eddie Maloney, Tommy Genovese, and Rickie Chaisson. The ransom note demanded $150,000. The money was paid and Frankie the Wop was released unharmed.

So Senter's bright idea was that he would whack his bookmaker, thus erasing his debt, and make it look like it was a botched kidnap by the same crew that took Frankie the Wop.

If Senter had done more research, he might have picked a Gambino relative that the Boss liked better. Manny was not Don Carlo's favorite. He wasn't good with money, wasn't an earner. His rackets refused to produce. Having his biological family member in his crime family was, for Carlo, like treading water. It wasn't getting him anywhere.

Manny went from being mildly troublesome to being a full-fledged problem for the Boss when he told Carlo that he wanted to divorce his wife so he could marry his blond girlfriend. Gambino, as Catholic as a bishop, said no divorce.

In addition to religious reasons, divorces had been proven bad for business. When Vito Genovese sought a divorce from his wife, she got on a courtroom witness stand and started to talk too much about her estranged husband's rackets.

Manny, who lived in Flushing, Queens, and always drove a late-model Cadillac, was now on his uncle's shit list.

On May 18, 1972, Manny Gambino called his girlfriend and told her he was going to New Jersey to meet a guy named Bob. On the morning of May 19, his wife got a phone call: "We got your boy. We'll call back at noon."

The phone rang at noon sharp: "We need $350,000 or else," the kidnapper said. "Drop off the cash at Molly Pitcher."

The wife, Diane, called Uncle Carlo, who thought about ignoring the problem but eventually ordered that the ransom be paid. What Senter didn't expect was that Manny's wife would want to barter.

Sure, she wanted to pay, and she wanted her husband to live, but $350,000 was simply beyond their means. She lied and said she didn't even know anyone rich enough to lend her that kind of money. He was going to have to accept less. She eventually talked Senter down to $40,000.

The first attempt to pay the ransom was botched. There was a failure to communicate. The kidnapper had intended that the money be dropped off at the Molly Pitcher rest stop on the New Jersey Turnpike. Instead, Manny's father, Joseph Gambino, took the money to the Molly Pitcher Inn, a bar in Red Bank, New Jersey.

Honest mistake, and the kidnapper gave Carlo Gambino a second chance to deliver the cash. The family received a handwritten note that read, "If you want him back alive, this is your last chance."

At this time, a Gambino captain, possibly a relative of the victim, was contacted by FBI Special Agent Anthony Villano. For once,

Villano said, we have a common objective, getting Manny back. Maybe we should work together. The Gambino representative told the fed to go fuck himself, but soon thereafter, after giving the matter some thought, a Gambino lawyer called Villano and asked what he had in mind.

The "kidnappers" sent Diane a message with instructions for dropping the ransom money. She said she was sending a man to make the drop for her. The kidnapper was concerned about a trap, but Diane said he shouldn't worry. The guy was coming alone.

The kidnapper replied, "Go to a telephone booth at Eighty-Second Street and Madison Avenue. There you will be given further instructions."

Diane's appointed money-dropper was a business associate of Tommy Gambino. He drove his own Cadillac. Hiding on the floor of the front seat was Special Agent Villano. Other FBI agents followed at a distance.

The Gambino rep called a given number from the phone booth on the Upper East Side and received additional instructions. The next contact spot was a phone booth at a gas station in New Jersey. At that location, the man received his final instructions. He was told to go to a particular overpass on New Jersey's Palisades Parkway, a road that runs north and south along the western bank of the Hudson River, and throw the money over a particular metal guardrail.

Villano notified his backup of the drop spot. As Senter waited underneath the overpass to catch the bag of cash, the FBI tried to figure out how to get from the top road to the bottom road. As it so happened, the Gambino rep threw the bag of money off the bridge, Senter caught it, and got into his van just as the FBI guys were coming down the road. The FBI did not catch Senter that night, but they did get a read on the license plate number on his rented van as he rushed from the scene.

For a time, police suspected that Manny himself was behind his own kidnapping, an attempt to extort his rich uncle. Then the story went that Manny Gambino was disappeared by a guy named Jimmy McBratney, so Senter's attempt to frame McBratney worked. It didn't fool police, but, as we'll see, it fooled John Gotti.

For a short time, police thought it was the President Street Boys who kidnapped Manny. Before going away for a decade, Joey Gallo had kidnapped a bunch of top guys in the Profaci family as a way to negotiate a more lucrative role in the family, so they had a reputation as kidnappers. But that was long ago, and my dad and the other Gallo crew members had no clue where Manny Gambino was.

When the press began poking around, the Gambino family gave the standard story regarding what Manny did for a living. He and his brother Thomas, they said, owned and operated Neptune's Nuggets, a company out of Bay Shore, Long Island, which produced a line of prepared baked clams, frozen clams, and shrimp. A former partner in the business told police that Manny had forced his way into ownership of the business and then milked it dry.

Diane had done as she was told and now waited in vain for Manny's release. Weeks passed and still no Manny. The van that had been spotted at the scene of the ransom drop had been rented by a Robert Senter, a name that meant nothing to the FBI.

Villano's research into Manny Gambino's personal life was intriguing. Though married with a family, Manny had fallen hard for what Villano referred to as a "showbiz blonde." The blonde said she wasn't going to put out anymore unless Manny made her and him a full-time thing. He wanted to leave his family and live in sin with his hottie. That sort of thing was discouraged by other members of his family.

"You want a mistress to fuck, that's OK," elders explained to Manny. "But you don't bust up your family because of it. You are a family man. Your Uncle Carlo has stayed faithful to his wife since the day they met. Gambino men are family men. If you leave Diane, it ain't gonna look good on your résumé, especially as you are a nephew of Carlo, *capisce*?"

On June 2, 1972, hopes of finding Manny Gambino alive were

dashed when his blood-drenched Cadillac was found abandoned in a parking lot at Teterboro Airport in New Jersey. These were the days before DNA technology, but lab analysis did reveal that the blood was the same type as Manny Gambino's.

The car was hauled to a federal facility where the glass was carefully removed and sent to Washington, D.C., to be processed in state-of-the-art fashion for fingerprints.

During this processing of evidence, Senter's thumbprint was found on the inside of one of the windows, closer to the center than to the edge of the pane. The location of the print was important because it meant he had, at some point, been inside Manny Gambino's car, most likely sitting in the driver's seat.

Another piece fell into place for the investigation when an FBI informant revealed that Manny had a guy working for him, collecting protection money from local businesses. In due course, the FBI developed evidence that identified not just Senter, but his accomplices in the potential murder. They included John P. Harrington, William J. Solin, and John Edmund Kilcullen.

On December 4, the same day Senter was taken in, Kilcullen surrendered. Both Senter and Kilcullen were held on federal bail of $100,000.

Senter's alleged partners in crime were an interesting bunch. Kilcullen was a thug, a bouncer/enforcer, absolutely typecast for his role. But Solin was a "former" CIA agent who claimed to work as a New York bartender.

Special Agent Paul J. Brana was assigned to investigate. Years later, he recalled his frustration and eventual satisfaction with the Manny Gambino case.

Before the arrests, Agent Brana bothered Senter every chance he got. He would haul him in and question him about once a week, just to make him feel crowded.

"I didn't take him to the police station to be questioned," Brana recalled. "But rather to a cheap hotel room that the FBI had commandeered, which psychologically was more stressful." When the stress maxed out, Brana purchased a six-pack of beer so Senter could wet his whistle as he tap-danced around the feds' questions.

Eventually the feds rolled up Senter and placed him under arrest. Now, under a more intense interrogation, he gave them a few revealing admissions right off the bat.

"The thing that I don't understand is how your fingerprint got on the inside of Manny's driver side window. You must've been in that car."

"OK, OK. I shot the guy, but you have to believe me when I say it was a fucking accident." He explained that there were extenuating circumstances. "We were in his car, and I was driving," Senter said.

"What happened?"

"He threatened my family's life over my gambling debt."

"What exactly did he say, as best you can remember?"

"He was on and on about the money I owed him. He was like, 'Hey, you don't come up with the money and your sister's baby is going to have problems.'"

"How much did you owe him?"

"It was $78,000."

"When did the gun come out?"

"Right then when he mentioned my sister's baby. I pulled my .22. I was afraid."

"After you pulled the gun, what did you do with it?"

"I stuck it behind Manny Gambino's left ear."

"While driving?"

"Yes. Then he lunged for the gun, it went off, and the bullet went into Manny's head."

"What did you do then?"

"I guess I panicked. Nothing I could do could bring Manny back, so I took him to a remote spot in New Jersey and I buried him."

"Where exactly did you bury him?"

"Would you like me to show you? Come on, I'll take you to the body."

And so, in the heat of July 1973, Senter got to go on one last road trip, to Colt's Neck Township, New Jersey. The location was decrepit, dark—a ghost town.

He took the feds directly to the spot. Trouble was, the FBI guys were all sissy boys and didn't want to get their shoes dirty, so they had to make a call to the New York office to find someone with a strong stomach and a shovel.

Special Agent Wayne Orrell, a Native American fed, crossed the river and sure enough, Manny Gambino's remains were right where Senter said they'd be.

The site of the shallow grave was a garbage-strewn clearing adjacent to the Earle Naval Ammunition Depot, in Monmouth County about sixty miles from New York City. The location was off Asbury Avenue in the town of New Shrewsbury.

The decomposed remains were wrapped in a blanket. Also found in the grave: yellow rubber gloves, worn by the Senter when he dug the hole, and a pair of eyeglasses, belonging to the victim.

The description of Manny's remains is chilling. His corpse had apparently stiffened with rigor mortis while sitting in a chair, and the unearthed cadaver was still stuck in that position.

It took a day for the remains to be officially identified as Gambino's. The cause of death was a bullet in the head. The body was identified through dental work, after an autopsy at the Monmouth County Medical Center in Long Branch.

After Senter's first appearance in Brooklyn Federal Court, a psychiatric examination was ordered by Judge George Rosling. Perhaps the thinking was that a guy had to be crazy to kidnap Carlo Gambino's nephew. Might as well just blow your own brains out—it amounted to the same thing.

With Senter's newfound notoriety, his wife changed her name to "Mrs. Gordon" and moved in with her mother.

As a team of U.S. attorneys prepared for the prosecution, they used further statements by Senter himself, along with info they culled from confidential informants, to put together a three-dimensional scenario for the crime, one they were certain would convince any jury.

The scenario said that Senter never had any interest in kidnapping or ransom, that this entire angle of the crime was merely a ruse to put the investigation on the wrong track, including the drop-off and pickup of the ransom money at the overpass.

None of that meant a thing, the prosecution's theory went. Senter had only one thing on his mind, and that was erasing his gambling debts. He used that debt to lure Manny Gambino to a secluded place. He said he had the money and wanted Manny to come pick it up.

"I got the money hidden in a place where no one'll find it," Senter promised.

And he took Manny to the abandoned naval base in Jersey.

Naturally, the lawyers on Senter's defense team had their own version of how Manny Gambino breathed his last. This one, almost everyone agreed, demonstrated a remarkable imagination. They said that the "kidnapping of Manny Gambino" was a hoax, perpetrated by Manny himself. Senter and the others named in the complaint, they said, were in on it as accomplices.

Manny, the lawyers argued, was a man with two families, one a wife and kids, the other a once-accommodating-but-now-complicated mistress named Nancy Masone.

And that business about sticking his .22 behind Manny Gambino's ear, that was all a gag. Nothing remotely that aggressive had been done, the defense team insisted.

The gun, they now maintained, had gone off while Senter was trying to transfer the weapon from one pocket to another. If there were forensic inconsistencies to that scenario, they said, it was probably because Manny had seen the gun when Senter first pulled it from his pocket and had made a desperate move to get out of the car, and that was what he was doing when the gun went off and a bullet lodged in his skull.

The defense might've seemed desperate, made up of whole cloth in a last-ditch attempt at getting Senter off, but the theory had an unlikely ally: Special Agent Villano, who said he was aware of Manny's domestic woes, that Manny wanted to leave his family and live with his mistress but had been told by dangerous folks inside the family not to do it, that it was exactly the sort of thing that Gambino men did not do. Manny had been desperate for an "out," and setting up his own fake kidnapping fit in nicely with the kind of wild thinking Manny was doing at that time.

Villano also investigated Manny's money troubles. Manny was having financial issues because of his attempt to keep a wife and a mistress happy simultaneously. He needed the money Senter owed him.

You would think that Villano's theory would've fallen apart as soon as Manny's body was found, but that wasn't the case.

Villano said, "The snatch began as a hoax. Manny Gambino worked out a scenario with his debtor [Senter] and two others. Midway through the plot, Gambino's accomplices began to have their doubts. They could see that, if things went sour, Manny Gambino would give them up, either on a Mob contract or to the Law. There was an argument in Gambino's Cadillac and Senter settled the dispute with a bullet in the back of Manny's head."

Villano's theory and the scenario being put forth by Senter's lawyers were similar but not identical. They agreed that the kidnapping began as a hoax, but Villano thought it was fear of being betrayed that caused Manny's death, while Senter's own story took a more direct route to the chase, claiming it was the gambling debt that made him pull a gun on the man he'd just "kidnapped."

On June 1, 1973, Senter pleaded guilty to Manny's murder. Did he kill a Gambino and live to tell about it? The answer is yes—but there *was* one attempt on his life in prison. On November 22, 1974, while Senter was housed in the Federal House of Detention on West Street in Manhattan, he drank a cup of hot cocoa that turned out to have strychnine in it. He was rushed to the hospital where doctors successfully pumped his stomach.

* * *

By the time the Law cleared Jimmy McBratney as a suspect in Manny Gambino's kidnap/murder, it was too late. John Gotti, a Gambino associate with absolute ambition, was given the contract to take out McBratney. Gotti and crewmates found McBratney in a Staten Island bar called Snoope's Bar and Grill.

Snoope's was not the ideal spot to do a crime. For one thing, compared to the dark dives of Manhattan and Brooklyn, it was lit like a movie set. You practically had to wear sunglasses to enter the place.

Plus, the joint was busy but not too busy. When it comes to doing crimes, the best venue is an empty room, no witnesses. The second best is a packed room, where nobody can see past the people crammed in around them.

But Snoope's was comfortably busy, and when Gotti walked in with that strut, it was like there was a spotlight on him.

At eleven p.m. on May 22, 1973, Gotti and his chums—fellow truck hijackers Ralph "Ralphie Wigs" Galione and Gotti's longtime sidekick, Aniello Dellacroce's nephew Angelo "Quack Quack" Ruggiero—tried to abduct the thirty-year-old McBratney with the intention of killing him in private. They approached him in the bar pretending to be cops.

Galione pulled his gun.

"You're under arrest," Gotti said, and grabbed McBratney hard by the arm.

"Hey, who are you?" McBratney said, one hand still on his drink.

"Police," Gotti said.

McBratney didn't buy that for a second.

"Let's see a badge," he said.

Well, Gotti and the others didn't need no stinking badges. Instead, Galione showed McBratney that his gun worked, as he squeezed off a shot into the ceiling, which brought a shrill scream from the young woman tending bar.

Gotti and Ruggiero tried to slap handcuffs on his wrists, at which time he began to fight. The other men, and one woman, at the bar all abandoned their stools and stood to one side as the struggle moved up and down the bar. Finally, in one corner, the three attackers managed to push McBratney up against a wall. Galione had had enough of this bullshit. While Gotti and Ruggiero held McBratney, Galione pulled his piece and blew McBratney away. As McBratney slid down the wall to the floor, the three men fled.

Word was that, despite the messy nature of the kill, taking place in public, committed by men who didn't bother to wear masks, Carlo Gambino was tremendously pleased. Don Carlo didn't like his nephew Manny, but Manny bore his name, and his death needed to be avenged. This was now done, and John Gotti would get the credit.

The barmaid identified Galione and Ruggiero from an array of photos soon after the shooting, and these men were quickly arrested. They had no idea who the third guy was—at first. But Gotti, being Gotti, couldn't shut up about the hit, couldn't stop bragging about it, and eventually boasted of the crime within earshot of an anonymous FBI informant.

Gotti was arrested on June 3, 1974, caught because of another anonymous tip, in a club in Maspeth, Queens, while having a chat with a hood named Anthony "Tony Roach" Rampino. Gotti was held on $150,000 bail, which his friends and family put up. He showed up for his court dates and took his medicine.

Galione, the man who actually killed McBratney, would have also gone to jail for the crime, had he not been himself iced a few days before Christmas in 1973. Galione, thirty-seven years old, was shot to death at three a.m. in the hallway of his apartment building on Shore Parkway in Bath Beach, Brooklyn.

The mistake bought Gotti four years in the pen for manslaughter—he "recklessly acted in such a way as to assist in the death of another person"—but he never did lose his taste for indiscretion. Those four years behind bars might've cut down on his street fun, but they did nothing to slow his rise in the organization. Whacking a guy, then doing the time while keeping your mouth shut, was yet another surefire way to impress the upper echelon.

* * *

Dominick "Mimi" Scialo was a Colombo capo who pushed people around in Coney Island. He was a big man, six-foot, two hundred pounds, and his headquarters were at the Italian-American Civic Rights League clubhouse on the corner of West Fifteenth Street and Neptune Avenue in Coney Island.

His claim to fame came in 1958 when he made the FBI's Most Wanted list for the murders of two Brooklyn juveniles who'd botched an arson job they'd been assigned.

He'd been arrested several times for murder but never convicted, this despite one of his victims naming him in a deathbed statement. He was under indictment for the January 9, 1970, slayings of two Coney Island garage owners, brothers Arthur and Joseph Dunn. The garage was the A&J Body and Fender Shop on Neptune Avenue.

Yes, he was a bad man—but he was an even worse drunk. And that was what did him in.

He knew he had a problem. He'd been seeing a shrink, trying to get a handle on his alcohol and anger-management problem. We know this because investigators for the New York State Joint Legislative Committee on Crime tailed him as he visited the doctor. We also know that the visits did no good.

During the holiday season of 1973, Carlo Gambino and friends were having dinner at a popular restaurant in Coney Island, when who walked in with a snootful but Mimi Scialo.

There was a large Christmas tree in the corner, the waitstaff wore Santa hats, and the whole place was done up with holiday cheer.

"Well, look, if it ain't the fucking godfather," the forty-six-year-old Scialo said when he saw Gambino.

"Mimi, maybe you should leave," the maître d' said, keeping Scialo away from Gambino's table. A couple of guys at Gambino's table stood up and looked like they were ready to whack Scialo right then and there.

Gambino whispered something, and they sat back down. Patience.

In January 1974, after the holiday season was through, Mimi

disappeared. Unaware of the disrespect he'd shown Gambino that night, investigators came up with other reasons why he might have vanished. The most popular was that he was trying to move in on loan-sharking, bookmaking, and policy rackets that were outside his turf.

The authorities held Scialo responsible for at least four murders, and several other shootings. One wounded guy who they thought was shot by Scialo was Larry Lampasi, who'd once been a President Street Boy but had gone with the Colombos during the second civil war. Lampasi was shot twice in the face but lived. Detectives also noted that Lampasi was a good friend of Carlo Gambino, and that Gambino was pissed off about him getting shot.

An FBI memo written at the time said that Scialo had been disappeared for "failure to follow organizational command." The Colombo-Gallo war was underway at the time, but it was hard for investigators to determine which side bumped off Scialo, as he'd done plenty to piss off everybody.

In October 1974, the FBI was listening in on a bug they'd planted in a Gowanus, Brooklyn, social club.

"You know, Scialo is buried in the basement of the club," one voice said.

"Who put him there?"

"The Undertaker. I can't stand it. It fucking bugs me every time I have to go down there."

The location was Otto's Social and Athletic Club, which filled two white-brick buildings at 494 and 496 President Street, the same street as Gallo headquarters but seven avenue blocks east, on the other side of the Gowanus Canal.

The FBI didn't know who the Undertaker was but assumed he was a guy whose specialty was getting rid of inconvenient stiffs. According to their files, the only gangster with that nickname was the Boss in Buffalo, Stefano "the Undertaker" Magaddino, but he was hardly a suspect in a Brooklyn murder.

Agents, armed with a search warrant, raided the club on Wednesday, October 9, interrupting about a dozen card players and a bocce game being played on the club's court.

Assisted by detectives from the office of Kings County District Attorney Eugene Gold, the FBI agents dug in the basement. About four feet below the dirt floor, they found two bodies, one of which, sure enough, used to belong to Mimi. The bodies were badly decomposed, one more than the other, but even the bones told a story, as one had a bullet hole in the skull. The other had two bullet holes in the skull and was encased in a plastic bag.

The medical examiner, Milton Wald, said that Scialo had been shot once behind the left ear in "typical execution style." Identifying the other corpse was tough because the hands and feet had been hacked off and remained missing. Investigators were hoping that dental casts taken at the Kings County Morgue might do the trick, but the second body remained unidentified.

The '70s were a time when guys started to get whacked because they *might* flip someday. Here's the story of the murder of forty-one-year-old Charles "Charlie Bear" Calise, July 7, 1974, who didn't have to rat to be whacked.

The Bear lived in Yonkers just north of the Bronx and was as wide as he was tall. He was five-nine and weighed 275 pounds, with most of that being muscle. He was called Charlie Bear, for one thing, because he was a bear of a man, but also because he was the son of Anthony "Teddy Bear" Calise, the late bookmaker. Charlie had recently gotten his name in the paper when he was alive, but he made the biggest news when dead.

Over Memorial Day weekend 1974, a combined force of law enforcement arrested four men, including Charlie Bear, on gambling charges. He'd been found in possession of records indicating he was taking in $1,500 a day in bets. The operation was run through a pay phone in a garage. He'd been arrested before but this time he was nervous. He was free on a "stiff probation" stemming from his previous arrest. Now he was looking at time, and the prosecution planned to use that to get him to talk. That was all it took. Gambino felt he couldn't take a chance that loose lips would sink the whole fucking ship.

Early on the morning of July 7, 1974, Charlie Bear's body was found face down in the back seat of a stolen Buick station wagon parked at the Clarkstown Plaza shopping center in Clarkstown, New York, northwest of the Bronx. He'd been shot five times in the face. He still had his ID on him, but no cash. Police knew right away that he lived on Forest Avenue in Yonkers.

The body was discovered at 3:58 a.m. by Rockland County Sheriff's Patrol during a routine check. The medical examiner, Dr. Frederick Zugibe, listed the cause of death as "Brain Destruction." Then he added, "(And severe bleeding)."

Seems to me if your brain is destroyed, don't mean shit if you bleed or not.

The man was killed, the doctor said, late Saturday night or early Sunday morning.

The district attorney knew all about Charlie Bear and told journalists that he was "involved in organized criminal activities in Westchester. This appears to be a Mob hit."

The Bear had been involved in gambling operations in Westchester and in northern sections of the Bronx. The shots came from a small-caliber gun.

Today we know that Father O'Neil, Aniello Dellacroce, killed Calise. He was the Gambino underboss who learned the tricks of the pro-killer trade straight from Anastasia.

Another guy who was hit because he might blab was Carmine Consalvo, a Gambino soldier and Jersey drug dealer. During the summer of 1975, he was facing charges of conspiring to smuggle $42 million worth of heroin—that was 528 pounds—into New Jersey and New York. Consalvo's apartment was owned by his wife's uncle.

Just the fact that he might flip was enough to put him on Gambino's hit list. He knew the jig was up. On September 7, 1975, the thirty-eight-year-old Consalvo fell from the twenty-fourth floor of the luxury Colony Apartments in Fort Lee, New Jersey.

Police ruled out any chances that it was an accident because the apartment's balcony had a five-foot-high railing around it. Police said, however, they could not rule out suicide as Consalvo had been suffering from depression.

A woman on the twenty-second floor said she saw Consalvo's body fall past her window and "there was no cry—there was nothing." The apartment appeared in good order and there was no sign of forced entry.

Consalvo's wife was in the laundry room at the time of his deadly dive. When she returned she found the apartment door locked. Whatever happened up there, Consalvo was no longer a risk to rat.

Three months later, Consalvo's kid brother, thirty-two-year-old Francis Consalvo, took a dive of his own. Francis was Aniello Dellacroce's bodyguard. His body was found on the roof of a one-story building on Lafayette Street in Manhattan. He had jumped, fell, or was pushed from the roof of a five-story building next door. Frank wasn't in the same kind of trouble as his brother, although he had been arrested a handful of times for assault and robbery.

Between the deaths of the two brothers, two more former Gambino soldiers with ties to Consalvo bit the dust. In October 1975, thirty-three-year-old George Adamo and twenty-eight-year-old Charles LaRocca were shot dead and left in a van in Brooklyn. They were former Gambino soldiers who'd defected to Carmine "Lilo" Galante and were reportedly the guys assigned to whack Carmine Consalvo.

CHAPTER 19
"Come to the Dixie. Bring Cash"

It was sometime in the early 1970s. I was a teenager. My father Ricky DiMatteo and my uncle, Joe Schipani, often had dinner at the Dixie Tavern, a bar/restaurant in the South Slope, corner of Fifth Avenue and Twentieth Street, owned by a Genovese capo named Todo Marino. They called my uncle Joe Shep. He was a made man in the Genovese family. Joe and Ricky would eat with Todo and his crew.

One night, I got a call from Ricky.

"Come to the Dixie," he said. "Bring cash. I'm playing cards later at the Gondola."

"Right away, Pops," I said.

That was the Gondola Restaurant, owned by Joe Marola, a guy my dad liked playing cards with.

When I got to the Dixie, I was guided into a back dining room, and I saw my dad and Uncle Joe sitting at a big table with many other guys. I went straight to Ricky and gave him the envelope. I generally scanned the faces and gave a little nod to anyone who looked back. But I didn't think much about who anyone was. I gave Uncle Joe a kiss and, my job done, turned to get out of there.

But Ricky spoke up. "Hold on, Frankie Boy. Meet the guys at the table."

So, I start shaking hands. "Pleased to meet you." Didn't think much of it, and then I came to an old man with a preposterous nose. Pulling my eyes away from it, I looked at his whole face: silver hair, warm brown eyes, a face that was erupting into a friendly smile. I swear to God my first thought was, *No way this is Don Carlo Gambino.* I shook his hand. I don't know what the expression on my face was. I hope I didn't look as stunned as I felt. What was I supposed to do? I didn't know if I should kiss him. Genuflect? I was just lost. I turned and went back to my dad.

"You need anything else, Pops?"

"You're done," he said. I left and went to President Street and found my best friend, Goombadiel.

"Goombi, I just fucking met Don Carlo."

"No shit, where?"

"The Dixie?"

"Your dad and Joe Shep was there?"

"Yeah."

"I figured."

I later learned that, after I left, Gambino asked who I was.

"That was my son," Ricky said.

"A recruit Ricky," Gambino said, and everyone laughed.

For the next few months, we went to the Dixie for dinner. I would walk in behind Ricky and Joe. The same men and you-know-who were again at the table. This time I made certain that I greeted Don Carlo *first.* First week I paid my respects but didn't sit at the table. I went over to the bar and waited, out of earshot. But the week after that, I headed toward the bar and Don Carlo spoke up.

"Come. Sit," he said. "Eat." He patted an empty chair next to him. He seemed frail. Again, his eyes and smile were warm and friendly. I felt like I was looking at a loving grandparent. But I couldn't forget he was still The Godfather.

He asked me if I spoke Italian.

"A little," I managed to say.

He smiled and spoke in his Sicilian dialect: "*Come stai* Frankie ragazzo, *vieni a sederti e mangiare qui, devi uomini buoni li per imparare questa vita se tieni il mese chiuso e gli occhi e le orecchie aperti, ma se usi il naso puoi sentire la puzza degli uomini cattivi.*"

I just looked at him. I only understood every other word—but Joe Shep later translated for me. In English, Don Carlo said, "How are you, Frankie Boy? Come sit and eat. You have two good men there to learn from. Keep your mouth closed, your eyes and ears open, but your smell will be your best friend because you can smell the stink of bad men."

I understood what he said—and I've kept it in mind ever since. When I encountered smelly or sweating men, I looked twice at them. I never trusted many people after that.

At that time, that little man at the head of the table was the subject of investigations by every branch of government there was. He had people poking into his affairs who worked for committees, bureaus, and services—an alphabet soup of federal pain in the ass.

During the late summer of 1972, the NYPD's former chief inspector told the U.S. Senate Investigations Committee, "Carlo Gambino is considered to be the Boss. He is suspected of being active in narcotics. He is in gambling, shylocking, labor racketeering, vending machines, criminally receiving stolen property, and alcohol tax violations. He is related to Tom Lucchese through marriage. He entered the country sometime around 1921 as a stowaway at Norfolk, Virginia. He is also suspected of smuggling aliens."

A month later, a report from the Federal Bureau of Narcotics and Dangerous Drugs said, "The Gambino brothers, Carlo and Paul, were reported to exercise control of the narcotics smuggling activities between Mafia elements in Palermo, Sicily, and the United States, on behalf of Salvatore Lucania (the late Lucky Luciano). During 1948, the Gambino brothers met with Lucania at the home of their relatives in Palermo."

Three weeks later, a report published by the Immigration and Naturalization Service read, "Investigation conducted by the Bureau of Narcotics revealed that during May 1948 some thirty-odd Sicilian aliens were smuggled into the United States. Investigators learned that Carlo Gambino was involved in the smuggling of these aliens and that some of the aliens, in turn, had been smuggling substantial quantities of heroin into the United States as payment for being brought into this country." (We'll be discussing Gambino's alien-smuggling business in chapter 21.)

That report also noted that the INS had been trying to deport Gambino back to Italy for thirty-two years. And amazingly they still hadn't given up. First it was World War II and then it was Gambino's bum ticker. It was always something.

OK, here's the part where Gambino saves my life. In 1976, I opened an after-hours club on Twentieth Street and Sixth Avenue—just up the block from the Dixie Tavern. I was twenty. One night, some neighborhood assholes came in and were giving me a hard time.

The first time I asked them to leave, I said it nice. I said please. They told me to fuck off. So, the second time I wasn't so nice. I told them to get the fuck out.

"We're with O'Neil," one of them said. That was Aniello Dellacroce, Gambino underboss, but really running things because Don Carlo was sick.

"I don't give a fuck who you're with," I said, and threw them out.

An hour later, my cousin heard a knock on the door. He answered it, and some guy hit him. We all ran out to help. The guys I'd thrown out were back, and they had brought help.

We all went around the block to a schoolyard to fight. As soon as the first punch was thrown the cops were there. I had a gun, which I heaved as far as I could.

When we came out of the schoolyard, we were held while police went in and found the gun, and we were all arrested. After two days in jail we got out because no one took responsibility for the gun. They couldn't hold six guys for one gun.

Next day, I got a call from Ricky.

"Meet me at the Dixie at six. We got a sit-down with O'Neil."

"OK," I said. I was shitting bricks. I got there at 5:30, met Ricky at the bar.

"Follow my lead," he said. "And be firm that you never said, 'Fuck O'Neil.'"

"Of course."

There was an incident many years earlier that now weighed heavily on my mind. On September 21, 1961, members of the Gallo crew beat the shit out of Aniello Dellacroce, who was a capo with the Gambinos at the time, while he ate at Luna, a tablecloth *ristorante* in Little Italy. Now he would have my fate in his hands.

Ricky went into the back. I stayed at the bar. After about fifteen minutes he came and got me. We went to the back room and there was O'Neil and the two guys I'd kicked out. One of them had a nasty smirk on his face.

On my best behavior, I shook their hands and sat down.

O'Neil spoke first: "I heard you said a really bad thing about me."

I told him just what happened. "I thought they were bullshitting me. And they really were being assholes. I said I didn't give a fuck who they were with, but I didn't mean it that way."

Thank God, he laughed.

O'Neil looked at me, and said, "I believe you, son, but let me teach you something. You were right, but in this Life you say the wrong thing it will make *you* wrong. And dead."

Then he turned to one of the assholes and made a small gesture. One of his bodyguards smacked the asshole hard in the face. That took the smirk off.

"Never use my name," O'Neil said, "and get the fuck out of Brooklyn."

He told me I had to close down my club. That was my punishment. I said thank you to O'Neil, shook his hand, and left. I went back to President Street and sat down with Blast, who chewed me out good. He sent me across the street to Roy Roy's club to ponder my sins.

"OK," I said, head bowed.

"And by the way, thank God that Carlo likes you."

I sat in Roy Roy's club and drank a Dewars. In a few minutes Ricky came in.

"The fix was in," he said. "Don Carlo gave you a pass, so O'Neil had to go light."

* * *

Two weeks later, I again went to the Dixie with Ricky and Uncle Joe. Gambino was there and called me over to him. I thought I was going to get chewed out again, but I didn't.

He said, this time in English, "Frankie Boy, you must learn this Life before you live it or it will chew you up."

"I'm really sorry about my mouth," I said. "It won't happen again."

He smiled and said, "Eat."

And that was the last time I saw him. Soon after that, he was so sick he was bedridden. When I heard he'd died, I felt really bad. For obvious reasons I liked him a lot. I understood his quiet power, and why he was respected and the don.

The story, however, doesn't quite end there. I ran into those guys from the beef two years later in Fort Lauderdale, Florida, at the Four O'Clock Club. I was in there with my friends Louie and Goombi. The second we walked in, I spotted them.

"We're fucked," I said. "Let me handle it."

They saw me and walked over. I put my "fuck you" face on. I didn't need to, though. Those guys wanted to shake hands, be friends, and buy us a drink.

I'm a guy with a suspicious nature and didn't buy it at first.

"If you are going to do it, do it now," I said.

"No, no, no, we're talking to a few girls over there, come join us."

And it was peaceful. We had a drink with them, and maybe even smiled a bit. Everybody tried to make light of the past, but I never got to the point where I trusted them, and I was very happy when we got out of there with nobody hitting nobody.

What were the odds? Small fucking world.

CHAPTER 20
Sinatra

IT IS IMPOSSIBLE TO TELL THE STORY of Carlo Gambino without mentioning Frank Sinatra. Sinatra was very important to the Italian people. He wasn't America's first Italian superstar—Rudolph Valentino wins that prize, with Joe DiMaggio also beating Frank by a few years—but he was the most important. He redefined "cool" for Americans, Italians and non-Italians alike, and of course he sang great. He went into acting and won an Oscar (for playing Maggio in *From Here to Eternity*), starting another long and successful career in film.

Truth be known, he wasn't the favorite singer in Red Hook for the simple reason that he refused to sing in Italian. We preferred Jimmy Roselli, who came to my engagement party (another story). Sinatra rose to the top of the showbiz world and stayed there for many decades, but there was always talk that he couldn't have done it without Mob help—including that of Don Carlo.

What was thought to be rumors became etched in America's collective mind when *The Godfather* movie came out. It included a scene where a Sinatra-type singer (played by Al Martino) comes to Vito Corleone to beg to have his career saved. Corleone (Marlon Brando) slaps him, tells him to be a man, and grants the favor that gives the guy's career a reboot. How much of that is fantasy is unknown. Mario Puzo and Francis Ford Coppola probably don't know.

Here's what we *do* know. . .

In January 1947, Sinatra got a phone call from Joe Fischetti, who was Al Capone's cousin. The pair had been friends for almost a decade. Frank dug the "Men of Honor" reputation of mobsters and mobsters dug Frank's glamor, a real-life teen idol, causing little girls in bobby socks to squeal with delight long before Elvis or the Beatles hit the scene.

Fischetti, who may or may not have been known by the nickname "Trigger Happy," was Chicago's top political fixer. You didn't get anywhere in Chi-town politics without an okay from Fischetti. He was also in charge of illegal gambling in the Windy City. He was one of the Fischetti Brothers, the youngest, and the one women liked the best—so he and Sinatra had charisma in common, as well.

During this phone call, Fischetti told Sinatra there was going to be a meeting in Havana, Cuba, in a few weeks to honor Lucky Luciano, who'd been deported to Italy after World War II.

Luciano's deportation was a backhanded reward for his help during the war, notifying the underground resistance in Italy to side with the American GIs and advising the Pentagon as to where to invade (Anzio, for example) to maximize geography. Luciano was no longer welcome in the United States, but Cuba was another matter.

Fischetti asked Sinatra if he wanted to attend the meeting and meet "The Man." Sinatra eagerly said he did.

On January 1, 1947, Frank requested a gun permit in California, at which time he was fingerprinted.

They asked him what he needed the gun for.

"I sometimes carry large sums of cash," he said.

A month later, Frank flew to New York, took care of some business, and taxied back to Idlewild (the airport that grew into JFK) for a flight to Miami Beach. He stayed in Fischetti's mansion on Allison Island.

On the eve of their departure for Havana, they visited the Colonial Inn in Hallandale, Florida, a carpet joint run by Meyer Lansky, and conveniently located next to Gulfstream racetrack. The Colonial and Lansky had their own patriotic World War II history. Lansky, in addition to being liaison between the Pentagon and Lucky Luciano's power, allowed an army signal corps unit to use the Colonial Inn in Florida as its headquarters, the gaming equipment pushed aside and cots moved in, turning the casino into a huge barracks.

After the war, it became a casino again, and it was hopping when Sinatra and Fischetti came to play. That night, in the Colonial's nightclub, Frank got up on stage and sang a couple of numbers.

The next morning—by this time it was February 11—Sinatra and Fischetti boarded a Pan American clipper bound for Havana. The men were photographed walking down the steps of the plane at the Cuban airport. Each was carrying an attaché case, which theoretically contained upward of $2 million in cash for Luciano.

In Havana, Frank met Luciano, Lansky, and Carlo Gambino in that order. The transfer of the attaché cases to Luciano (or one of his boys) went unrecorded. It was some meeting, and the suspicion is that all the bigwigs who were there came with an attaché case. Gambino, a smiley guy to begin with, was all grins as he met the rail-thin singer with the big ears. In addition to those already mentioned, those who grinned as they shook Sinatra's hand were Albert Anastasia, Willie Moretti, Vito Genovese, Frank Costello, Little Augie Pisano, Joe "the Fat Man" Magliocco, Joseph Bonanno, Joseph Profaci, Joe Adonis, Tony Accardo, Carlo Marcello, and Santo Trafficante. There were other mugs there, not-so-famous guys but powerful, like Joe "Doc" Stacher, who controlled the coin-operated machines of Newark on Lansky's behalf.

Doc later told a Sinatra biographer, "The Italians among us were very proud of Frank. They always told me they had spent a lot of money helping him in his career."

Mob support of Ol' Blue Eyes dated back to when he was the lead singer of Tommy Dorsey's band. Luciano was a big fan—which is how Sinatra got the invite to the Havana conclave.

It was only days before the powerful gossip columns in America's daily newspapers began to hit Sinatra hard with the Mob rap. One guy wrote that Sinatra had a habit of making friends with "cheap hoodlums."

Sinatra reportedly raged when he read that and threatened to smack the writer next time he saw him—which was at a Hollywood nightspot called Ciro's. The writer came in and Frank punched him behind the left ear, sending the scribe tumbling to the floor.

"If I see you again, I'll kill you," Sinatra said.

The FBI followed Sinatra and kept a thick file on him for the next forty years. The bureau being the way it was, denying that the Mafia existed and paranoid about communism, showed that authorities were concerned not with his mobbiness as much as with his support for anti-racist initiatives and other liberal causes.

The one thing that tied Sinatra and Gambino together in the minds of the public was a photograph taken on April 11, 1976, at the 3,500-seat Westchester Premier Theater in Tarrytown, New York.

Frank was performing at the dinner theater, and the upper echelon of the Gambino family was in the audience. The theater was a Mob venture, built for $5.3 million. Because of all that Mob money, everyone taking a skim, it was impossible for the venue to pay its own bills and it was seemingly always on the verge of bankruptcy.

Booking Frank at the venue was a moneymaking move, because they knew they could charge top dollar for tickets and the place would sell out. Frank did two shows. Gambino and his boys enjoyed the show, finished their dinner, and were having coffee when a man came to their table and whispered in Gambino's ear.

"All right, now we go see Frank," Gambino said, and the men at the table, who included, among others, Paul Castellano and Jimmy "the Weasel" Fratianno, stood as one.

Backstage, Sinatra greeted Gambino with a kiss and a hug. A photographer was present and the famous photo was taken. Seven men stood in back, while two sat on chairs in front. The back row consisted of Castellano, Gregory DePalma, Sinatra, Frank Marson, Gambino, and Fratianno. In front were the godfather's brother Joseph Gambino and Richard "Nerves" Fusco.

Gambino reportedly, with the help of Jimmy the Weasel, had convinced Sinatra that, if he performed for free in Westchester, he would be allowed in the exclusive brotherhood called the Knights of Malta and be awarded the Maltese Cross, which had only been given to seven hundred men during the thousand-year existence of the secret society.

After performing his two shows gratis, thinking the money was going to the Knights of Malta, Sinatra had his picture taken and was told by Gambino that he had earned a favor. Was there anything he needed?

Sinatra said there was. He had a bodyguard at one time named Andrew "Banjo" Celentano who was planning to write a tell-all book about Sinatra. Could someone have a talk with Banjo and explain to him that he was a *jadrool*, a fool. Gambino smiled. The book was never written.

That's our last glimpse of Sinatra in Gambino's world, but the theater stayed in the picture for a while longer.

In the late spring of 1978, Boss Anthony "Nino" Gaggi, fifty-three years old, was indicted by a Manhattan grand jury for an alleged fraudulent scheme to force the Westchester Premier Theater into bankruptcy.

He was taken down with nine others, many of whom had not previously been considered Mob-connected. Unable to sell 275,000 shares of stock in their theater, Gaggi and his codefendants were said to have fraudulently made it appear as if the shares had been sold.

They were also said to have bribed investors to "buy" their stock with under-the-table refunds, and were also allegedly skimming off the theater's proceeds. The whole scheme smacked of white-collar crime, country club style.

In country clubs, they didn't refer to the WASP Mafia. They simply called it the good ol' boy network. It was one of the WASPs who'd gotten caught with his hand in the cookie jar, and he was ratting out the others, including Nino. For the feds, this case was a bonus.

They'd been listening to Vegas when they caught drift of the Westchester Theater scam. During the trial that fall, Gaggi's lawyer John Mitchell tried to convince a jury that Gaggi had nothing to do with the theater, but the government presented witnesses that claimed Nino was a "secret investor."

The trial earned headlines in November when a sacred name was first mentioned: Frank Sinatra. A photo of Sinatra and Carlo Gambino was introduced into evidence. The owners of the theater, secret and otherwise, had apparently discussed bringing Sinatra in as an investor. Jimmy "the Weasel" Fratianno testified, the San Francisco boss and former hit man escorted to and from the witness stand under heavy armed guard.

In December, even before the jury was charged, motions to acquit because of lack of evidence were filed by the various defense attorneys. Seven of the motions were denied, but Gaggi's was not. He was a free man.

CHAPTER 21
Gambino's New Sicilian Secret Society

SOME HISTORY-CHANGING DECISIONS were made when Don Carlo was alone, sitting and thinking, eyes twinkling, then hard, then twinkling again, Mona Lisa smile on his thin lips. Even as an old man, one of his favorite things to ponder was the homeland.

Gambino believed in the sacred power of Sicily.

Here in America the real gangsters, the Sicilian-born gangsters, were dying off, many gone for years now, many gone because Don Carlo decided it was time for them to go, but what was left?

There was nepotism and sons of gangsters wanting to follow in their fathers' footsteps. There were smooth-faced men, damaged by American mediocrity and too soft to be any good on the street.

There were American meatheads, vicious and animalistic, but without discipline, just as apt to kill a neighbor because of a loud party—or a guy in a bar who looked at his *goomada* wrong—as carry out a Commission-sanctioned hit. No discipline. America had become a permissive society, and young American gangsters didn't listen to their elders, and they had little or no respect for what had come before.

Then, the idea. Don Carlo's mysterious little smile grew just a little bit larger. Eureka! What the American Mafia needed was a fresh influx of Sicilian blood.

To accomplish that, Gambino put recruiters to work back in the old country. Smuggling Sicilians into the country was nothing new, even for Gambino—but now he was going to go full tilt and build an army. Sicilians with special skills were promised a better life and smuggled into America by the hundreds, maybe thousands.

The promises of a better life were always sincere, and in most cases worked out, as there was lots of money for a gangster to make in America, a hell of a lot more than in Palermo.

So, Gambino, who had diminished the power of the other four crime families in New York and forced them to be subservient, was now in charge of a new battalion of men, all doing his bidding in one way or another, men who no one knew anything about.

The headquarters for the human smuggling operation was a barbershop on Mulberry Street in Little Italy, sort of an Ellis Island where Gambino kept track of the men he'd smuggled in, so he'd know who to put where. Often, these guys were wanted by police back in Sicily, sometimes in more than one country, so they were assigned new identities.

No one is sure how many Sicilians Gambino smuggled. Estimates go to two thousand, sometimes recruited as individuals and sometimes in teams.

For example, a crew of counterfeiters was brought in who were experts at making cheap replicas of expensive watches. Their front was the Garofalo Swiss Watch and Movements Company, with offices in Times Square and a warehouse in Little Italy.

Watches weren't the only thing they counterfeited there. You could get a blank Social Security card, a fake driver's license. The warehouse, it was later learned, served other Gambino operations as well: porn (both mags and eight-millimeter stag films), and "slugs," which were blank coins that could be used in coin-operated machines.

The fake watches were sold by other Sicilians of Gambino's choosing, who impersonated pilots for an Italian airline. They would go into bars, claim to be short on money, and sell their seemingly expensive watch at a discount price. They didn't just operate in New York, either. You could get a counterfeit watch from an Italian-speaking pilot in Atlanta, Chicago, L.A., and Miami, as well.

We know about the op because it was raided by the NYPD late in 1970. The most controversial item found was the slugs, because coin-operated machines were Mob-owned. Police found the guy in charge of the counterfeiting ring was thirty-year-old Bruno Pennisi, fresh from Sicily.

NYPD intelligence became aware of the influx of Sicilian mobsters, and because of the slugs, assumed that they were working outside the parameters of the American Mafia.

It was a first in organized crime, whole criminal enterprises being manned entirely by hoods who had no record or documentation of any kind inside the U.S. The Mob rosters the cops had carefully built, the charts that graced the walls of task force offices in an attempt to understand the enemy, were useless against these guys. Those rosters were badly out of date, anyway, and had not been significantly updated since the early 1960s.

If apprehended, the new Sicilians gave fake names, and there was no way to tell who they really were.

One international hood who became part of Gambino's new secret society was Tommaso Buscetta, a longtime Mafia hit man. It wasn't hard to figure out how he became part of Gambino's new Sicilian army, as he was a friend of Don Carlo's cousin Rosario Gambino.

Buscetta was public enemy number one in Sicily, where he was wanted for his part in the car-bombing deaths of seven policemen and a number of civilians. After what became known as the Ciaculli Massacre, Buscetta allegedly fled to South America and entered the U.S. through Mexico. Belief was that he was in the U.S. to do what he did best, blow guys away.

Buscetta was no match for American law enforcement, however, as it turned out. In June 1970, he was strolling through Brooklyn when a crew of feds, state cops, and NYPD took him in. After Italy inexplicably failed to follow up on a request for extradition, the feds took him to the southern border of Arizona and ordered him to return to Mexico.

CHAPTER 22

End of an Era

As Gambino lay on his deathbed, there were still at least six law enforcement agencies actively investigating him: New York Police Department (file number #8-128760), Federal Bureau of Investigation (file number #334450), Immigration and Naturalization Service, Internal Revenue Service, Federal Bureau of Narcotics, and the Waterfront Commission. They didn't know it, but time had already run out on those efforts.

At some point Gambino made his final trip to his Oyster Bay gardens, and took to his bed. One of Don Carlo's last visitors was Big Paulie Castellano, who solemnly pledged to his cousin, his brother-in-law, his best friend for fifty years, that he would carry on for him, and keep the Gambino family healthy and strong.

Don Carlo had tried to keep his own sons out of the business. He correctly predicted the ravages of the new RICO laws, the Law's new capability to put hoods away for many years, and he decided he didn't want his boys to spend their lives in jail. (It didn't completely work. Tommy could not be dissuaded and eventually lost five years to RICO.)

The new law allowed the government to prosecute gangsters for being part of a criminal enterprise, rather than for a specific crime. Plausible deniability fell apart under the new law.

Gambino felt he had no choice but to name Big Paul as his successor. He was the man he trusted the most, the first man he met in

America, his first cousin and his brother-in-law—you couldn't get closer than that.

Carlo and Big Paul had been young men when they started up their first cover business, the meatpacking joint on Quentin Road north of Marine Park.

The best man for the job would be Father O'Neil, Aniello Dellacroce, but he was in jail. And besides, Big Paul was like a brother. Dellacroce was Gambino's friend but he also had many enemies. Too many.

Could Paul hold the ship together? Don Carlo knew he'd be in the next world before he learned the answer to that question.

The doctor, a stethoscope still hanging from his ears, said, "This is it."

The family was summoned.

The family gathered at bedside.

Under covers up to his chin, he looked to weigh about fifty pounds. The room became crowded. All three of his sons were there, with their wives. Dr. and Mrs. Sinatra (Gambino's daughter, Phyllis). Big Paulie remained in the room and was joined by his brother Peter, plus Kathryn's sister and her husband from downstairs.

The TV was on, showing the Yankee game. The Yanks beat the Royals in the Bronx, 7 to 6. Thurman Munson went three-for-five. Game over, the TV was turned off.

Gambino's heart gave out and he died, at 1:45 a.m. on October 15, 1976. He died peacefully in his bed at his Oyster Bay home with his family at his side. It seemed like he had been an old man forever, yet he was only seventy-four.

Two doctors signed his death certificate, one from Brooklyn and one from Queens. Cause of death: myocardial infarction in combo with arteriosclerosis. A heart attack killed a man whose heart was already very sick.

In charge at the funeral, and as interim boss until the Commission decided what to do, was Gambino's consigliere, Joseph N. Gallo, who lived in Astoria, Queens, and preferred to conduct business behind closed doors. Joseph was low-key and had only one criminal conviction on his record, as he was fined fifty bucks for gambling in 1946.

Gambino's body was placed on view in a $7,000 bronze casket beginning at two in the afternoon on October 16 at Cusimano & Russo funeral chapel, a Spanish-mission-style building on West Sixth Street in Gravesend, Brooklyn, twelve blocks west of Gambino's Brooklyn home.

Because of a combination of security reasons and the expected heavy attendance, all four chapels in the funeral home were reserved for Gambino. The partitions between the chapels were removed to form one large room.

There were flowers everywhere. Stefan's Florist in Lawrence, Long Island, delivered six arrangements; the displays were more than a thousand dollars.

Early attendees were cousin Paul Castellano, Gambino captain Carmine "the Doctor" Lombardozzi, Colombo underboss Joseph Brancato, and Colombo soldier Joseph LaRosa.

A man-mountain bouncer was stationed at the front door to the funeral home. Those he recognized were admitted without question. Others were asked if they were family. Those who said no were not allowed in.

The guy at the door was one of a team of humongous security guards who also functioned as pallbearers, ushers, etc., ready to leap into action if there was anyone showing disrespect.

The casket, held by men of very broad shoulders, went into the church followed by Gambino's daughter, Phyllis, and her husband, Tom. Next in were Gambino's sons: Carl, Joseph, and Thomas, then Carlo's brother, Joseph, followed by nieces, nephew, and grandchildren.

The Cadillac hearse took the body from the funeral home to the church at a pedestrian pace, and the route was lined with spectators, many in tears that the Great One was gone.

It couldn't be said that Gambino didn't charge tax, but many a poor Italian immigrant in Brooklyn had Gambino to thank for the fact that they weren't living under a bridge.

The funeral Mass was celebrated at Our Lady of Grace Church, site of his wedding and Kathryn's funeral, around the corner from the Ocean Parkway home.

Some ballsy reporter asked one of the OLG priests, Father Richard Lavecchia, if Don Carlo was a "communicant of the church."

"That was his definition, not ours," the priest said. "He will receive the exact same liturgy that anyone else would receive. Nothing will be different, either for the bad or the good."

The head OLG priest, Father Dominic Sclafani, officiated at the funeral Mass. As befitting the dead man's low-key style, the funeral was large but lacked the fancy production that had sent other godfathers to their final resting place.

Don Carlo's procession included a flower car, the hearse, thirteen limos, and seventeen private cars. The motorcade stretched out to two blocks long. The parade continued beyond the seventeen private cars because an estimated four hundred members of the press were on hand from around the world. There were also cops, feds, photographers, neighbors, curious people, etc.

The feds were human facial-recognition machines and made lists of the known hoods at the funeral. Joseph N. Gallo. Paul Castellano. Gambino captains James Failla and Salvatore Avarello, etc.

But no one could identify one mourner, and it was clear he didn't want to be ID'd. He was about fifty years old, short, stocky, and sharply dressed—and sat in the church with his face hidden behind a black silk handkerchief.

The same man, similarly masked, had been to the funeral parlor on both nights of the wake. He wore a glistening pinky ring and reportedly sipped scotch from a cocktail glass, which was automatically refilled each time it was empty.

The mystery man drove the reporter from the *Daily News* crazy. The *News* had been the Mob's tabloid of choice since forever. Reporters from the *News* were used to knowing things the *Post* reporters didn't, so a guy in a mask drove him crazy. He followed the guy to his limo and jotted down the plate number.

The limo was a rental so the reporter called and asked who had rented that car. "Oh, that was Dr. Boris," the limo rental guy said, and offered no other info. The reporter talked to an FBI guy he knew.

"We've been trying to identify this guy for two or three days now," was all the fed had to say. "We still haven't been able to get a clear look at his face. We noticed when he arrived at the church, he hopped out of his limo, moved quickly through the crowd to the church entrance. The bouncer met him halfway and then cleared the path for him to cut the line and enter the church."

The reporter next talked to a member of the NYPD organized crime task force. "You know, this guy is starting to get on our nerves. We've used up more film on the Masked Marvel than we have on some of the top capos in Gambino's family. It's going to be embarrassing if it turns out he isn't worth it." (To wrap up this "mystery man" story, an NYPD detective later told the *News* reporter that surveillance had finally managed to get a photo of the man with his mask down. Trouble was, they still didn't recognize him.)

When the funeral service was over, the pallbearers carried the bronze casket back to the Cadillac hearse and the cortege headed for Middle Village, Queens, to St. John Cemetery. Again, the pace was slow and streets were lined with mourners.

Ignorance was bliss. No one knew the damage the little man had done to Brooklyn, the very real scourge he'd put on huge sections of the borough with a public stance against the babonia and a junk supermarket open for business.

Gambino's body was interred in a marble vault in the main cloisters of St. John Cemetery, the same graveyard as Lucky Luciano. Usually, by the time a funeral gets to the cemetery, the mourners have dwindled down to close family and friends. But on Gambino's big day, about three hundred mourners made the trip to Middle Village.

So many people were still paying their respects that they were packed like sardines into a small chapel. More prayers were read, at a snappy pace because there was no air. The prayers were selections from the Book of John and the Book of Psalms, including the twenty-second and twenty-third Psalms, and read by Father Joseph Cataldo.

"I am the Resurrection and the Life. He who believes in me even if he died shall live, and whoever lives and believes in me shall never die."

Father Cataldo wrapped it up with the Lord's Prayer and sprinkled the casket with holy water.

Mourners were given red carnations and red roses, then walked past the casket where they placed the flowers in two large gold-colored vases. The casket was moved to the fifth floor of the cloisters and placed in its vault, directly above Kathryn.

Interestingly, at the time of Don Carlo's passing, a prognosticator on Long Island predicted that Carmine Galante, subject of my book *The Cigar*, was most likely to fill the massive void left by Gambino's death.

That guy needed to shine up his crystal ball. It was true that Galante envisioned a one-family system with him as father, but it was uncertain at best that he could pull that off.

As we now know, Galante didn't live to pull off anything, shot dead on the patio of Joe and Mary's Italian-American Restaurant on Knickerbocker Avenue in Bushwick. But at the time, the theory was taken seriously enough that cops took action. If Galante was going to take advantage of Gambino's peaceful death by bumping off the fathers of the other families, then those guys were in imminent danger.

Police in New York and New Jersey, and on Long Island staked out the homes of major mobsters. An informant told an NYPD detective that the recent death of Andimo Pappadio of the Luccheses, gunned down in the driveway of his Lido Beach home on Long Island's South Shore, also served to make Galante's ascension easier.

Everyone agreed that it had been a long time since Carlo Gambino could be considered active. Sure, if you were lucky you'd meet him like I did, sitting at a table speaking softly, offering wisdom, and sipping coffee, but he'd been slowing down for a while.

More and more he was happy without the hubbub of being a boss. He liked staying at home. When he passed, his Long Island neighbors were saddened. He was "one of the nicest gentlemen" they'd ever met.

One neighbor said, "I saw him the night before last. He was in bed. I stayed maybe five minutes. He was looking bad. He offered me a cup of coffee. He always did."

A reporter asked the neighbor if they'd ever discussed Gambino's criminal career and he said, "We never discussed that. It never came into the discussion. He was just a neighbor like you would have."

In Gambino's obituary, which was extensive, it was noted that he was survived by three sons, Thomas, Joseph, and Carl, and one daughter, Phyllis Sinatra. Every paper that ran the obit noted that Mrs. Sinatra was married to a Brooklyn doctor and not a Hoboken crooner.

When Don Carlo passed away, John Gotti was in jail, serving time for the McBratney hit. He got out a year later and was almost immediately straightened out, with Paul Castellano officiating. In record time, Gotti was promoted from soldier to capo by Dellacroce, now fully in charge of the vicious Bergin Hunt and Fish Club crew in Ozone Park, Queens.

The FBI put a lot of resources into watching the transition of power after Gambino's death. Chaos plays havoc with the best of well-oiled machines. With things in a state of flux, guys were apt to make mistakes.

In late October 1976, only days after Don Carlo's passing, a meeting was held in a private residence in Brooklyn, and several Gambino capos were there:

- Nick Patti, from Ansonia, and a close friend of Gambino's. Once, after one of Gambino's many heart attacks, Patti was the first man allowed to visit.
- Frank Piccolo, who'd been mentored by Patti, became the

most powerful Gambino capo in Connecticut. He was whacked in 1981.

- Ettore "Terry" Zappi, aka Tony Russo, a Gambino cousin and Oyster Bay neighbor who came up through the ranks and was promoted to capo soon after Anastasia's death.
- Frank Perrone, who we met earlier. His bachelor party made the papers.
- David Amodeo, top Gambino man in the Bronx.
- Joe N. Gallo.

The meeting lasted for three hours, and it was agreed that Big Paul and Joe N. Gallo would run things. The toughest part was deciding how the money would flow.

They eventually agreed that all future payments would go to Gallo and he would "keep Castellano aware of all financial interests." There was even a comment to the effect that having Castellano and Gallo in charge would keep the cops happy, since Castellano was "more civilized" than Dellacroce, who frankly scared the shit out of everyone, cops included.

In November, the feds overheard conversations to the effect that there had been a movement to make Joe N. Gallo head of the Gambino organization while Gambino was still alive, in bed but still breathing. This idea was eventually nixed—by Gallo himself, apparently—and Gambino was allowed the dignity of remaining Boss until his natural death.

There was also talk that Gallo and Castellano in charge might be only temporary, that O'Neil might be made boss when he got out of jail and if he still had his wits about him.

It was believed whoever ran the Gambino family would not be "exerting his influence" over the other families the way Don Carlo had.

In December 1976, with Dellacroce now out of jail, there was another meeting at a private residence in Brooklyn. Dellacroce, Big Paul, and Gallo personally greeted every hood that showed up. Big

Paul said he had been "nominated" to head the Gambinos, and he was appointing O'Neil as his underboss and Gallo as consigliere.

Castellano said that the family was one—he held his hands clasped together—there was no friction, and he, Dellacroce, and Gallo were in charge. Castellano said that Don Carlo's "rules" against dealing in drugs, bombs, or kidnappings still applied.

He gave them a business update, the borgata—he pronounced it *brugad*—was moving into Atlantic City, which was opening up for gambling, and there was a whole boardwalk of hotels and casinos to horn in on. He then assigned various capos to travel out of town to inform the leaders of Mob families in other cities of the new Gambino leadership.

"Inform him that I am the new boss here, and I wish him the best," Castellano said.

It painted a pretty picture of unity. Reality was very different. While Gambino had spent his last years running the new Sicilian Secret Society, the Gambino crime family split into two distinct factions.

Brains: stock market fraud, money laundering, that sort of thing—which was run by Big Paulie Castellano.

And Brawn: run by Father O'Neil, Aniello Dellacroce. Old-fashioned street rackets. Gambino made it clear that Big Paulie would be his successor but would have next to nothing to do with Dellacroce's street operations.

It is unclear if Carlo Gambino, sick in bed much of the time, realized that he'd left behind a crime family that only he was holding together. Once he was gone, a split became inevitable.

The Brawn side was appalled that Don Carlo had chosen Big Paulie. Father O'Neil was a legendary mobster, as tough and psychopathic as they came. Big Paulie, on the other hand, well, he was Don Carlo's brother-in-law. Castellano's operations were so clean that he saw himself as a legitimate businessman, with a copy of *The Wall Street Journal* under his arm.

What kept the peace was that Gambino had it set up so the two sides didn't interact much, and Dellacroce wasn't around. Back in jail, he had a heart attack that put him in the intensive care unit of the Bellevue Hospital prison ward. Some figured that Dellacroce would get better, get out of jail (which would occur on December 27, 1976), and take over the Gambino clan. But it didn't work out that way.

Gambino was the first godfather to pass after the faddish popularity of the movie *The Godfather*, in which Marlon Brando, as Vito Corleone, died of a heart attack, just as Gambino would. The fictional character enjoyed nothing more in his old age than sitting in his garden, and that was the way Carlo also preferred to spend his final weeks.

Because of the movie, all things Mob were now showbiz in the public eye. It was estimated that 80 percent of the people who came out for Don Carlo's funeral were strangers, the public, out to see a mobby spectacle. All that was missing was the glorious soundtrack. Cue "The Godfather Waltz" by Nino Rota.

Self-proclaimed experts were convinced that Gambino's death meant an end to all restraint when it came to organized crime selling heroin in America.

A fed narc agent told a reporter, "When Gambino died, the last restraints on Mob involvement in dope trafficking were removed. Now they're all scrambling for position and trying to regain narcotics territory taken over by black and Hispanic groups."

"Dellacroce was one of the scariest individuals I've ever met in my life, and I've met them all. Dellacroce's eyes were like he didn't have any eyes. Did you ever see 'Children of the Damned'? His eyes were so blue that they weren't even there. It was like looking right through him."

—Joseph Coffey, former New York Mob investigator

"Of all the gangsters that I've met personally, and I've met dozens of them in all of my years, there were only two who when I look them straight in the eye, I decided I wouldn't want them personally mad at me. Aniello Dellacroce was one."

—Ralph Salerno, former New York Police Department detective

CHAPTER 23
Dellacroce

IF YOU'VE BEEN WONDERING WHY there has been so little about Aniello Dellacroce so far, that's because I saved him for his own chapter. He was the guy who didn't get to be a father, even though he deserved it. And he deserves his own chapter.

Dellacroce was born March 15, 1914, to Francesco and Antoinette Dellacroce in New York. He had one brother, Carmine, and was the uncle of the Quack Quack brothers, Angelo and Salvatore Ruggiero.

Before his Gambino days, in the 1930s, Dellacroce was a part of the Mangano crime family. He soon became a protégé of underboss Albert Anastasia. He learned to be ultraviolent from the master. (Dellacroce earned the lifelong nickname "Father O'Neil" after clipping a few goons while dressed as a priest.) Once Anastasia became boss, he appointed Dellacroce caporegime with his own crew. Later, Dellacroce bought and set up shop at the Ravenite Social Club, Mulberry Street, in Little Italy.

At the end of August 1956, Dellacroce was arrested in the Ravenite along with several others as part of an organized crime crackdown. He was charged with consorting with known criminals and possession of a blackjack, and held on $500 bail for trial in Special Sessions.

The club was a popular hangout, and Dellacroce headquarters. After Anastasia's murder in 1957 and Carlo Gambino became Boss,

Dellacroce's allegiance shifted smoothly. Dellacroce had been a strong Anastasia supporter. But he was also an old-school mobster who believed in loyalty to the family and its boss, who now was Carlo Gambino. If Dellacroce had not been so loyal, even to the man who whacked his mentor, Gambino's reign as Boss of Bosses would have been severely jeopardized.

In 1965, Gambino appointed Dellacroce to underboss. Dellacroce replaced sixty-seven-year-old Joe "Banty" Biondo in that position. Biondo had been a trusted underboss for years. But Gambino began to suspect Biondo was skimming where he shouldn't ought to skim. Sam the Plumber told Don Carlo he thought Biondo wasn't kicking up like he was supposed to, especially when it came to the Long Island waste management industry.

Gambino assigned spies to keep an eye on Joe Banty's "books," to watch the money, and they reported back that tribute money was remaining in Banty's stuffed pockets.

The spies also reported back to Don Carlo that Banty's personal life was a mess. He'd left his wife and was shacked up with an underage hooker. A lot of powerful gangsters have looked the other way when it came to who was fucking who, but Gambino was notoriously moral when it came to the sanctity of marriage.

Gambino felt that Banty's private life made the borgata look bad. In April 1965, Banty received a phone call and was informed that the Boss wanted to see him. Banty said he would be right there, but he stood Gambino up, a move that caused Gambino to have a temper tantrum, something those close to him had never seen before.

Gambino's morality went both ways. Another boss would have whacked his underboss for pissing him off that way, but Gambino thought Banty was too much of an old-time member of the brotherhood to be hit. Banty and Gambino had worked together for thirty-five years.

Some say Gambino didn't hit Banty out of kindness. Others thought Banty's life was spared because Gambino thought he still had earning potential. Maybe he'd be able to squeeze another couple of dollars out of the guy.

Gambino assigned seven of his officers to, all at once, go and have a chat with Banty. They were to "gauge Banty's attitude." They reported back that Banty was mostly old and tired. Gambino told his underboss that he was to retire immediately and Banty said OK.

In June, Gambino was recorded having a meal with Sam the Plumber, during which they discussed Banty.

"He's on the shelf," Gambino said. He added that he was thinking of making cousin Paul Castellano, his wife's brother, his new underboss. That news brought some grumbling from Gambino's other officers. They thought that Castellano was a pretty good butcher, but not up to being underboss. Don Carlo, they felt, was showing favoritism.

Gambino listened and withdrew the suggestion. Also in the running was Carmine Lombardozzi, but his Wall Street magic had worn off, and he was another guy who liked broads too much for Gambino's taste—and thus Neil Dellacroce became the new underboss. Dellacroce was the most dangerous and loyal of men.

As Gambino's power grew, so did Dellacroce's. Being underboss to the Boss of Bosses arguably gave him more juice than the bosses of other families. He wasn't just the underboss of the Gambino family, he was the underboss of everything.

Along the Jersey shore the Law was playing havoc with the Genovese guys who ran those docks. A lot of them were in jail: Ruggiero Boiardo, Angelo "Gyp" DeCarlo, Anthony "Little Pussy" Russo, and John "Johnny Coca-Cola" Lardiere. Still out and about were Pasquale "Patsy Ryan" Eboli (Tommy's brother), and Frank "Funzi" Tieri, but they weren't enough. Across the board, power slipped, and the Gambinos filled the void.

It wasn't just the Gambinos, either, moving in on the Genovese rackets. The Bonannos, although weakened by Bonanno's exile, were aggressive, as well, behind the efforts of Philip "Rusty" Rastelli.

I wrote a lot about Rastelli in my book, *The Cigar*, about Carmine Galante, Rastelli's archenemy, who also wanted control of the Castellammarese (Bonanno) faction. Rastelli had issues that had nothing to do with being a gangster. He and his wife had whatcha call a *tumultuous relationship*. They took turns shooting each other! Rusty, the widower, had better aim.

In charge of poking around the other families looking for weak spots to exploit was Dellacroce. Gambino treated Dellacroce like a son.

Dellacroce, on Gambino's behalf, was moving in on Sam the Plumber's operations in Connecticut. According to FBI memos at the time, "Gambino's family runs just about everything in New York and the surrounding areas." Dellacroce was highly mobile, if not inconspicuous. He did business, driving himself in organized crime's hottest car, a fire-engine-red Caddy ragtop, with whitewall tires and interior.

On September 26, 1966, as part of a combined state and federal investigation subcommittee, Dellacroce and twelve other Mob bigs responded to a subpoena and showed up to testify for a Queens County grand jury. Joseph Colombo was there. Carlos Marcello, who ran New Orleans, was there. Tommy Eboli, Frank Costello, both on hand.

The only no-show was Carlo Gambino, who called in sick. The hearing was delayed when someone called the courthouse and said, "There's a bomb planted on the fifth floor. Those thirteen fellows will not live to testify."

After a long search during which no bomb was found, Dellacroce was asked to come back on October 3. Which he did. His testimony consisted of name, rank, serial number, and the Fifth Amendment.

Dellacroce's name made the bold type in Charles McHarry's "On the Town" column in the *Daily News* on May 22, 1967. McHarry wrote that his sources told him Dellacroce was on the payroll of a Newark soft drink firm at $200 per week.

"Question is, as what?" McHarry asked.

The item didn't seem like much. But it was enough to launch an investigation into the Royal Crown Bottling Company of Newark, New Jersey.

For the next few years, it seemed like Dellacroce was always on some witness stand or another, taking the oath to tell the whole truth and then taking the Fifth. But sometimes it was the questions he was asked that mattered. Nobody expected him to answer, but the question alone might cause trouble in Dellacroce's paranoid world.

Dellacroce was called before the New York State Joint Legislative Committee. General counsel of the committee, Edward J. McLaughlin, asked, "Isn't it true that you recently advocated to other underworld figures that Carlo Gambino was too ill to run things anymore and he should be replaced by Joe N. Gallo?"

Dellacroce took the Fifth. To answer no would perhaps be to admit to consorting. That "underworld figures" expression was dynamite.

McLaughlin asked another question: "Isn't it true that Joe N. Gallo was to be merely a figurehead as Boss of the Gambino family, and that you yourself had your sights set on being Boss?"

Dellacroce took the Fifth.

Dellacroce missed the days when authorities always asked questions that seemed to come from left field and you could tell that they didn't know their asses from a hole in the ground. Now they had picked up on some of the lingo, knew some of the structure. They knew the military ranks, the Five Families, the Commission. It bugged the shit out of him.

One person interested in this interrogation was Carlo Gambino. He made it clear that he did not believe McLaughlin's allegations regarding Father O'Neil. On the other hand, when it came time to decide who he wanted to succeed him as godfather, Dellacroce or Paul Castellano, those two questions, unanswered, were not going to help Dellacroce's case.

Dellacroce was eventually convicted on five of the counts, and on September 8, 1971, he was sentenced. Despite a plea by Assistant

District Attorney Kenneth Conboy to have the defendant receive the maximum sentence, Justice Jacob Grumet gave Dellacroce only one year in jail (actually five sentences of one year each, to be served concurrently).

Appeals delayed matters for a while, and Dellacroce was a free man during that process, but at the beginning of June 1972, he began serving his term on Rikers Island. He only served four days before his lawyers appealed again and arranged to have him released during that process.

One of Dellacroce's capos was Carmine "Charley Wagons" Fatico, who ran his rackets out of the Bergin Hunt and Fish Club in Ozone Park, Queens. Fatico was a native of East New York. Although he could be tough when he had to be, he was known mostly as an earner. They called him Charley Wagons because in his youth he was an expert at hijacking trucks. His brother Daniel was also a Gambino soldier and often was in on Charley Wagons's operations.

Fatico was born in 1910 and had been arrested regularly since he was in his late teens. He beat people up, stole stuff, and took bets. Looking back, one of the most striking aspects of Fatico's operation on behalf of the family—then still being run by Albert Anastasia—was that there was this twelve-year-old kid hanging around, doing favors for tips, trying to learn the ropes. His name was John Gotti. He started hanging around when Fatico still had his HQ in East New York, and he made the move when Fatico moved his clubhouse to the Bergin Hunt and Fish Club.

Gotti first got his name in the papers when he was involved in a rock-throwing rumble against a black gang in Brownsville, Brooklyn, at the corner of Eastern Parkway and Broadway. The white kids were standing on the street and the black kids were on the roof of a three-story frame house on Stewart Street. Gotti, who lived at 2282 Dean Street, was held with four others, three white, one black, on $500 bail. Also arrested was Dellacroce's nephew Angelo "Quack Quack" Ruggiero, who would stay at Gotti's side through thick and thin. Gotti and Ruggiero had to appear before a judge in "adolescent court," charged with malicious mischief.

Quack Quack was with Gotti again, as was brother Gene Gotti, the next time John made the papers, arrested in an FBI roadblock for hijacking a truck full of furs, $94,000 worth, in December 1967. Gotti, at that time, was living at 311 Eighth Street in Park Slope, Brooklyn. That cost him more than four years of freedom. By 1972, Gotti, just thirty-one, had just finished doing a stretch in Lewisburg Federal Penitentiary for hijacking a truck packed with cargo from a Northwest Airlines flight and was running gambling ops for Fatico in East New York, a poor neighborhood that was actually in East Brooklyn.

The following year, when Fatico was busted and had to stay away from the Ozone Park club, he promoted the just-made Gotti to capo. Gotti would now report directly to Aniello Dellacroce. In that capacity, Gotti frequently commuted from Ozone Park to Mulberry Street where he would hand over the envelope and brief Dellacroce in person in the Ravenite Club.

Fatico managed to stay out of prison but underwent several long trials, and he never got back to the position of responsibility he'd had when he put Gotti in charge of his old crew. He lived to 1991 and died at eighty-one of natural causes.

Dellacroce didn't have to go very far to go to his club, the Ravenite. He lived on Mulberry, almost directly across the street. He lived in a building that appeared from the outside to be a run-down tenement, the sort of place where you might find tubs in the kitchens. But Dellacroce's apartment was luxurious, as if it were on Central Park West.

As for the club, the best way to describe it was "inconspicuous." It was so quiet and dark on the outside that people passed it daily without being aware that it was there.

Dellacroce was at the Ravenite on August 1, 1972, when a "small-time thug" and heroin dealer named Carlo Lombardi fired four pistol shots into the club. At first it was thought Dellacroce was the target. Turned out Lombardi's beef had nothing to do with Dellacroce. He was having trouble with Carmine Consalvo, whose brother was Dellacroce's driver and bodyguard.

Lombardi burst into the club and confronted Consalvo, as Dellacroce and others watched in disbelief. Lombardi managed to squeeze off four shots before he was grabbed and disarmed. After escaping, with a bleeding cut over the eye, Lombardi fled to Beekman Downtown Hospital. He was followed by men shouting, "You'll be dead in a week!"

At the hospital, Lombardi allowed himself to be cleaned up and bandaged but refused stitches.

After that, there was always a lookout on the sidewalk on Mulberry Street between Spring and Prince Streets. In 1972, if you wanted to drive past the Little Italy club at pedestrian speed, someone was watching, license numbers were jotted down, and, through multiple contacts at the Department of Motor Vehicles, identities were supplied. If you came into the club uninvited you'd be tossed out on your ear. If you came into the club and caused a fuss, the penalty was death.

Gambino was informed that Carlo Lombardi had shot up the Ravenite and "was acting like a new Crazy Joey." Don Carlo gave the thumbs-down.

Lombardi, clearly out of his fucking mind, headed upstate where he acquired a machine gun and practiced using it. On August 10, he returned to Little Italy and—with the sidewalk guard goofing off—again barged into the Ravenite, this time with his new little friend.

All of that practice didn't do him any good once he was again inside the Ravenite. The gun jammed and wouldn't fire. This time he managed to flee without being beaten up.

Lombardi probably should have moved to Timbuktu, but instead went only as far as the Catskill Mountains—Old Route 17 in the small village of Thompson, New York—where he stayed at a resort with a twenty-two-year-old woman known mostly for her tits. That setup lasted about a week. There was a knock on their motel door, and it was a couple of boys from the Ravenite.

Lombardi and his brunette girlfriend went for a ride to a dark and lonely country road. They were kicked out of the car and shot. Lombardi was hit twice in the head and died on the spot. The young woman was shot in the neck and, though bleeding heavily, she stayed still until the gunmen left, and survived the incident. The young woman was given twenty-four-hour police protection in the hospital.

In the vicinity of Lombardi and his girlfriend at the time of the abduction was Lombardi's lifelong friend, twenty-seven-year-old Joseph Fucillo, who was recognized during the hit and put on a list to be dealt with later.

Fucillo lived until October 17, 1972, when he was shot five times and killed while backing his 1968 Dodge down the driveway of his home on Seventy-Second Street in Bensonhurst, Brooklyn. Fucillo had pleaded guilty just the day before to possession of one ounce of heroin, involuntarily thrust into the "might sing" category.

Because the Lombardi kill took place during the bloodiest days of the Colombo-Gallo war—Lombardi's death was less than twenty-four hours before the fiasco at the Neapolitan Noodle—the 1973 attack on four innocent businessmen due to mistaken identity—authorities at first thought this might have been part of that. After investigating, police realized that Lombardi had nothing to do with either President Street or the Colombo family.

The Noodle incident—which was the President Street Boys fucking up—in which innocent men were shot and killed during a hit attempt on members of the Colombo family, caused a public fuss, which caused Police Commissioner Patrick Murphy to say he was going to "run the mobsters out of town."

Gambino hated the publicity that the Noodle killings caused. He hated collateral damage, he hated bad press, he hated anything that made politicians declare war on organized crime. Gambino said that the Gallo crew needed to be broken up. They needed to be separated and scattered. Gambino said that the others could take the guys they wanted, but he wanted John "Mooney" Cutrone to come work for him. Someone asked what would happen to Mooney if he didn't want to come and work for him. Don Carlo made a thumbs-down gesture and then changed the subject.

Lombardi, the "new Crazy Joey," died at age twenty-nine. He was a hothead and never expected to live long. He'd been questioned by police in connection with at least two murders and had seven arrests on his record dating back to 1961, crimes ranging from homicide to grand theft auto.

While Dellacroce was in city jail, his legal woes deepened. In 1972, he was indicted on federal tax evasion charges, conspiracy, and for filing a false income tax return for 1968.

It was all pure white-collar bullshit. The government claimed Dellacroce failed to pay $68,000 in income tax on 22,500 shares of stock in Yankee Plastics, and other investments.

Prosecuting Dellacroce on the tax charges was Special Assistant United States Attorney William Aronwald, who in 1971 joined the Justice Department's Joint Strike Force Against Organized Crime, in Manhattan. Defending Dellacroce was Herald Fahringer of Buffalo, New York.

Sitting at the defense table with Dellacroce was a pair of codefendants: Martin Goldman, fifty years old, former president of Hoffman Products in Newark, and fifty-four-year-old Michael Catalano.

The government claimed that Dellacroce in 1968 reported $10,400 in gross income while his actual income was $134,150. The key evidence in the case was surveillance tape made inside the Ravenite Club.

The bugs were placed secretly but following a court order, so the resulting recordings were allowed into evidence. Many witnesses were asked pointed questions, based on conversations on those tapes.

One tape contained a conversation between Dellacroce and Brooklyn gangster Tony Leone, a Bonanno soldier:

"I've had complaints about you," Dellacroce said. "You are only a soldier. It could be fatal if you disobey your boss. You are to keep what I say secret. The old man [Gambino] does not want any trouble."

A key prosecution witness was Frank Terranova, a guy who had been living under an assumed name and federal protection. Aronwald called for a conference with the jury out of the room. He then told the judge and the defense, "The prosecution has learned from an informant that Dellacroce had out a murder contract on Terranova. So, we're asking that certain questions not be asked. Certain questions might risk his life."

"Like what?" Fahringer asked.

"Don't ask him where he lives or his current occupation."

"I see no reason . . ."

Manhattan Federal Judge Arnold Bauman ruled that the witness would not have to answer any questions that might risk his life.

Dellacroce's defense pointed out that Terranova was facing charges of his own, regarding kickbacks while working as a federal purchasing agent, and was presumed to have improved his circumstances by testifying against Dellacroce.

With that all hashed out, the jury came back in and the direct examination of Terranova finally began. Terranova told the jury how he had given Dellacroce 22,500 shares of Yankee Plastics stock in exchange for an assurance that the company's employees would not strike. In other words, no raises.

The jury inferred that Dellacroce had threatened Terranova with labor unrest and settled for the Yankee Plastics stock, which was extortion. Terranova added that he had met with Dellacroce three times in the Ravenite to discuss how to make the deal so they wouldn't have to pay income tax.

Despite the restrictions on their questioning, defense attorneys worked over Terranova pretty good under cross-examination, trying to shake his credibility and make him appear opportunistic. Terranova admitted to lying under oath and to paying no federal income tax in 1969 and 1970.

On January 24, 1973, the jury of eight men and four women deliberated for three hours and twenty minutes before convicting Dellacroce and his codefendants on all charges. When the verdict was announced, Catalano's wife completely melted down in hysterics. None of the defendants registered emotion.

Aronwald used his conviction of Dellacroce as a main theme in his reelection campaign. Dellacroce's prison term kept him away for Gambino's death and factored in Paul Castellano's promotion to Boss.

Legal troubles piled on. Dellacroce became a target in a grand jury probe into Mob infiltration of legitimate businesses. He was again hauled before a grand jury where he refused to answer questions. So that he couldn't plead the Fifth, the feds granted him immunity. Now if he refused to answer a question, he was in contempt of court.

Aronwald again questioned Dellacroce, this time about Dellacroce's crime ventures in the Dominican Republic. Dellacroce said he had no idea what Aronwald was talking about.

Regarding how he made money, Dellacroce testified that he didn't. He said he had borrowed money to live on for the past few years. He'd also spent some of his savings. Asked who had lent him money, Dellacroce refused to answer.

"Isn't it true that you once said to one of your minions that you are 'merely a soldier' and have to obey orders?"

Dellacroce refused to answer.

"Isn't it true that you have kept company for twelve years with a woman who is not your wife?"

Dellacroce kept mum.

Before he was dismissed, Dellacroce had refused to answer twenty questions and was subsequently charged with twenty counts of contempt of court, charges that came with a possible penalty of $1,000 and one year in jail per charge.

During his trial, fifteen of the charges were dropped. These involved questions applying to Doris Campbell, his *goomada* of twelve years. Supreme Court Justice Jacob Grumet didn't think it right that a married man should go to jail for a year because he refused to answer a question about his girlfriend.

It went on and on. Dellacroce's name came up in court regarding a completely different matter, more white-collar bullshit. He was a named-but-not-charged coconspirator in a case about a $100,000 stock deal.

The indicted coconspirators were Joseph "Joe Paris" Guarnera of Glen Ridge, New Jersey, who operated a wig business and was Carlo Gambino's nephew; Frank "Frankie Butch" Guglielmini of Brooklyn, and James "Jimmy No Neck" Cavera of Staten Island. They bought stock, it tanked, they wanted their money back, and threatened physical harm if they didn't get it.

Cavera was quoted as saying, "We'll put you in a cast from your heels to your nose."

On March 12, 1973, Judge Arnold Bauman sentenced Dellacroce to five years in the fed pen for not paying his income tax. Dellacroce wore a black suit to the sentencing hearing, his face frozen into a perpetual scowl.

Afterward, William Aronwald gloated to the press, calling Dellacroce "a major crime figure" whose "lifestyle supported this theory." Dellacroce, the prosecutor added, "has lived the life of a professional hoodlum all his life."

On May 25, 1973, Dellacroce appeared in court, seeking bail. He was still serving his time for contempt and had not yet begun his five years for conspiracy and tax evasion.

Judge Arnold Bauman gave Dellacroce a scolding instead.

"You are a top-level hoodlum, a danger to society, a menace to the community, a parasite who lives off the lifeblood of honest people. And, by George, I'm not going to be the one to admit you to bail pending appeal."

The judge then addressed the public. "If Aniello Dellacroce can walk the streets of New York City on bail, then the language of the statute is less than meaningless. If ever it is meant to apply to anybody, it was meant to apply to the Aniello Dellacroces of this world."

On the morning of June 16, 1973, Dellacroce's son, twenty-two-year-old Armond Dellacroce, was strolling through Little Italy, only feet from his home on Mulberry Street, heading north toward Houston, when he heard a gunshot and felt a sting in his right leg. When police and an ambulance reported to the scene, Armond said he did not know who shot him and had no idea why anyone would want to shoot him. Law enforcement, on the other hand, had a theory that the shooting was connected in some way to the future leadership of the Gambino crime family.

"We believe the shot was meant as a warning to Aniello Dellacroce, who is in jail," one cop said.

With Gambino on the wane, there was a lot of talk. Who would—or could—fill Gambino's shoes as the Boss of Bosses? Bettors handicapped their programs. It seemed unlikely that he'd come out of the Bonanno family, which was the weakest of the five, although the Bonannos included Carmine "Lilo" Galante, who was as ruthless as they came.

Galante was the only hood who had admitted aloud that he wanted to become super-don. Galante came out of prison looking to make up for lost time. He had run a lucrative heroin-importing pipeline, and he wanted that power back.

While he was away, Italian mobsters, along with black and Hispanic gang members, had chipped away at the trade. Galante had a dozen Mob guys whacked, and up to forty black and Hispanic drug dealers—clearing the table for his reemergence at the top of the heap.

Then Galante had lunch on Knickerbocker Avenue in Bushwick, Brooklyn, and assassins blew him away, dead with his cigar still in his mouth. All that ambition failed to make Galante bulletproof.

As long as Gambino breathed, Father O'Neil was the favorite to take over the Gambinos, and possibly more. Then Don Carlo passed, Dellacroce was passed over, and the vicious killer took the slight with unexpected grace.

CHAPTER 24
Gemini Lounge

GAMBINO'S DEATH SIGNALED the end of an era. Nothing would ever be the same again. Without him, what were the chances of the center holding? Slim. There were bound to be fissures in the family.

Without him and his extreme but very real set of scruples, a sense of tradition, of civilization, there were segments of the big Gambino operation who made pigs of themselves. The deadliest operation run by the Gambino crime family was a massive auto-theft effort that was run by Roy DeMeo out of a Brooklyn bar called the Gemini Lounge, built on a corner lot on Flatlands Avenue, with a slaughterhouse back room where scores of victims were offed and dismembered.

It started when Gambino was still alive but spun out of control after he was gone.

During the heyday of the DeMeo crew, they carried out business differently from other professional killers. For them, murder was the first choice. They didn't just kill men who had somehow wronged them or failed to pay back a debt. They killed anyone who was viewed as "bad for business."

Other gangs sent out gunmen to hunt down the subject, fill him with lead, and run away. Chaos often reigned as murder scenes were filled with uncontrollable and unpredictable elements.

But DeMeo didn't do it that way. His boys scooped the guy up and dragged him into a tavern known as the Gemini Lounge.

The bar had previously been known as Phil's Lounge, but Phil got himself into debt with Roy and, instead of cash, Phil paid off by giving Roy the bar. Although Roy was the actual owner, on paper the bar belonged to an Irish guy named Charles Doherty.

The Gemini Lounge was a common name for nightclubs beginning in the mid-1960s, as Gemini was the name of the NASA manned space program, the missions between the Mercury and Apollo flights. The Gemini missions sent a pair of astronauts into orbit, sometimes more than one capsule at once, so they could practice the docking maneuvers that would be necessary to land a man on the moon. Doherty, however, was not influenced by the space program when naming the bar. He named the joint after his own astrological sign.

Doherty's brother John was an NYPD cop assigned to the understaffed Auto Crimes unit—a familial relationship that came in handy when deciding which streets to hit on any given night. In exchange for looking the other way, John the cop was said to have been bribed upward of $1,000 a week.

There was nothing hot-shit about the bar, which sat on an acutely angled corner. It was dimly lit, as all good joints should be. Alcohol and darkness are the keys to romance—that and Jimmy Roselli records. There was a TV on the wall at one end of the bar. And on the stool under it sat a bookie taking bets on horse races or other sporting events.

The bar sat at a complicated corner. Coming together directly in front of the building were Flatlands Avenue, Troy Avenue, and East Forty-First Street. Cars heading northeast on Flatlands might see no traffic coming on Troy Avenue. and think they had clear sailing, only to be crushed by a speeder coming down East Forty-First, with the bar causing the blind spot. Cars heading southwest on Flatlands might see no traffic on East Forty-First and be nailed by a car on Troy. The traffic flow at that unexpected hub was further complicated by Avenue L, which starts at East Forty-First and cuts across Troy a few paces farther east, forming a triangular park space out in front of the bar. The obtuse and acute angles are unlike the right angles one finds at Brooklyn's gridded intersections. In the Flatlands, streets are so old they had Dutch names, and meandered around hills that hadn't been there for three hundred years.

The bar was long enough for ten stools. Along one wall was a pinball machine, a jukebox, and a tiny stage in one corner where a rock band could play as long as it was smaller than a quartet and none of the musicians were overweight.

Above the bar was a framed front page from the *Daily News*, October 5, 1955, celebrating the Brooklyn Dodgers' World Series victory, their only world championship. The cover read, "WHO'S A BUM!" It featured a cartoon of a happy hobo drawn by Leo Edward O'Mealia.

When DeMeo business was not being done, the bar functioned as a public house. Anyone could come in for a drink. DeMeo hired a retired firefighter to run the place for him. This differentiated it from the clubhouses of most crews. Most of those places were private clubs, which meant you couldn't get in unless you belonged. At the Gemini Lounge you never knew who you were going to run into, but the clientele tended to be blue collar.

Other than the members of DeMeo's crew, wiseguys didn't go there. It didn't have a reputation as a Mob joint. In fact, if you asked around you'd've been told that it was a cops and firemen bar.

DeMeo was in there quite a bit, so if someone needed to meet him or make a payment, that would be the first place to call. If Roy wasn't around, the bartender would know where he could be reached. DeMeo kept the place dimly lit and had a favorite table in the back, on a two-step riser, so he couldn't be seen from the street but he could keep an eye on everything that went on in his joint.

Not everyone was completely oblivious to the bar's mobbiness. Casual visitors noticed that the members of Roy's crew acted differently from others who'd stopped in to have a drink. They spoke in code, sometimes only partially verbal, using only a handful of verbs and even fewer nouns. If they needed to have a conversation involving complete sentences they'd retreat through a door in the back and carry on in private.

Guys were in and out all the time at any hour, but Friday night was when the crew had their official business meeting, so if you wanted to catch them all together they were like clockwork.

For those who knew what went on there, the Gemini Lounge was known as the Horror Hotel. As one informant described DeMeo's victims, "They checked in, but they never checked out."

The back apartment was rented by Joseph Guglielmo, nickname Dracula. He earned the name by being the guy who happily cleaned up the blood from the guys who were iced in his apartment. Even those who didn't know all of what went on in Dracula's apartment had noticed that he sure painted his apartment frequently. Why the hell would a small apartment behind a bar need that many coats of paint? It was a mystery.

There was a phone in Guglielmo's apartment but it was merely an extension of the bar phone.

Although Guglielmo was considered by the younger members of the crew to be a doofus, a sad burnout case, he had tremendous value. He could cook a sauce and prepare an *al dente* pasta. Because the Gemini Lounge was a public room and not a social club, there were times when the boys didn't want to discuss business in front of thirsty strangers and so naturally the meeting took place in Guglielmo's apartment. And they ate. It was there, sitting at and standing around the kitchen table, that Roy would hand out everyone's cut.

It was in this apartment that guys were iced, disassembled, and packed up for disposal. The apartment was also used to nail broads by gang members who needed a convenient private space.

This dismembering business—the crew called it "disassembling"—was messy, certainly, but hardly chaotic. DeMeo had worked as a kid as a supermarket butcher, knew how to get the job done, and taught his boys well.

One trick was to shoot the hood near a tub, so the blood could be drained from the body before it coagulated. Bodies were sliced into six parts—two legs, two arms, a torso, and a head. The pieces were bagged and either went to the dump off the Belt Parkway, off the Canarsie Pier into Jamaica Bay, or into the ocean.

The most disturbing murders committed at the Gemini Lounge took place during the summer of 1977, known in Brooklyn as the Summer of Sam, because David Berkowitz (and perhaps others, calling themselves the Son of Sam), was shooting white kids parked on lovers' lanes and had everybody in a fucking uproar.

We'll pick up the story on Wednesday, July 20, 1977, at nine p.m. Nineteen-year-old Cherie Golden was in tears as she came home to her house on East Tenth Street in the Midwood section of Brooklyn. With her was her boyfriend, thirty-five-year-old Johnathan W. Quinn from Farmingdale, New York, on Long Island.

Cherie's grandmother took one look at Cherie's swollen eyes and asked, "What's wrong?"

"Johnny's going away," Cherie said. She had big brown eyes and had once won a Twiggy look-alike contest.

The grandmother nodded sympathetically, but she didn't really understand what Cherie was talking about. Maybe the boyfriend was moving. Maybe he was being transferred with his job. All she understood was her granddaughter was very sad. The guy was too old for Cherie, anyway. She'd be better off without him.

Johnny's reality was much worse than a simple transfer. John Quinn had been convicted of auto theft and was due to appear the next day for sentencing in Nassau County Court, in Mineola on Long Island.

While Quinn waited downstairs, Cherie ran up and took a shower. She changed into a pair of cutoffs and a white T-shirt with red and blue stripes on it.

"Ready?" Quinn asked.

"Ready!" Cherie said with perfect posture and a toothy smile, demonstrating that she'd stopped crying.

"We just got one stop to make, a quick stop at a bar on Flatlands Avenue," Quinn said.

"Okay," Cherie said. She kissed her grandmother goodbye and ran out the door. She and Quinn climbed into his silver Lincoln Continental and drove off into the Brooklyn night.

Cherie's grandmother may not have known what Johnny Quinn did for a living, but the NYPD did. They understood Quinn was a member of one of the more profitable auto-theft rings in Brooklyn. If things went the way the crew feared, Quinn was going to lead the cops directly to them.

In addition to the auto-theft stuff, which was impressive enough, the Nassau County District Attorney's Office had linked Quinn to a stock-theft ring reportedly headed by seventy-four-year-old mobster Arthur "Artie Todd" Tortarello and responsible for $25 million worth of security thefts.

Quinn had a record that showed he'd been in on many Nassau County rackets over the years. The DA sure would love to flip a guy like that.

Now things were coming down fast for Quinn, and his teenage girlfriend was feeling blue. It was their last night together maybe, at least for a long time.

Johnny might have told Cherie some sketchy details regarding what he did for a living, and she may have helped him, or ridden along, on simple tasks and errands, but we know for certain that he had not been completely honest with her. For one thing, he'd failed to mention his wife and six kids in Farmingdale.

What their plans were, we'll never know. The couple did have an apartment they used in Manhattan. Johnny told Cherie it was their love nest. He told everyone else it was his fuck pad. Whatever it was called, they didn't make it there that night. Their first and only stop was the Gemini Lounge.

"How come we got to go there, Johnny?"

"I got to drop off a package. Plus, there's a surprise."

"What kind of surprise?"

"For you."

Her eyes lit up.

The "surprise" was that someone told Johnny that they had a

Porsche for sale, perfect for his little girlfriend to drive around in while he was in jail, a reminder to everyone that she knew a guy.

After he dropped off his package, which contained phony blank documents and some VIN-making tools, he and Cherie were going to take a look at the car. Hard to say now if there ever was a Porche. Probably not.

Quinn pulled up to the bar and told Cherie to stay in the car while he took care of business.

"Hurry up, I'm ready for my surprise," she said.

Quinn was only in the joint for a matter of seconds before he was shot in the back of the head with a .32 handgun.

Only then did one of DeMeo's boys look out the window. There was Cherie Golden in Quinn's car, sitting demurely in the passenger seat. The decision was quick and heartless. Time for her to go. DeMeo ordered two of his killer crew to take care of it, so they went out front with big smiles on their faces.

She was a young girl who should have had her whole life in front of her, but at that moment all those boys saw was a girl who knew too much and had come to the end of her rope. Such a waste.

"Johnny said you were out here, beautiful, but too shy to come in," one of them said. He was in motion. Her eyes followed him as he walked around the front of the car.

"Hey," Cherie said brightly. "I heard there was going to be a surprise for me."

"There sure is," the killer said. He circled around to the driver's side of the car and held Cherie's attention as the other hit man came up on the passenger side and shot her three times in the head—twice in the back of the head and once, when her upper body whipped around, in the face.

The men put their heads on swivels to see if there had been any witnesses. One of the beauties of the Gemini Lounge was that out front there were no near neighbors. A guy would need binoculars to ID a face. Experience taught that most people were smart enough not to look anyway.

The first killer said, "Go ask Roy if he wants her disassembled."

"Right." In a minute the other returned. "Roy says dump her whole. He wants to send a message."

Less than two hours after the couple was last seen by Cherie Golden's grandmother, at 11:30 p.m. on July 20, John Quinn's lifeless body was discovered dumped in the street on Seaview Avenue and Father Capodanno Boulevard near a remote corner of Ocean Breeze Park on Staten Island.

On Friday, July 22, Cherie's mom called Detective Joseph Tepedino at Brooklyn's Lawrence Avenue station to report her daughter missing. She told the detective that Cherie was with an older man she'd been seeing.

"I'm afraid they've run off together or something," the mom said.

"What's his name?"

"John Quinn."

The mom was informed that her daughter had been seeing a hood, a married man—and a dead one at that. The chances of getting Cherie back were slim.

On Sunday, July 24, a lady from the Gerritsen Beach section of Brooklyn called the NYPD and reported an abandoned car on her street. Gerritsen Beach is a tight cluster of beach houses separated only by the narrowest streets in the five boroughs, a place where any extraneous car would be an irritant. The car in question was a silver 1976 Lincoln Continental Mark IV, parked on Lois Avenue between Noel Avenue and Frank Court.

Police approaching the vehicle knew what they had. Flip a coin to see who pops the trunk. Everyone else stepped back and covered their noses and mouths. But the trunk held no body.

"Wait a second, it's in the front, jammed underneath the dashboard," a cop observed.

They taped off the tiny street. Folks on Lois Avenue could stand on their upstairs decks and look down on the gruesome action.

The medical examiner arrived and pulled loose clothing off the body, tossed there casually to make it less obvious to outside observers.

It was the body of a young female. The medical examiner double-checked that the car had only been abandoned for a couple of days. He was surprised by the level of decomposition. It looked like dental was going to be the only way to get a positive ID. The body had melted in the car oven, baked by the July sun. It was doubled up and stuffed in place, creating a haunting misshapenness.

One of the loose pieces of clothing found atop the body was a white T-shirt with blue and red stripes on it. The body was still wearing a pair of cutoffs, but was naked from the waist up. It was barefoot, toenails painted pink, but a pair of flip-flops were found in the car.

Beneath the body, Detective Joseph Polizzi found bloodstained blank documents for transferring ownership of a car.

Several spent cartridge cases were found on the dashboard, directly above the body. The body was taken to the Kings County morgue. Dental records were used to positively ID the remains as those of Cherie Golden.

Cherie's parents offered a $10,000 reward for information leading to the arrest and conviction of their daughter's killer. A phone number was listed for witnesses to call—but no one ever did.

DeMeo lived out on Long Island. Every day he made the commute into Brooklyn. On his way to and from he would stop at Broadway Freddy's Diagnostic Center, which was run by Roy's childhood friend Freddy DiNome.

Freddy's second home was the drag strip. His racing name was Broadway Freddy. He was good enough to get his picture in the papers a few times. One year his racing income was in the six figures, racing in Englishtown, New Jersey, Lebanon Valley, and other strips in his dragster, which he called "Saturday Night Fever."

He had remained a drag-race driver even after he started working for Roy. Once, the crew went to the racetrack to watch, and Freddy was in a bad accident. His car burst into flames but Freddy got out of the car, on fire. As track personnel hit him with the fire extinguishers, Freddy calmly waved to the crowd to assure them he was OK. It wasn't until Freddy had a particularly bad accident, an almost fatal crash, that he gave up racing and became a full-time hood. One thing was for sure, the money was better. Best guess is that Freddy, by all accounts illiterate, was making $20,000 a week by stealing cars and committing insurance fraud—that is, falsely reporting stolen cars and starting fires.

Freddy DiNome was five-nine with a crooked nose and looked like he'd been sent by central casting. He grew up near Ebbets Field in the Brooklyn neighborhood known now as Wingate, but then as Pigtown because until the second half of the twentieth century, that was where the pig farms were. He couldn't read but was a genius around cars.

He worked on his racers at his Brooklyn auto shop. He was never happier than when he was under a car, and this came in handy when your enterprise was stealing cars. Freddy could render them untraceable and sell them overseas.

Roy DeMeo quit his last legit job, working at a dairy, when he was twenty-two. After that, he and Freddy stole cars and worked their way up and down Avenue P as breaking-and-entering men.

It is difficult finding eyewitness accounts of activity in and behind the Gemini Lounge. Most witnesses are dead, the others tight-lipped. But we do have this from Freddy DiNome:

Freddy said he was pitching quarters outside Dracula's apartment when a car pulled up. In it was a frightened passenger named Frank Amato, who was the cheating husband of Big Paul Castellano's daughter.

Two men escorted Amato into the building. Inside was at least one young man who was there specifically to make his bones. Afterward, DiNome heard that the guy chickened out, didn't have the guts to pull the trigger, so DeMeo took care of it himself, with a machine gun. There was a pause and then the door opened and DeMeo himself invited DiNome inside, where he saw the dead Amato in the shower.

They cut him up and handed the parts out to DiNome, who wrapped them up in garbage bags and small boxes that were loaded into a van. DiNome drove the van to a boatyard at Sheepshead Bay where he met his brother Richie. They moved the boxes and bags onto the boat, went sixty-five miles out to sea, and dumped the various parts of Frank Amato into the ocean.

Patrick Presinzano was thirty-three years old and a thief. His fatal mistake came when he stole jewelry from a woman who was the wife of a man who knew Roy DeMeo. The guy went to Roy, like he was Vito Corleone or Carlo Gambino, and asked for him to settle his beef for him. Roy considered the guy a friend and so it was done.

It goes to show the madness on the streets at the time. Partially, it was just the vicious times, but the movie *The Godfather*, such a great movie, gave these guys a new sense of entitlement, the feeling that they could do whatever the fuck they wanted and it all remained somehow glamorous and romantic.

This kill was problematic for the crew. One of the drawbacks to acting like the Godfather is that there were real dons out there who don't like it. You don't act like a boss until you're a boss. That was the feeling. This wasn't the first time Roy had been too big for his britches.

Presinzano's body was found lying in the street at Boynton Place and Avenue X in Sheepshead Bay, Brooklyn, on March 23, 1978. The location was at the ass-end of Brooklyn, remote to all through traffic, back by the MTA yards where they parked the out-of-service subway trains.

It looked like he'd been thrown out of a moving car. His throat was slit. He'd been shot four times. His pants and underwear were pulled down to his ankles.

It's unlikely that when hitting this guy, Roy and his crew realized that the jewel thief was the son of a Bonanno family capodecina named Angelo "Moe" Presinzano. Maybe the crew thought that bumping off Presinzano would get lost in the shuffle. Who could keep track of all the whacking that was going on?

When the meat wagon picked up Presinzano's stiff, it was the fifth gangster they'd found in the previous two days, and one of them got more than its share of attention. That was Salvatore Briguglio, a Teamsters official suspected of involvement in Jimmy Hoffa's disappearance, and who was recently indicted for the murder of Anthony Castellitto. He'd been shot to death by two men on a street in Little Italy.

Also that day, police found the badly decomposed body parts of Genovese capo Pasquale "Paddy Mac" Macchiarole. The parts were in several plastic bags and wrapped in canvas, stuffed into the trunk of his 1977 Lincoln Continental. The car was in a supermarket parking lot at Skidmore Avenue and Rockaway Boulevard near the Canarsie Pier. (This case bears many of the earmarks of the Gemini Method.) Macchiarole, who once had extortion charges against him dropped when the guy he'd been extorting was shot to death, had been missing for three weeks from his Elmhurst, Queens, home. Then serial thief Americus Scotese was shotgunned in Midwood while walking his dog. In Manhattan, Anthony Cuomo was gunned down in an East Side café.

And so on and so on. Presinzano's murder didn't get much attention.

Among the DeMeo crew that hung out at the Gemini Lounge was Mickey Hammer, an enforcer who, when reminding customers that they were late on their loan payments, would use a hammer to shatter the guy's knuckles.

Another of the boys was Henry Borelli, who was an accountant and expert at keeping two sets of books, one to keep the government happy. His job was not an easy one as cash transactions were frequent, and frequently private.

Another was Chris Rosenberg. He was Roy's right-hand man, the second in charge. Chris was manager of Roy's auto-theft op, twenty-three years old in 1974, and drove a conspicuous automobile. You always knew ahead of time if Chris was at the Gemini Lounge, because you'd see his white Corvette parked out on the street, usually on the Troy Avenue side.

Roy and Chris Rosenberg met in 1966 at a gas station when Chris was sixteen years old. He was a little guy who desperately wanted to be a big guy, a Jewish kid who dreamed of being Italian. So, he wore platform shoes and tried to act just like Roy, going as far as referring to himself as Chris DeMeo. (Chris was not his real first name either, which was Harvey, but he wanted to eliminate any notion that he was Jewish.)

When Roy met Chris he was dealing nickel bags of weed, so Roy lent him the money to deal in larger quantities. After a while, he added coke and ludes to his menu. He used his drug money to purchase his own chop shop, which he called Car Phobia Repairs. The name must have been a very inside joke, as it mystified everyone.

In and out of the Gemini on a regular basis was Dominick Montiglio, Nino Gaggi's nephew, a guy in his early thirties who came back from Vietnam with his nerves shot. He had a lot of psychological pain that he had tried to self-medicate with physical painkillers, and the result was heroin addiction.

He regularly pestered his Uncle Nino to secure him a full-time job with the crew, but no such position was ever offered because he was a junkie. That didn't keep him from hanging around with his drug-addled eyes and ears open.

Montiglio started out as a promising guy. He had talent. As a teen he'd been a singer with a deep, soulful voice that allowed him to cover songs originally recorded by black groups. Montiglio's group, The Four Directions, played dances and weddings.

They worked their way up to nightclubs and warmed up for Little Anthony and the Imperials and The Shirelles. They sang backup on the Mitch Ryder and the Detroit Wheels hit "Sock It To Me (Baby)." They appeared on a couple of TV shows, but that was their peak.

Further success would have needed a Mob push that Gaggi wasn't willing to give, so at age seventeen, Montiglio's showbiz career was through. He enlisted, went to Vietnam, and in true Forrest Gump fashion earned a Silver Star by taking out an enemy sniper and carrying a wounded Green Beret to safety. The war left him shattered, with nightly nightmares in which he tried in vain to hold on to human entrails, slimy guts that kept slipping through his fingers.

The Quinn-Golden murders had been Roy's idea and caused a major fuss, both with the public and with Big Paul Castellano. If it had been just Quinn it would've been no big deal. A hood getting whacked might make the papers, especially if a photojournalist could snap a shot of the corpse, but no one gave a rat's ass.

But the girl's murder, that was a different matter. People cared—and the fact that it was first thought of as Son of Sam shit, then as Mob shit was embarrassing to a lot of important people, guys on both sides of the street.

Not that Big Paul grieved with Cherie's parents, but he knew bad press when he saw it. Violence against women was frowned upon, especially that summer with a psycho killer on the loose.

The murders earned the crew more publicity than they wanted, for sure, but it came with fringe benefits. Tough guys looked at it differently from other people. If they could off that pretty little girl, they could off anyone—and DeMeo began to take on contracts for a price. You got someone you need hit? Roy could make him—or her—disappear. No muss, no fuss. The crew became professional hit men. It didn't pay as well as stealing cars, but it was fun.

In October 1979, Big Paulie ordered a hit on Khaled Daoud and Ronald Falcaro, two guys who might have been ratting to the cops about their car racket. DeMeo took the gig and brought two of his best killers with him to carry out the contract.

The victims were kidnapped, taken to a darkened auto repair shop in Canarsie, and shot. Daoud was a stationary target but Falcaro made a run for it—which bought him two extra seconds of life.

The men then stripped down to their underwear, pulled out

knives, and began to disassemble the bodies. It was hard work, and it gave the men a healthy appetite, so while the pieces of the two men were being bagged for dumping, DeMeo called out for pizza.

After eating, the men threw the bags of body parts into a garbage truck, which took them to the Fountain Avenue dump, not far from the housing development then known as Starrett City.

The DeMeo crew stole cars, of course. But stealing the cars only got the process started. Those autos were then altered so that they could never be traced to their previous owner. In essence, by providing the auto with a brand-new set of identifying markers, the crew transformed it into a new car, one that traveled abroad for sale without the slightest visible taint.

In order to change the cars in a way that would fool everyone, the DeMeo crew acquired the assistance of an employee of General Motors. This guy smuggled out of his car-making plant blanks and stamps used to create each car's identification tags.

Once the tags were stamped and placed on the car in Canarsie, the car appeared legitimate and new in every way and would be loaded onto a cargo ship without raising a single red flag.

And it was a good thing because a red flag might've led to a search of the automobile in question, a level of scrutiny that the DeMeo crew presumed would not be there. So confident were the thieves that their product would pass as legitimate and make it to the Middle East unsearched, they put contraband like American cigarettes and pornography in each trunk.

Those who hung with Roy were often impressed by the compartmentalization of his brain. He was a guy who could be a loving husband and dad one minute and kill without hesitation the next.

Some thought he had a strong sense of business and simply saw the business world as a brutal one and the domestic world as a loving one. But a look at his background indicates a predilection to chilly behavior. His mother was a cold and bitter woman, so there certainly seemed a chance that some of Roy's cold heart was inherited.

It seems likely that psychopaths are born and not made, but those who become killers have things in common, and one of the key indicators is a smothering yet unloving mother, who looks outwardly to be doing her motherly duties but who feels nothing for her children, only the burden of responsibility. The child is often an unwary and unwanted recipient of the bitterness she feels toward the father.

All right. Enough shrink talk. Roy was all in when it came to the cars, but it was the violence that got his blood flowing. That was something they all had in common. They all got a boner off it, all the brutality, the attack on human sensibilities. Wasn't that the ultimate toughness, after all, to be knee-deep in human gore and call out for pizza?

The victims came now sometimes in pairs, sometimes without names. There was the guy who came into the bar on a Saturday night to hear the band that was playing. Enjoying himself, he had a few too many, became loose of lip, and called Roy a motherfucker to the pretty bartender who promptly ratted the guy out. Roy took him out to Roy's car, shot the guy in the head, drove away, and came back without him. Nobody knew who that guy was, just that he'd been there and then he was gone.

There were a couple of victims, guys lured to the bar and dispatched in the usual fashion, and nobody remembered their names, either. Roy was doing a favor for some guys in the city. Who were they? Nobody remembered. No one was keeping a list. If they ever knew the names, they forgot.

There were few hoods in the Gambinos more aggressive and violent than John and Gene Gotti, but even they knew better than to attack the DeMeo crew. The Gottis were a little bit afraid of them.

The Gemini crew was "an army of killers." The Gemini Lounge had basement entrances on both the Flatlands and Troy sides, and down there Roy kept not only guns and ammo but hand grenades and other explosive devices. He was ready to go to war, should war come.

Gary Gardine has to be a nominee for the stupidest fuck on the whole fucking street. By the end of 1978, everyone who came out from under the rock knew you didn't fuck with anyone in connection with Roy DeMeo, who was hitting guys who looked at him funny.

So, what does Gardine do?

He took three pounds of pot from Chris Rosenberg and never paid for it. What did he think was going to happen? What happened was they found his body on November 30, 1978, somewhere in Brooklyn in the trunk of a burning car.

In January 1979, Peter Waring and thirty-four-year-old Paul "Paulie Pinto" Dordal were busted on cocaine and weapons charges. The crew was good at reading tea leaves by this time. It was Waring's second arrest, yet he was freed by police almost immediately, way too quick. Something was up. On February 7, suspecting that Waring had informed the police, Dordal was invited to the Gemini Lounge, where he was subjected to the Gemini Method.

On October 1, 1979, Roy sent Nino Gaggi and fifty-eight-year-old Peter Piacenti to pick up sixty-four-year-old James "Jimmy the Clam" Eppolito, an old-time cigar-chomping hood, and his thirty-four-year-old son James, Jr., and bring them to the Gemini Lounge for a "sit-down."

The younger Eppolito had infuriated Big Paul when he allowed himself to be photographed with former First Lady Rosalynn Carter. That normally would not be a capital crime, but Mrs. Carter had been duped into supporting a bogus UN charity—the International Children's Appeal—that the Mob was using to launder money, so a photo of the lady and a hood exposed the business.

The elder Eppolito had also pissed off the crew by telling Big Paul that Nino and Roy were moving drugs in big quantities. Senior squealed to the boss because Junior had been ripped off on a coke deal. Big Paul sided with Nino and Roy, and the Eppolitos were dead meat.

The idea was to bring the pair to the clubhouse for the usual treatment, but they never got there. Eppolito, Sr., got wise to the deal and tried to make a run for it. Nino shot them right there on the road, one inside the car and one outside. No regard was given to passersby who looked on in horror. Most of those witnesses turned their heads and kept their lips zipped.

One did not.

The Eppolitos' bodies were found shot in a car just off Brooklyn's Shore Parkway at Brighton Sixth Street. Both men had been shot multiple times in the head.

The witness who couldn't let it go was twenty-year-old Patrick Penny, who had just happened to be passing by. Penny was a career burglar with scruples who lived on Twentieth Avenue in Bensonhurst.

Penny was a baby-faced towhead who would've blended in on the surfers' beach more than with the hoods of Bensonhurst. Penny was with two women who begged him to forget what he'd seen, but he was determined to do the right thing.

Penny happened upon an off-duty housing cop named Sergeant Paul Roder, who lived in the Flatlands section of Brooklyn not that far from the Gemini Lounge. The housing cop didn't go to the police station but rather pursued the shooting suspects, who had fled on foot.

The cop and witness caught up with the shooters a short distance away at Coney Island Avenue and Neptune Avenue. The moonlighting cabbie was packing, identified himself as a police officer, and ordered the running men to stop.

Gunshots were exchanged. Gaggi was shot in the hip, and Piacenti in the neck. They were captured and charged while still in serious condition at Coney Island Hospital with the killings of the Eppolitos as well as the attempted murder of Sgt. Roder. They were indicted five days later.

This looked like the end for Gaggi, who had skated out of trouble a few years earlier because he'd invested in a suburban theater. Now he was in real trouble. Gaggi's troubles destabilized Roy DeMeo and his hold on an increasingly ambitious crew. Gaggi had been stealing cars before some members of the crew were born, and his wisdom was going to be missed.

Roy called an emergency meeting of the crew in Dracula's apartment, at which they discussed what, if anything, could be done to help Nino Gaggi. There was a witness—he could be eliminated, it was agreed.

The subject then turned to ways to take care of Gaggi's family, because that was what you did when a brother was in trouble. It was agreed that envelopes of money would be delivered to Nino's wife, but the deliveryman had to be surreptitious, maybe cut through a few backyards, to avoid surveillance by the law.

The cops questioned Penny, whom they knew because he'd once done time for burglary. Now, facing police questioning once again, Penny was starting to think it was smarter if he didn't see what he said he'd seen. In fact, he was starting to think he hadn't seen anything at all.

The police said, nonsense, it happened right in front of you, and you described it perfectly. Cops understood it wasn't Penny's eyesight that was failing, it was his nerve.

At first the police tried to keep Penny safe by stashing him in a motel, but he didn't like it and kept running away. Cops found him, and this time they arrested Penny, charged him as a material witness, and threw him in jail to await the trial. Penny was desperate to get away. Once, when he was let out of his cell and taken to the district attorney's office for a meeting, he tried to escape out the window.

A DA's investigator remembered feeling sympathetic: "I saw him sitting here in the office one day, and I remember thinking I wouldn't want to be in that kid's shoes."

Then, members of the Gemini crew went to see Robert Penny, the witness's brother. They said they would pay Patrick $50,000 if he developed a sudden case of amnesia—and that sealed the deal. Penny saw nothing.

Eventually, of course, all of the indiscriminate whacking made Castellano mad. This wasn't the way the Gambino crew should act. It was DeMeo's turn to be taken out. On January 10, 1983, forty-three-year-old Roy DeMeo was called to a meeting at a home-turf bodyshop. Nino Gaggi and other members of DeMeo's crew were there.

In situations like this, when Paul Castellano was trying to figure out who was loyal and who wasn't, he would have someone very close to the target do the hit, to prove that he didn't need to be whacked, as well. Castellano told Nino Gaggi that he had to do it.

As DeMeo sat down for coffee, Nino stepped up and shot him—but his nerves got to him: he twitched and shot Roy in the chest, merely wounding him. The others calmly pulled their own weapons and finished the job.

As it so happened, Roy was clipped on his daughter's twenty-second birthday. DeMeo had never missed one of his kids' birthdays, ever, so on the night of January 10, when Dad didn't come home, his family knew immediately that something was wrong.

His son called one of his dad's friends. "He doesn't miss cake," he said.

It turned out DeMeo had already missed one appointment that day. He was expected for a meeting with his uncle, a law school professor who was to advise him regarding an impending grand jury investigation into the DeMeo crew. In reality, evidence revealed, Roy had instead gone to a Catholic church and confessed his sins to a priest, preparing his soul for the ever after. He knew about the concern that he was going to cut a deal with prosecutors and throw the Gambinos under the bus.

DeMeo's 1983 maroon Cadillac Coupe DeVille was found eight days later in the parking lot of the Varuna Boat Club on Emmons Avenue in the Sheepshead Bay section of Brooklyn.

The car was towed to the local stationhouse and searched by detectives with the Organized Crime Control Bureau. In the trunk, underneath a crystal chandelier, was DeMeo's frozen body, hands and feet bound. His head was wrapped up in his leather jacket. He had been shot in the head and behind both ears. Just like Anastasia, there was a bullet wound in his hand, a through-and-through stigmata caused when he put his hand up in front of his face in a vain attempt to shield himself. At the time of his death, DeMeo's reputation might've been as a madman who killed a lot of people, but his only arrest had been a DWI.

Investigators agreed that they would've found the body sooner because of the smell, except the weather stayed below freezing, so very little decomposition had taken place.

Police were blunt with the widow when they paid the call to notify. "Roy's dead," they said. "We found him in the trunk of his car. We found his car abandoned on a Brooklyn street. We received a complaint. A store owner complained the car had been parked there for days. We towed the car in and then popped open the trunk. Your husband was inside."

"Where is he now?" the pale widow inquired.

"Still in the trunk. We're waiting for him to thaw before we take him out."

The widow shuddered. Her knees buckled.

"Are you sure it's him?"

"Yeah, our guys recognized him. We still need a positive ID."

"I can't."

"Doesn't have to be you. Just a family member. Here's the address of the morgue."

The morgue was on Clarkson Avenue in East Flatbush, between Brooklyn and Kingston Avenues. Roy's son Al went there on a frozen January morning to identify the body. The most disturbing thing about Roy's remains was that rigor mortis had developed while the body was bent into a ball to fit inside the trunk of the car, and the body had stayed that way for ten days. The medical examiner had thought that the frozen body they recovered would return to a more natural posture when it thawed, but that didn't happen. The body still looked as if it had been through a compactor, and Al DeMeo would always remember his father's limbs being horribly bent.

There were other disturbing aspects to the body, as well. The skin was a deep purple hue, there was that hole in his hand, and one shot had blown out an eye.

The son positively identified the body, and even as he was still gazing in shock at this monstrosity that had once been his father, police peppered him with questions, clearly believing that Al knew who'd done it. But Al had nothing to say.

Funeral arrangements were made at a church in Massapequa in which the beautiful stained-glass windows had been donated by Carlo Gambino. It was decided that Roy's remains would stay hidden inside a closed coffin.

The funeral director later revealed that the FBI had wanted to bug the parlor for Roy's visiting hours, to place electronic surveillance devices everywhere including on the coffin itself, but that he'd turned them down flat. They threatened to hurt his business—extortion is legal when the feds do it—but the undertaker stuck to his guns.

At the church, the parking lot and the street in front were peppered with feds in cars sticking telephoto lenses out the window. Whether they didn't want their picture taken, or had just turned their backs on Roy, whatever the reason, none of the gang from the Gemini Lounge showed up at his funeral.

From the church, the body was taken by solemn procession to St. John Cemetery in Middle Village, Queens. After another brief ceremony with mourners and a priest in the cemetery chapel, Roy was put in the ground and covered up.

Dracula and son Al picked up Roy's Coupe DeVille from the police impound lot. They found the vehicle under a layer of fingerprint dust. That would be easy to clean. More difficult to clean would be the trunk, which reeked from the pool of coagulated blood that remained in it. Also in there were the discarded latex gloves that the CSI people had worn while going over the car.

That turned out to be Dracula's last act in support of his buddy Roy, the guy who'd made life livable after his long stretch in stir had left him addled and unable to survive on his own in the real world. The instant Roy's car was out of the impound lot, police acquired a search warrant for Dracula's apartment.

The next day, Al packed Dracula up, gave him some cash, and put him on a plane out of New York City—although Al later wrote that he didn't know Guglielmo's destination.

Nobody ever saw Dracula again. When the feds finally made their indictments, Dracula Guglielmo's name was there, but he was listed as "missing." The Law thought he was dead. But, if Al DeMeo is telling the truth, there's a chance Guglielmo lived out the remainder of his life somewhere, maybe in a bare-lightbulb room over a dive strip joint. I'd like to think there was a happy ending.

Guys who made up crews back then weren't all geniuses. Some were barely getting by. They did things only when they were ordered to do so. Otherwise, they just sat around watching cartoons on TV and counting flowers on the wallpaper. So, without Roy to give orders, some guys floundered.

Police arrested one member of DeMeo's crew because they thought they could break him. They put him on ice and let him cool, trying to get him to turn. They raided his house and, most disturbingly, found a poster-sized photo of the guy naked with his dick out. He wasn't completely flaccid either, maybe half-staff.

While DeMeo's son Al was still a teenager, they came after him. They thought he knew shit, and apparently he did because years later he wrote a fucking book. The seventeen-year-old was driving down a highway at night when four cars in formation forced him off the road. Al broke his windshield with his head and rolled out of his car with his gun in hand. Men in masks attacked him and beat the shit out of him anyway. They pistol-whipped his face and fractured his eye socket. He underwent eight hours of surgery, but his eyesight was spared.

“This Life of ours, this is a wonderful life. If you can get through life like this and get away with it, hey, that’s great. But it’s very, very unpredictable. There are so many ways you can screw it up.”

—Paul Castellano

CHAPTER 25
Icing Big Paulie

THE ORIGINAL INTENT, when naming Castellano as BOSS, was for Dellacroce to maintain control of all the blue-collar rackets: auto theft, murder, robbery, hijacking, extortion. His gift was his ability to terrify.

Dellacroce didn't complain about being passed by. He faithfully pledged his loyalty to Big Paulie. Because Dellacroce was a team player, the system worked. Then came Father O'Neil's legal and medical problems.

In early 1985, Dellacroce was indicted along with other leaders of the New York families as part of the Mafia Commission Investigation, maximum RICO bullshit.

Dellacroce was indicted separately on federal racketeering charges stemming from his New York and Long Island crews over the previous eighteen years.

Then Dellacroce got sick and was unable to attend either of his trials. On December 2, 1985, Aniello Dellacroce died of brain cancer, at the age of seventy-one. Like Don Carlo and Lucky Luciano and Carmine Galante and Roy DeMeo, Father O'Neil was interred at St. John Cemetery.

Adding insult to injury, Castellano neither visited Dellacroce when he was sick nor attended his funeral. His absence at the funeral caused a bad buzz, as many mafioso dignitaries were there, and there was much discussion of Castellano's absence and what it could possibly mean.

According to an FBI memo, Big Paulie didn't go to Dellacroce's funeral out of fear.

"There are too many rats in this family," he said, according to fed surveillance. He thought he'd be shot if he went. Turned out, it made no difference. He was going to be shot anyway.

When Castellano failed to go to Aniello Dellacroce's funeral, he'd signed his own death warrant. In fact, he only had days to live.

Exactly two weeks after Father O'Neil bought the farm, Big Paulie breathed his last, as well. Looking back on it, it's amazing Castellano lasted as long as he did. Once Don Carlo was gone, Big Paulie had lost his best friend.

Young John Gotti, a man with little or no sense of history, was saying things like, "This guy ain't Cosa Nostra."

In addition to big-time problems within his own crime family, Castellano had other worries. The Gemini Lounge in East Flatbush was busted, and RICO laws meant Castellano could go away for what Roy DeMeo and his crew had been doing, which as we know was stealing shitloads of cars, running a slaughterhouse for human beings, and splashing around in the blood on Dracula's apartment floor.

The Gambino family thrived without Don Carlo for a decade by separating brain and brawn. But that all came to an end when Dellacroce died. That left Castellano alone at the top of the Gambino heap, a position he lacked the persona to maintain. Castellano had to leave that big house on Todt Hill sometime.

Castellano started going out a bit more. He had to come out anyway because he was on trial in Manhattan Federal Court. But he came out to conduct business sometimes, too.

It was December 16, 1985, a chilly, gray day. Court was not in session, but Castellano decided to have a meal in the city. Silver Bells, Christmastime in the city, sidewalks filled with folks on their way home from work, and others with colorful shopping bags. On the corner, a Salvation Army Santa was ringing his bell. Perry Como was coming out of a loudspeaker somewhere.

It was 5:30 p.m., rush hour. Castellano and his right-hand man, forty-seven-year-old Thomas Bilotti, had just gotten out of a car after it pulled up in front of Sparks Steak House on East Forty-Sixth Street.

Three gunmen in trench coats and black fur hats that made them look Russian, holding semiautomatic handguns, approached Castellano and Bilotti on foot with long strides. All three gunmen began firing at once. It sounded as if a pitched battle were going on in the street.

According to legend, John Gotti himself, the future Boss, along with his own right-hand man, Sammy "the Bull" Gravano, were in a car at the end of the block, watching the action. One of the hit men was believed to have been John Carneglia.

Both men were shot in the face and went down. Big Paulie lay dead on the sidewalk in front of the restaurant, his hand lying under the Lincoln's open door, his half-smoked cigar, still smoldering on the sidewalk, six inches from his fingers. The still form of Bilotti was in the street. One of the hit men approached Castellano and fired one more shot into his head at point-blank range, the coup de grâce.

Shell casings for a .32-caliber and a .380-caliber gun were found scattered on the pavement. Each victim had six holes in his head. It was the most spectacular hit since Albert Anastasia took his last shave twenty-eight years earlier. Police found that neither of the victims was packing.

The gunmen then ran eastward and were seen still on foot running down Second Avenue. One eyewitness said that one of the fleeing men was talking into a walkie-talkie as he ran.

Another eyewitness saw the men getting into a black Lincoln Town Car on Second Avenue. The witness even got the number off the car's New Jersey license plate, and police learned that the car was a rental.

Regarding the double homicide, the FBI had a primary suspect. His name: John Gotti, forty-five years old, of Howard Beach, Queens, a Dellacroce confidant. Speculation was that Gotti had hit Castellano because he felt Big Paulie was not respected by the troops and was hurting the family's earning power with his indecisive leadership style.

Orrrrrr Gotti simply wanted to rise to the top of the Gambino family and was moving up a rung on the ladder the old-fashioned way, by taking out a guy above him. Perhaps it was the notion that Castellano was keeping too much of the Gambino profits, taking money out of the pockets of soldiers and capos in order to make improvements on his Staten Island mansion.

Or all of the above.

Gotti had never hidden his disdain for Don Carlo's brother-in-law, whom he referred to as a "fat *stronzo*." The tabloids were filled with Gotti's name the day after Castellano and Bilotti were whacked. He was strutting around, grinning from ear to ear with new power. It wasn't even a fucking mystery.

It was the beginning of a love affair between Gotti and the press. Gotti wasn't going to stop pushing until he was on top, and once on top, he would be the highest-profile gangster since Al Capone.

At the time of his death, Big Paulie was in deep shit, having been overheard by fed surveillance saying stuff he shouldn't have said. Ironically, one of the tapes the government would have used against Castellano was of him griping about Sparks Steak House. Not about the food, which is always great. Castellano complained that Sparks wasn't paying him, and the steak house was going to have to be closed unless the owner paid up.

You could feel Don Carlo rolling over in his grave.

In fact, Gotti had all the old mobsters spinning in their graves. It was supposed to be a secret fucking society and Gotti loved notoriety. He always knew where the camera was and had a big smile for all the little people watching him on TV or reading about him

in the newspaper. He was cheerful and exuded both confidence and menace.

From the point of view of familial power, there was a solid reason why Gotti would make a better father than Big Paulie, who was one of a herd of big-time hoods looking at long RICO bids. Castellano had been facing charges based on the crimes of Roy DeMeo.

Gotti was a ruthless, tough man, everything Castellano wasn't. Gotti was a gangster's gangster, and blasting his way to the top was in the time-honored tradition of the brotherhood.

Cops wandered around in the street outside Sparks with their heads down, cursing into the blacktop. This was one of those double homicides that police didn't want any part of. The homicide detectives could analyze the forensics, blah blah blah, all they wanted, but they weren't going to get any closer to nailing the guys who did it. So, they just got downright weird.

About two weeks after the carnage outside Sparks, the NYPD publicly stated that their thinking was that Bilotti was the main target of the hit. The man who was initially referred to in the press as "Castellano's chauffeur," they said, was actually a powerful guy who had the Boss's ear.

The cops said they figured there was a faction in the Gambino family that thought Bilotti was working his way into an underboss role. They felt Gotti was afraid of Bilotti because, in case something happened to Castellano, Bilotti would be boss, and Gotti couldn't let that happen.

It wasn't even an interesting theory.

Clearly Big Paulie was the primary target and Bilotti was just a pleasant side kill. By taking out both at once, Gotti had removed multiple problems. The upper echelon was dead on East Forty-Sixth Street, and John Gotti was going to proclaim himself Boss and see if anyone had the balls to tell him he wasn't.

No one did.

* * *

To show how non-secret the secret brotherhood had become in the years since Gambino's death, the funeral parlor where Big Paul was laid out was under siege by reporters, both newspapers and TV stations, all pushing and crowding, trying to get a clear view of something.

Guys wondered out loud: Would John Gotti be showing up to pay his respects? A Castellano family spokesman said, "No way. Family only. Which means you leave now."

But they didn't leave.

The day they interred Castellano was strikingly dissimilar to the day Don Carlo was laid to rest. Back then, there was respect. Today, there were no weeping immigrants, just newshounds on the scent of a big story, crawling like profane vermin over the sanctity of the Roman Catholic ceremonies.

Big Paul was buried in an unmarked grave, its location only known to the closest friends and family, somewhere in Moravian Cemetery in the Dongan Hills section of Staten Island, not far from Castellano's Todt Hill mansion.

The FBI put a tail on Gotti twenty-four seven. They knew that he was having lots of meets with other Gambino officers, just to make sure everyone understood which way the wind was blowing.

There were meets in Ozone Park in Queens, meets in Little Italy at the Ravenite. Gotti came to the top spot with his own underboss, Sammy "the Bull" Gravano, a man who would be true to Gotti right up until the moment he sold him down the river.

Among those who needed to have the new situation explained to them was Joe N. Gallo, a very powerful man who'd been Gambino consigliere for a generation, and James Failla, the aging tough guy who'd been backup to O'Neil.

Gotti became known as the Teflon Don because authorities couldn't make charges stick. Gotti's trials came out in his favor. In 1985, he was on trial for assaulting a guy named Romual Piecyk, but after Gambino thugs cut Piecyk's brake lines and phoned him with regular death threats, the victim decided not to press charges.

In 1986, Gotti was in a federal courtroom on trial for racketeering. This time he was granted no bail. They figured that with Gotti locked inside a fed cell he wouldn't be able to intimidate witnesses and jury members.

It didn't work.

Gotti had plenty of pals on the outside and managed to place a friend of the Gambino family as Juror Number Eleven. When it came time for deliberations, Juror Number Eleven argued so aggressively for acquittal that the other jurors feared for their safety, and they came back with a verdict of not guilty on all counts.

Gotti was next arrested in 1989 and charged with beating up a labor union official outside the Ravenite Club on Mulberry Street. In January 1990, he was acquitted.

Despite a constant effort by law enforcement to take Gotti off the streets, they didn't manage to convict him of anything until 1992, when he was done in by an electronic surveillance device, a bug in the Ravenite, and a betrayal by Sammy the Bull.

The feds and the NYPD raided the Ravenite on December 11, 1990, and arrested Gotti and Gravano. Gotti was charged with five murders: Castellano, Bilotti, Robert "DB" DiBernardo, Liborio Milito, and Louis Dibono.

It was the death of DB that had a strong personal effect at our house. The porn king Robert DiBernardo was a friend of my dad and at my house for breakfast twice a month. DB made his bones with the DeCavalcante crew from New Jersey, and later became caporegime in the Gambino family. DB was a well-respected capo and a good earner.

In addition to his pornography distribution operation, Star Distributors in the city, which he co-owned with Teddy Rothstein of Oceanside, he was also involved in labor unions and other legitimate businesses. He was intelligent and articulate. Many guys thought he would make a great boss one day.

Officially, DB was vice president of Star Distributors. On paper, he was listed as a suit-and-tie corporate officer, but on the street where it mattered, he was the Man, the absolute last word regarding Star and its business decisions.

DB was first arrested in 1980 in what was called a $700 million smut racket. A year later, he was convicted by the feds of transporting obscene material across state lines. That case went all the way to the Supreme Court, which upheld DB's conviction. His legal status would remain up in the air for the rest of his life, what there was of it.

DB's one flaw, and it turned out to be a fatal flaw, was he was a loner. He came and went on his own, no posse, no entourage. He paid his tribute, but he had his own mind. He expressed his own opinion, which could be dangerous, especially in a family that was in major upheaval after Big Paul Castellano was gunned down.

DB became a victim of his own success. Guys in the ranks grew jealous of DB's position; some owed him a lot of money. Those closest to the new Boss, John Gotti—namely Sammy "the Bull" Gravano and Angelo Ruggiero—began to conspire against DB. They had Gotti's ear and they filled it with negative stuff about DB. Gotti became convinced that DB had been bad-mouthing him, saying he was an ineffective leader.

Gotti came to see DB as a threat to his power. DB had no love for Gotti, but he stuck with him. In June 1986, DB was called to a meeting in the basement of Gravano's drywall company in Bensonhurst.

DB came to my home to speak to Ricky about being called in.

"Don't go. Or, bring someone with you," Ricky advised.

"Why?"

"If you've been heard grumbling, that's enough," Ricky said.

DB smiled and said, "Don't worry. I make all their money for them."

He had his coffee with us and left. Only a few weeks earlier he'd knocked on the door and asked Ricky how they blew up the car that Frank DeCicco was in. Ricky said remote control.

So, DB went to his meeting at Gravano's drywall company alone, and there, he was without ceremony shot in the back of the head by Gravano's main shooter, Joe Paruta. Then they disposed of him in such a manner that he would never be found.

* * *

DB was gone, the fourth Gambino man to be offed since Gotti took over. Thirteen days after DB's disappearance, FBI agent William Noon testified in Brooklyn Federal Court that Gotti not only had Big Paulie whacked, but his childhood pal Angelo Ruggiero, O'Neil's nephew, also gave the green light to the hit on DB. Ruggiero was the one on trial, and his lawyers called the accusation uncorroborated hearsay, which didn't mean it wasn't true.

Here's proof of just how fragile everyone's position in the Mafia is: DB was a guy who seemed to have everything going for him. He had the respect of just about everyone around him, and he was one of the highest earners—two traits that should offer you some longevity in the Life. And he was whacked.

After the 1990 arrests, Gravano was originally Gotti's codefendant. When the prosecution played audiotapes recorded in the Ravenite, among the tidbits they picked up was Gotti saying nasty and insulting things about the Bull.

Hearing that, Gravano decided he no longer had anything to be loyal to. Fuck Gotti. Fuck omertà. Gravano agreed to testify against his old pal Gotti in exchange for a spot in the Witness Protection Program.

The jury took only fourteen hours to decide Gotti was guilty on all charges, and that was the last Gotti saw of freedom. He was sentenced to life in prison without the possibility of parole.

In 1998, he was diagnosed with throat cancer and had the tumor removed in the U.S. Medical Center for Federal Prisoners in Springfield, Missouri. The operation was thought to be successful, but the cancer came back two years later, and Gotti returned to the federal hospital, where he died on June 10, 2002, thus closing the curtain on the glory days of the Gambino crime family.

EPILOGUE
Other Gambinos

IN THIS FINAL CHAPTER we'll take a brief look at others with the Gambino name. Some of them, to varying degrees of success, carried on the tradition brought to America from Palermo by the great Don Carlo. Gambino believed in the power of Sicily, but America came to believe in the power of that name. Gambino. In the twenty-first century, a rap star would take the name. It *meant* boss.

TOMMY GAMBINO

Carlo's eldest son, Thomas Francis Gambino, was born on August 23, 1929. He went into the Life, became a made man in the family that bore his father's name, and did all right for himself. There was power in that name, and he knew it. That power radiated past organized crime and into the legit world, as well.

Despite his lifelong work in the rackets, Tommy had managed to survive the RICO purge with just a five-year sentence for racketeering. He'd never been in jail before that and didn't go back after his release in May 2000.

When Carlo Gambino's friend Tommy Lucchese died in 1967, Tommy Gambino moved in and took over the garment district, which stretches over forty square blocks in Manhattan.

One lesson Tommy learned from his dad was, if you are going to run a business, run every aspect of it. So, when it came to dressmaking and the like, Tommy was in charge at all levels, from owning manufacturing firms to running the trucking firms that moved the garments from factory to warehouse, from warehouse to store.

If anyone tried to get in on the action—that is, have dresses made at a non-Gambino factory, transported in a non-Gambino truck, or sold in a store that Gambino didn't approve of—there was trouble.

Tommy Gambino was typical of first-generation Americans who were mobsters' sons. When Meyer Lansky sent his son to West Point, it became the thing to do, and Tommy Gambino went to the New York Military Academy, not far from the U.S. Military Academy at West Point.

Tommy did not, like his old man and his grandfather, marry his first cousin to keep the power inside the family. But in 1962 he didn't stray far from the fold when he picked a wife, either. He married Tommy Lucchese's daughter, Frances. She was, as they say, the marrying kind—a graduate of the Sacred Heart Convent School, practically a nun!

When the two families, Gambino and Lucchese, joined in marriage, the resulting wedding was huge, with upward of one thousand guests on hand and two godfathers holding court. (The to-do is said to have inspired the lengthy wedding sequence at the beginning of *The Godfather.*) Both families were from Palermo and their friends mingled well.

Tommy Gambino was a guy who knew every aspect of every racket he ran. But his success was miniscule compared to that of his old man. Unlike in the movie *The Godfather*—in which new bosses were determined by lineage, like kings and queens, rather than by democratic vote, like popes—Tommy Gambino did not rise to the top when his father died. He remained a caporegime, while Big Paul and then John Gotti ran the family.

An FBI surveillance device once picked up Tommy baring his soul to his Uncle Paul, looking at life with a combination of regret, pride, and more than a twinge of frustration: "I never had a chance to do something I want to do. I always did it for my family, for my children, for my father and mother. When I spoke, I always asked myself, how does this affect other people?"

Along with the ability to keep lots of moving parts straight in his mind, Tommy had something else in common with Don Carlo: he was low-key and did not believe in mixing emotions with work. Cold-blooded killing, if you thought about it, was the only way to go. Hot-blooded killings often resulted in regret. The crime family he worked for already bore his name, so there was no reason to strut around like fucking Mussolini.

Tommy was happier behind closed doors than he was in the spotlight. This not only fit his temperament but also his philosophy, which was *never get your name in the newspapers*. Notoriety was counterproductive. It was a lesson that John Gotti didn't or couldn't share.

Staying out of the limelight had other fringe benefits. It was far easier for law enforcement and politicians to ignore you when you weren't in the headlines.

Along with a philosophy of life and reserved demeanor, Tommy had something else in common with his dad: he was not a womanizer. Very odd in a world where hoods all had wives and girlfriends, the Gambino men were faithful husbands, fathers, and grandfathers. They were the very definition of family men—and they did their best to always keep the unpleasant aspects of Mob life away from their homes and their children's schools.

When John Gotti took over the Gambino crime family, he was protective of Tommy Gambino. Tommy was like his old man—didn't get his hands dirty—so Gotti made sure to protect Tommy from harsh realities. For a guy who never rose above capo, Tommy Gambino was a very rich man, with a luxury apartment in the Lenox Hill section of Manhattan, and a mansion summer house on Long Island's North Shore.

Following his 1995 conviction, Tommy attempted to demonstrate what a good citizen he was by donating $2.5 million to the bone marrow transplant center at the Long Island Jewish Medical

Center. Despite his frontline efforts to aid the treatment of leukemia, he served his five-spot.

On October 3, 2023, he passed away at the age of ninety-four. His presence on the earth with his legendary name and quiet power was a throwback to the American Mafia of the twentieth century.

JOSEPH GAMBINO

The son of Carlo Gambino who did not go into the Life was Joseph, known as the easygoing brother, who applied his intelligence to excelling in the legitimate business world and became a millionaire. He was legit, but that didn't mean he didn't use his name to establish clout. Nobody was going to try to rip off Joseph Gambino.

Although he co-owned some businesses with his brother Tommy, it's said that he ran the legit end of those operations, while Tommy handled the extortion, etc. He couldn't have been completely oblivious. Everyone knew that if a non-Gambino truck driver even tried to park his rig on a Gambino street, he was going to get his tires slashed. It figures that Joseph knew it, too.

Carlo sent his son Joseph to NYU, but he dropped out before graduation to work for Consolidated Carriers Corporation. That company had a stranglehold on garment district trucking until the 1990s when federal racketeering charges forced its breakup.

The feds wanted Joseph's ass, but no matter how much surveillance they slapped on him, he never said anything incriminating. The closest they came to overhearing Joseph issuing a threat was when an undercover agent wearing a wire came to him for a job interview.

"Two rules," Joseph said. "No drugs. No stealing. If you get caught we don't call the cops. We take care of it ourselves."

It was slim evidence but an up-and-coming assistant district attorney named Eliot Spitzer, who later was drummed out of politics over a sex scandal, had a hard-on to indict anyone named Gambino, and so Tommy and Joseph both were tried for illegal restraint of trade. The case didn't go to trial. The brothers' attorneys managed a no-jail deal with the prosecution and paid a $12 million fine to make the charges go away.

Joseph died in 2020 at the age of eighty-three.

ROSARIO GAMBINO AND THE CHERRY HILL GAMBINOS

Rosario Gambino was Don Carlo's cousin, who was smuggled into the U.S. in 1962, when he was twenty. Rosario was caught and deported as an illegal alien but promptly married a U.S. citizen and reentered the country with his legal green card.

Like Don Carlo, Rosario was straightened out in Sicily and came to the U.S. premade. He had two brothers, Giuseppe and Giovanni, who also had their buttons and came over on the same boat as Rosario.

The brothers settled in Cherry Hill, New Jersey, and immediately put together a crew for illegal enterprises. They called themselves, appropriately enough, the "Cherry Hill Gambinos," taking advantage of their famous surname.

Rosario was a friend of Tommaso Buscetta, who at the time was the most wanted man in Sicily, for blowing up a bunch of Palermo cops. Buscetta turned rat in 1984.

In April 1970, Rosario and a crew were working a protection racket in Brooklyn. He got in trouble one day when he was working over a Brooklyn coffee shop owner who didn't have the envelope. When a man in the shop tried to intervene, they beat him up, too. Trouble was, the Good Samaritan was an off-duty cop, who had the Sicilians arrested. Rosario got off with a hundred-dollar fine and no jail time.

In 1972, Rosario was rolling in dough. He bought a house for his dad, Tommaso, and another for his brother Giuseppe, and a third for himself. All were in nice sections of Jersey. Best bet is that the money came from Rosario's participation in the "Pizza Connection" operation, in which billions of dollars' worth of babonia was smuggled into the U.S. using pizzerias as a front. Many of those pizza parlors were owned by the Cherry Hill Gambinos. Sure, they made pizza, but they also stored and moved heroin. The op ran from 1975 until 1984, when it was busted.

Rosario was put in handcuffs and led away. When police searched Rosario's office, they found something they hadn't expected: dozens of copies of confidential intelligence reports on organized crime figures. The documents were seized and the paper dusted for prints. On the documents were found the fingerprints of bad cop Louis Eppolito.

Eppolito was NYPD, but he was born in East Flatbush and had Mob blood running through his veins. His dad, Ralph, was "Fat the Gangster." He had an uncle called "Jimmy the Clam." Eppolito was already in trouble when his prints were found in Rosario Gambino's office, accused of being a Mob hit man while off duty.

Based on that arrest, and all those pizza boxes packed with heartbreak and death, Rosario was convicted on narcotics charges in 1984 and was sentenced to forty-five years behind bars. He went directly to the Federal Correctional Institution, Terminal Island, in L.A.

In 1999, Rosario's children gave President Bill Clinton's half brother, Roger, a Rolex watch and a check for $50,000 in exchange for his guarantee that he could get Bill to pardon their father. It's unknown what became of the watch, but Rosario didn't get his pardon.

Rosario went away only until 2007, half of his sentence, when he was transferred from prison to an immigrant detention center in California.

In May 2009, Rosario, now sixty-seven years old and in a wheelchair, was deported back to Italy. Rosario had protested his deportation, saying he would be tortured in Palermo because of his notorious last name. What actually happened when he arrived in Rome was he was arrested and within minutes was in jail—wheelchair and all. And, now in his eighties, he's been in and out of jail ever since.

ACKNOWLEDGMENTS

The authors would like to thank the following persons—some gone, some still around—and organizations, without whose help the writing of this book would have been impossible: Keith Brenner, the Brooklyn Farmacy & Soda Fountain at Henry and Sackett for the best egg cream in town, Anthony Deluca, Rick Erickson; editors James Abbate and Stephen Smith; our literary agent Doug Grad; Green-Wood Cemetery; Joseph Guagliardo, Holy Cross Cemetery; Liza Katz, Senior Reference Librarian, Center for Brooklyn History, Brooklyn Public Library; Jennifer Maloney; and Tony Nap.

And Emily, Chris, Krissy, Matthew, and Frankie Boy. And to the others, who wish to remain anonymous, our heartfelt thanks.

Acknowledgments

SOURCES

Books

Davis, John H. *Mafia Dynasty: The Rise and Fall of the Gambino Crime Family.* New York: Harpertorch, 1993.

DeMeo, Albert. *For the Sins of My Father: A Mafia Killer, His Son, and the Legacy of a Mob Life.* New York: Broadway Books, 2002.

Kelley, Kitty. *His Way: The Unauthorized Biography of Frank Sinatra.* New York: Bantam, 2010.

Maas, Peter. *The Valachi Papers.* New York: William Morrow Paperbacks, 2003.

May, Allan R. *Gangland Gotham: New York's Notorious Mob Bosses.* Santa Barbara, California: Greenwood, 2009.

Meskil, Paul, and James Pierre. *Don Carlo: Boss of Bosses*, 2nd Edition. Windsor, Connecticut: Ironworks Publishing Company, 1973.

Mustain, Gene, and Jerry Capeci. *Murder Machine.* New York: Random House, 2012.

Raab, Selwyn. *Five Families: The Rise, Decline, and Resurgence of America's Most Powerful Mafia Empires.* New York: Thomas Dunne Book, 2016.

Periodicals

Asbury Park Press
Boston Globe
Brooklyn Citizen
Brooklyn Daily Eagle
Camden Morning Post
Montpelier Evening Argus
Nashville Banner
New York Daily News
New York Post
New York Times
Newsday
Philadelphia Inquirer
Santa Fe Morning Herald
The Village Voice
Westchester Magazine
Wilkes-Barre Times Leader
York Dispatch

Websites

Academic-accelerator.com
ameshistory.org
britannica.com
clydeships.co.uk
crimelibrary.org
dea.gov
fbi.gov
history.com
mafiahistory.us
nationalcrimesyndicate.com
nationalWW2museum.org
sunsentinel.com
thenewyorkmafia.com
wearepalermo.com

FURTHER READING

NEW YORK
Five Families

GENOVESE FAMILY

TOP HOODLUM, Anthony M. DeStefano
Frank Costello, Boss

THE DEADLY DON, Anthony M. DeStefano
Vito Genovese, Boss

CHIN, Larry McShane
Vincent Gigante, Boss

GAMBINO FAMILY

LORD HIGH EXECUTIONER, Frank DiMatteo and Michael Benson
Albert Anastasia, Boss

CARLO GAMBINO: BOSS OF BOSSES, Frank DiMatteo and Michael Benson
Carlo Gambino, Boss

MOB KILLER, Anthony M. DeStefano
Charles Carneglia, Soldier

GOTTI'S BOYS, Anthony M. DeStefano
John Gotti, Boss; Salvatore Gravano, Underboss; Gene Gotti, Captain; Angelo Ruggiero, Captain; Charles Carneglia, Soldier; Tony Rampino, Associate

LUCCHESE FAMILY

JIMMY THE GENT, Anthony M. DeStefano
Jimmy Burke, Associate

THE BIG HEIST, Anthony M. DeStefano
Jimmy Burke, Associate

BONANNO FAMILY

THE BONANNOS, Joe Pistone and Larry McShane
Joe Bonanno, Boss; Philip Rastelli, Boss; Carmine Galante, De Facto Boss; Joe Massino, Boss; Vincent Basciano, Boss; Michael Mancuso, Boss

KING OF THE GODFATHERS, Anthony M. DeStefano
Joe Massino, Boss

THE CIGAR, Frank DiMatteo and Michael Benson
Carmine Galante, De Facto Boss

COLOMBO FAMILY

OLIVE OIL KING, Frank DiMatteo and Michael Benson
Joe Profaci, Boss

CARMINE THE SNAKE, Frank DiMatteo and Michael Benson
Carmine Persico, Boss

LITTLE VIC AND THE GREAT MAFIA WAR, Larry McShane
Vic Orena, Acting Boss

SONNY, S. J. Peddie
Sonny Franzese, Underboss

THE PRESIDENT STREET BOYS, Frank DiMatteo
Joe Gallo, Captain; Albert Gallo, Captain; Larry Gallo, Soldier

MAFIA HIT MAN, Frank DiMatteo and Michael Benson
Joe Gallo, Captain; Carmine DiBiase, Associate

PHILADELPHIA

BRUNO FAMILY

MAFIOSO, George Anastasia
Angelo Bruno, Boss

PITTSTON

BUFALINO FAMILY

BUFALINO, Charles Bufalino
Steve La Torre, Boss; Calogero Bufalino, Boss; Santo Volpe, Boss; Russell Bufalino, Boss; William D'Elia, Boss

GENERAL

THE LANSKY LEGACY, Meyer Lansky II and S. J. Peddie
Meyer Lansky; Las Vegas; Cuba

OPERATION UNDERWORLD, Matthew Black
Sicily; World War II

GANGSTERS VS. NAZIS, Michael Benson
Meyer Lansky; Benjamin Siegel; Mickey Cohen; Murder, Inc.; World War II

MAFIA SECRETS, Gianni Russo and Michael Benson
Gianni Russo; The Godfather; Hollywood

RED HOOK, Frank DiMatteo and Michael Benson
Brooklyn Mafia

THE FBI'S WAR AGAINST THE MAFIA, Frank Storey
Mafia Commission Trial; Bruno Family; Pizza Connection

THE DON, RJ Roger
Five Families; Mafia Commission; National Crime Syndicate

THE MAFIA'S GREATEST HITS, David H. Jacobs
Mafia Murders; National Crime Syndicate

IN THE GHOST SHADOWS, Peter Chin and Everett De Morier
Chinatown, New York City; Ghost Shadows Gang

MEET THE KELLYS, Chris Enss
Machine Gun Kelly; Kathryn Thorne

DILLINGER'S GIRLS, Chris Enss
John Dillinger

INDEX